BLACK-OWNED

BLACK-

TINY REPARATIONS BOOKS

THE REVOLUTIONARY LIFE

OWNED

OF THE BLACK BOOKSTORE

CHAR ADAMS

Tiny
Reparations
Books®

An imprint of Penguin Random House LLC
1745 Broadway, New York, NY 10019
penguinrandomhouse.com

Tiny Reparations and Tiny Reparations Books & Design are
registered trademarks of YQY, Inc.

Permissions appear on pages 261–262 and constitute an extension of the copyright page.

Book design by Jenni Surasky

LIBRARY OF CONGRESS CATALOGING-IN-PUBLICATION DATA
has been applied for.

ISBN 9780593474235 (hardcover)
ISBN 9780593474259 (ebook)

Printed in the United States of America

1st Printing

The authorized representative in the EU for product safety and compliance is
Penguin Random House Ireland, Morrison Chambers, 32 Nassau Street,
Dublin D02 YH68, Ireland, https://eu-contact.penguin.ie.

For my father, Charles R. Wilson Jr.
No life is wasted, nor is any life without legacy.
May this book be a part of yours. Rest in peace.

CONTENTS

BLACK-OWNED

INTRODUCTION

I LOVE TO TELL PEOPLE'S STORIES.

That's often what I say when people ask how I came to write about Black bookstores, let alone the first full-length historical account of the businesses. And what I say is true: my career and passion as a journalist revolve around telling people's stories, crafting compelling narratives out of people's experiences in ways they may not have been able to themselves. It began with an article I read in *The Atlantic* in 2018: "The FBI's War on Black-Owned Bookstores." Joshua Clark Davis, a history professor at the University of Baltimore, wrote about the surveillance and espionage the FBI heaped on Black independent booksellers, or "activist entrepreneurs," during the Black Power era. This war on Black bookstores was a reminder of the ways law enforcement worked to diminish Black literature and political movements throughout US history. My interest was piqued. When I finished the article, I couldn't help but think about the booksellers. I was curious about their experiences. I wanted to know about their lives under FBI surveillance and what it meant to sell Black literature at such a politically turbulent time in the country. Did agents visit their stores?

What books were they most excited to sell? How did Black locals react to having such overtly countercultural businesses in their communities? I had questions. So I set out to get answers.

I began interviewing every Black bookseller from the era I could find. I started with Yvonne Blake, who runs her father's sixty-five-plus-year-old shop, Hakim's Bookstore, in Philadelphia. Then Judy Richardson of Drum and Spear, perhaps the best-known activist bookstore during the Black Power movement. I was soon sitting with booksellers from stores founded in the '60s, the '90s, and beyond. I ended up publishing my own article about my findings in February 2020: "Black-Owned Bookstores Have Always Been at the Center of the Resistance." Booksellers shared their accounts of run-ins with law enforcement in their own words. I was proud to tell their stories. Most of what has been written about Black bookstores is strewn across old, defunct newspapers, obscure books, journals, and government documents. All of which were difficult to find. There was no singular place to learn all I wanted to know about them. I was shocked to find that no complete book existed about Black bookstores' history, struggle, and cultural impact. I wanted to piece together these scattered stories, and uncover this information, and determine what lessons we could learn from the past to inform the future. Even then, I hadn't imagined that I would be the one to write this book. I was simply following my curiosity. Growing up in West Philadelphia, I had no idea that Black bookstores existed, let alone that the famous Hakim's Bookstore was just a short drive away from my home. I loved to read, though, and longed for instant access to books about people like me—a young Black girl with a disability. Learning about Black bookstores has thrust me into a world I didn't know existed all those years ago. I'm making up for lost time.

My research and interest in Black bookstores took me to many places and introduced me to more people than I can count. Whether they were serving as meeting places for Black Power groups and peddling socialist and Marxist literature in the 1960s or holding discussions about the Rodney King beating in the 1990s, or providing gathering places for people protesting George Floyd's murder in 2020, Black bookstores have always been at the center of Black resistance in one way or another. I am proud to share the first comprehensive history in this book. This book is organized chronologically, laying out the life of Black bookstores from when the first shop opened in the nineteenth century, and then focusing on the businesses' most active and successful eras: the 1960s, the 1990s, and the 2020s.

I made a great effort to include and highlight as many Black bookstores as possible in this book, whether they were massively influential or known only to a local few. But I know there are several bookshops not mentioned, both existing today and in the past. Still, they are all part of the tree that is the Black book ecosystem. Shops like Uhuru Bookstore, which existed in Greensboro, North Carolina, in the 1970s, and the Hub, a Kansas store that operated for about ten years starting in the 1960s, aren't heavily featured in the book. But they meant a lot to the communities they served. Details about Marcus Books, among the oldest of the nation's still-existing bookstores, are spread throughout the book.

I fashioned *Black-Owned* as a series of vignettes with historical accounts and information mixed in. It takes readers back in time, bringing those stories to life, allowing readers to see staff stocking bookshelves, to hear tense conversations with law enforcement, and to feel the disappointment of a store's closure. It is more than a historical account; it is a collection of vivid stories intended to stick with readers long after they put the book down. Stories a person could get lost in.

As far as estimates go, the country had a dozen Black-owned bookstores at the start of the '60s, and that number grew to 75 by the middle of the '70s. While approximately 200 stores operated in the '90s, there were only about 54 operating by 2014. The numbers would remain dismal for years, until today, when there are at least 130 Black-owned bookstores operating in the United States. These are all best guesses, though. There is no official entity keeping track of the number of Black bookstores, so there's no way to know for sure how many existed at any given time in the country's history. Best estimates—usually ballpark numbers—come from old articles, news clippings, and brief mentions in books. Despite this lack of clarity, it's certain that the political turmoil of the 1960s and '70s brought about more Black bookstores than the country had seen before. Historical recollections have consistently portrayed Black-owned bookstores as tangential, and even unimportant, to Black radical movements—or hardly mention them at all. But I sought to address this gap in living history. To understand the Black social and political movements that have shaped our history, we must understand the role Black bookstores have played in them—as well as the role they continue to play as we press forward into a new and uncertain future.

Six shops operating in major cities at the time were era-defining, model bookstores: Drum and Spear in Washington, DC;

National Memorial African Book Store, run by Lewis Michaux, in Harlem; Liberation Bookstore, run by Una Mulzac, in Harlem; Hakim's Bookstore, started by Dawud Hakim, in Philadelphia; the Aquarian Bookshop, run by couple Alfred and Bernice Ligon, in South Central Los Angeles; and Marcus Books, founded by couple Julian and Raye Richardson, in Oakland, California. Marcus Books grew out of Julian's Success Print Co., which he opened in the 1940s in San Francisco. He and his wife founded Marcus Books, named after Marcus Garvey, in 1960 and moved the store to Oakland, where it became one of the most influential Black bookshops in the world. These booksellers all ran mission-driven bookstores rooted in politics and worldviews that opposed the status quo. Black people, usually those with more radical politics, often invoke the words of Fred Hampton, Ella Baker, Malcolm X, Huey P. Newton, and the like during major political and social movements. I believe these activist booksellers of the 1960s and '70s should be mentioned in those conversations, too.

Though many of these booksellers were born decades apart, had different experiences, and had different goals, they all operated from a similar set of principles. First, they existed to counter racist or whitewashed education and discourse. They were hubs of learning at a time when mainstream literature, television, and film portrayed Black people as violent, uneducated, lust-filled, subservient noncitizens. This was a time when schools presented limited and condescending versions of Black history—if they taught Black history at all. These booksellers cared more about their mission and their communities than they cared about profits. Second, most Black booksellers wanted their work to mobilize readers. They hoped that, once educated through books, readers would join in Black liberation movements. They wanted to go beyond just providing communities with Black books—they wanted to develop a new generation of freedom fighters. Third, Black bookshops were gathering sites and meeting places for local political groups, intellectuals, and citizens involved in Black liberation movements, as many institutions, much like today, worked to stamp out Black history and restrict education. Last, and perhaps most important, Black booksellers wanted to build community. From Harlem to Los Angeles, booksellers viewed their work as a way of disrupting the rugged individualism that defined America. Black bookshops fit snugly in the tradition of important Black community spaces like churches, salons, and barbershops, but represented new, public political spaces, too. Their bookshops were not only ideological hubs but centers for relationships and political education where people could sit, read, and think together. Even people who weren't much interested in politics and current events found in Black bookstores places of solace and comfort, where they could hang out with friends, do homework after school, or simply "stay out of trouble." It was a time of renewed racial pride and optimism for Black communities in the country.

This period didn't last long, though: only about twelve years at the most. The Black Power and Black Nationalist movements, novelties to most Americans, were suppressed and lost their steam. So too did the surge of support and passion for patronizing Black bookstores. While Black bookstores' influence might have faded in the short term, these bookseller activists deepened the foundation previous Black booksellers had laid and served as a blueprint for those who came after them. Black bookstores were now synonymous with Black liberation and advancement, no matter their numbers. Black bookstores wouldn't see this much success again until the 1990s. The Black Power imagery of past decades spread through rap music, Black movies, and TV shows, igniting a fire in young Black people who were already infuriated by poverty and police violence. A renewed interest in Black history and radical movements meant that Black books were popular again. And not just history titles and biographies, which are often marketed toward men, but Black romance novels and fiction about Black women's lives. Terry McMillan's *Waiting to Exhale* and *Serenade* by Sandra Kitt were flying off bookshelves, while young Black men clamored to watch *Boyz N the Hood* and *Higher Learning*. Figures like Oprah, Jesse Jackson, and Virginia governor L. Douglas Wilder signaled better representation for Black people on television and in politics. At the same time, heightened poverty and violent displays of overt racism further proved that Black life in America wasn't much better than it had been in decades prior.

Shops like Eso Won in Los Angeles and Black Images Book Bazaar in Dallas ran the show during the '90s. Black bookstores of this time weren't overtly tied to radical movements or radical organizations like Drum and Spear or Liberation had been, but, as ever, booksellers found their shops to be inherently political whether they intended them to be or not. They held lectures, education sessions, and simple gatherings at their stores for Black locals to talk about the country's political climate. After a decades-long lull, another surge of Black bookstores came in 2020. After white vigilantes and police killed Ahmaud Arbery, Breonna Taylor, Tony McDade, and George Floyd in the first half of the year, the country was propelled into yet another racial reckoning. And the United States was reminded that Black bookstores are important centers of support, understanding, and activism in times of trouble. The estimated 120 Black bookstores operating at the time kept their stores open as long as they could before Covid restrictions locked down businesses everywhere. Booksellers stayed up late filling online orders from new customers seeking titles by Black authors and about racism.

The brief but overwhelming increase in business over that summer was bittersweet for Black booksellers. They knew they owed their fleeting success to Arbery's, Taylor's, McDade's, and Floyd's deaths. It was a truth they wrestled with all summer and for years after, and nagging questions quickly accompanied the grief. Why did it take death to spark an interest in Black books? Would this newfound interest last more than a few months, or would readers just move on to the next thing? Would anything change? Even as they endured this inner turmoil, booksellers met the moment as best they could. They held virtual community meetings to support other Black businesses and marched with protesters when they weren't fulfilling orders. They let Black kids sit in front of their closed bookstores to use their Wi-Fi for virtual school and allowed Black teens and adults to use their front steps as meeting places to plan their marches and protests. There were mixed emotions, moments of overwhelm, sadness, and joy, but ultimately booksellers' belief in the transformative power of books held true.

||| ▰▰▰▰▰ |||

Black-Owned is a collection of stories about Black bookstores spanning US history, from the unprecedented and radical nature of their earliest years during slavery to the communal model forged in the Black bookstore's turbulent adolescence, and to the continuing evolution of popular shops that have withstood the test of time or picked up where their predecessors left off. For Black people in America, the business of bookstores has always been about much more than selling books. This became clear enough as I studied the Black book industry. But I was still curious about the origins of this radical tradition. Activism and protest through literature seemed to be inherent in Black bookselling culture—this common communal theme and mission-driven posture had to come from somewhere.

My research led me to a single man: David Ruggles.

CHAPTER ONE

FIRST OFFICER OF THE UNDERGROUND RAILROAD

David Ruggles (left, center) stands alongside fellow abolitionists in "The Disappointed Abolitionists," an 1838 illustration by Edward W. Clay.

I'D NEVER EVEN HEARD OF DAVID RUGGLES BEFORE I BEGAN researching bookstores. And neither have many of the booksellers and book lovers I've spoken to since. The more I read about Ruggles's exciting and radical life, the sadder I became that so few people knew his story. Ruggles was a nineteenth-century abolitionist who helped enslaved people through the Underground Railroad, published anti-slavery pamphlets, and ran the country's first known Black bookstore. This news was unsurprising given what we know about Black people's tenacity and ability to fight systems of oppression in the face of adversity. But I was not prepared to learn the details of his life: the story of a man who weathered racist beatings, an attempted kidnapping, and years of targeted attacks, all for the liberation of his people.

Ruggles was asleep in his home on Chapel Street in Manhattan on December 28, 1836, when he heard loud knocking at his front door. Banging. He rushed to the door to find a group of white men trying to force it open.

"Who is it? Who's there?!" Ruggles demanded. It was the city marshal. He wanted to talk about something very important, he said. It was between 1 and 2 a.m.

Ruggles wasn't a fool. His work as an abolitionist, peddling anti-slavery literature and spurring crowds of Black New Yorkers with electrifying speeches, made him a consistent target for men like the ones outside his door. Men who were more than happy to comply with a federal order to capture runaway slaves who made it to free states and return them to their masters in the South. Ruggles knew their MO: arrest an unsuspecting Black person, haul them to jail, put them in front of a judge without a jury, and have them sold into captivity. He told the city marshal to come back at a decent hour. The marshal, and his gang, stormed off. But Ruggles knew they'd return. This marshal, D. D. Nash, was among a group of local police who gleefully kidnapped Black men, women, and children and sold them into slavery in the South.

Nash, along with Tobias Boudinot and the countless city officials who shared a disdain for Black people, terrorized New York's Black populace. Ruggles knew Nash very well, and he knew he was in trouble. Ruggles had recently published an article letting the public know about a newly docked slave ship in New York and its captain. The story caused an uproar and local kidnappers, who supported the captain, wanted revenge. Nash soon returned with his crew, this time bringing the equally notorious police chief Jacob Hays. They forced their way into Ruggles's home, drawing guns and knives on the hysterical landlady. They lunged for Ruggles and tried to grab him, making their problem with him clear: "We will learn him to publish us as kidnappers!" Ruggles narrowly escaped. It wasn't his first quarrel with kidnappers, and it wouldn't be his last. By this time, in 1836, Ruggles had developed a reputation as a charismatic abolitionist who could inspire almost any crowd to action. He'd opened the nation's first-known Black bookstore just two years earlier, in May 1834, as a home for both anti-slavery literature and his activism. Ruggles's shop was located at 67 Lispenard Street, in what is now known as Manhattan's Tribeca neighborhood. It sat in the elite St. John's Park neighborhood, a Madison Avenue–esque shopping headquarters filled with wealthy white people, many of whom shared anti-slavery sentiments—including the Tappan brothers, Lewis and Arthur, who helped bankroll the Anti-Slavery Society.

But the bookstore wasn't far from New York's Five Points neighborhood, a working-class area of Black, German, and Irish communities. Five Points was consumed by poverty, which many outsiders equated with crime and debauchery. The prevailing image of Five Points as a slum where one would certainly need a police escort reflected the biases people held toward the poor and working-class population. Ruggles made it his goal to reach as many people in Five Points as possible, in addition to serving residents in the Fifth and Sixth Wards. As Ruggles immersed himself in New York's abolitionist scene, it became clear to everyone he encountered that not only was he unafraid of going places known for danger—he intended to. Ruggles sold anti-slavery and anti-colonization publications to customers for as little as twenty-five cents per month. He considered his shop an intervention for young Black people who needed community and an educational home. To Ruggles, knowledge was vital for developing what he believed was the moral virtue necessary to thrive in society. And his shop, and later the accompanying reading room, was a site of "observation, reading and reflection." He wrote of his high hopes for the business, telling the public in an advertisement that a "centre of literary attraction for young men whose mental appetites thirst for food" would keep them from the "allurement of vice which surrounded them on every side."

This wasn't Ruggles's first foray into bookselling, though, or running a business in general. He'd been exposed to entrepreneurship since he was a child. Born in Connecticut to free parents, Ruggles was one of eight children. His father was a respected blacksmith and his mother a renowned cook in their town of Bean Hill, about a mile from the center of Norwich, Connecticut. His parents instilled in him a deep pride and strong work ethic, both of which would come to characterize his life as an activist. Though the family was poor, they lived in a small, close-knit, elite society that produced congressmen and senators. He was surrounded by abolitionists or those who, at the very least, questioned the morality of slavery. From an early age, Ruggles was aware of the evil of the slave trade and lived an integrated childhood, going to school and frequently playing with white people. Ruggles later wrote fondly of his formative years, in which he swam, climbed trees, and went ice-skating with his friends. By the time he was a teenager, Ruggles had a sturdy education, strong abolitionist politics, and a sense of self-respect and esteem modeled by his parents. He saw militant Black abolitionism during his teen years as a mariner before moving to New York at age seventeen with some cash in hand, ready to join Black New York's lengthy history of anti-slavery efforts.

In Norwich, he was exposed to small businesses like grocery shops, lending libraries, and bookshops that published weekly newspapers. When he was eighteen years old, Ruggles followed suit in his new home, opening a grocery shop at 1 Cortlandt Street in Lower Manhattan, in the heart of the city's central business district. There he sold "butter and books," and hired a pair of brothers who'd escaped slavery to help him run the store. Although the neighborhood didn't boast a large Black population, Ruggles advertised to Black communities through notices in *Freedom's Journal*, the nation's first Black-owned-and-operated newspaper, and delivered groceries to "any part of the city." He stocked the store with goods from other free Black people, supporting the free produce movement that boycotted goods made by enslaved people.

Eventually, anger at Ruggles's success boiled over. Someone broke into the store and "after taking $280, various articles, and destroying others, attempted to set the place on fire," according to a December 1829 report in the *New-York Spectator*.

A watchman was able to put out the fire, but the store was

destroyed. It was a setback for Ruggles—the journalist wrote that Ruggles's "prospects ha[d] been totally blighted"—but it was by no means his end. Dejected, Ruggles took a break from entrepreneurship and dove into the abolitionist movement. He worked as an agent, delivering speeches and organizing other abolitionists, for *The Emancipator*, an anti-slavery newspaper. It was a dangerous endeavor: traveling across the Northeast to meet with activists, publishers, and white people sympathetic to the abolitionist movement. There was joy and passion in Ruggles's work, sure, and he would need it to get through moments when his life and well-being were under attack. One night in January 1834, while traveling from New York City to Newark, New Jersey, a stagecoach driver wouldn't let Ruggles ride inside with the white passengers even though he'd bought a ticket like everyone else. Ruggles refused to ride outside in the cold like the driver ordered. The driver roughed him up before he and the white passengers banded together to push Ruggles out of the stagecoach and into the street. Ruggles had experienced similar violence before, but it hurt, nonetheless. Battered and angry, Ruggles could have turned around and gone home to lick his wounds. But he chose to continue, walking to Newark in the cold instead. This only made Ruggles even more passionate; though born a free man in the North, he felt an even deeper connection to Black people in the South.

After a year traveling as an activist, he was inspired to ditch the groceries and focus solely on literature for his next business venture, a bookstore. William Lloyd Garrison's *Liberator*, as well as *The Emancipator*, praised the new bookstore and publicized Ruggles's efforts in enough articles to draw both the curiosity of

New York's Black community and the ire of ardent racists. Slavery advocates immediately hated Ruggles, working to sully his name, and one even called his store an "incendiary depot" in an 1835 public notice, writing, "Let him be Lynched!" Ruggles's vision for America's first Black bookstore—whether he knew it was the first—is one still recognizable in bookstores today. That is, it was never *just* a bookstore. It was inherently a site that enunciated a pattern of Black activism and prioritized community. Understanding the scandal of a Black bookstore during the burgeoning abolitionist movement of the early 1800s means understanding the circumstances in which Black people lived at the time. Anti-literacy laws barred enslaved people from learning to read or write and made it a crime for people to teach them. Black people in the South were largely unable to travel, assemble in groups, or found churches, schools, or social groups. They could be jailed, beaten, branded, or killed for breaking any of the numerous restrictions implemented to enforce social control.

Reading, writing, loitering, "vagrancy," and showing public affection were among the long list of these regulations. Black people in Northern cities weren't allowed to use public libraries or participate in white-run literary activities—and risked their safety and freedom if they tried. This inequity would persist well into the twentieth century. In the North, where free Black people were somewhat active participants in American society, Black individuals largely lived in poverty, suffered severe illness, and had shorter life expectancies. They were also at near-constant risk of kidnappers like D. D. Nash. In the midst of all this: a Black bookstore. Historians say Ruggles's bookstore was likely a central location for the rising young Black people who graduated from the African Free School. Any educated Black person in New York City in the 1830s likely stopped at the store.

The space demanded that Black people gather, read, and learn—all acts that were still largely forbidden in many parts of the country and, therefore, inherently radical. The riots that Ruggles faced as he opened—and reopened—his store were by no means unusual. Simmering racial tensions caused New York to frequently erupt in violence, as leaders in the slave-owning South worked hard to squash abolitionism. Of course, literacy and the distribution of radical literature played a key role in the conflict. In 1835, then-President Andrew Jackson even banned the US Postal Service from delivering any pro-abolition publications in the South. Hatred of abolition stretched across racial lines, too. Just a few years earlier, in 1833, a white student was publicly whipped in Nashville, Tennessee, for simply having abolitionist writing with him as he traveled. Another white man, the abolitionist newspaper editor Elijah P. Lovejoy, was persecuted for his publication's writing in the early 1830s. A few years later, he would be murdered by a white mob in Alton, Illinois.

For Ruggles and those who fiercely opposed slavery, abolition was just as much about combating the institution through writing and speeches as it was helping enslaved people one by one. Abolitionists of the time understood that even the most peaceful antislavery efforts could lead to their deaths—even something as simple as selling abolitionist literature in a bookstore. Ruggles mainly sold abolitionist pamphlets and journals in the store, along with a sprinkling of books. He also sold stationery and paper supplies, and he bound books. Just a few steps from pamphlets by

Maria Stewart, a Black woman abolitionist and women's rights activist, visitors could find Lydia Maria Child's all-but-banned antislavery collection, *The Oasis*. The store had a printing press and Ruggles put it to use, publishing his own pamphlets about abolition. Black people who couldn't read or write would come into the store begging Ruggles to help them write letters and make sense of legal documents. Ruggles diligently pored over them. Some were wills from white people who left property to their Black servants, only to have family members try to cheat them out of it. This was the only place of its kind in New York. Just one year after he opened the bookstore, a mob of angry white people set his office, just feet away from his store, on fire. A week later, a racist mob camped outside the burned office for three nights to intimidate Ruggles and anyone looking to buy his books or seek his services. Local anti-abolitionist newspapers reported on the fire with articles full of joy and implied threats.

But none of this stopped Ruggles. He turned to *The Liberator*, writing a notice of his own. He condemned the attacks on his character and offered the public $50 for any information leading to a conviction of the person (or people) who set fire to his store and $25 to anyone who could name even one of the men who had gathered in the mob outside his office. These were bold words for a free Black man in a city crawling with white people happily plucking Black people off the street and shipping them into bondage. A few years later, in 1838, Ruggles expanded his store to include a reading room. Around the city, the numerous existing reading rooms only allowed white people and most catered to an all-male clientele. Ruggles's reading room existed alongside a string of literary societies that Black people founded in the 1800s as places for Black development and education, with some specifically dedicated to Black women. They were in direct opposition to major white societies, some even run by progressives, and libraries that shut Black people out. Ruggles openly complained about the segregation. Black people deserved "access to the principal daily and leading anti-slavery papers, and other popular periodicals of the day," he reasoned. And he was determined to provide them with just that.

That same year, he launched the *Mirror of Liberty*, the country's earliest Black magazine. The publication was devoted to reports on local anti-slavery work and what Ruggles termed "practical abolition," which called for the immediate aid and freedom of all enslaved people. He printed and sold the magazine out of his store and at other anti-slavery stores. It encompassed Ruggles's anti-slavery work, including poetry, essays championing women's rights, local news about the abolitionist movement, and reports from one of the many anti-slavery groups Ruggles worked with. Along with spreading anti-slavery writing, Ruggles made it his mission to protect Black people from kidnappers. Long before Malcolm X called for Black people to secure their freedom "by any means necessary," Ruggles was declaring Black people's right to use force for their protection and liberation.

"Whatever necessity requires, let that remedy be applied," he wrote in an 1836 report about a kidnapping. "Come what may, anything is better than slavery."

||| ▓▓▓▓▓▓ |||

As time has passed, we've learned about pillars of the abolitionist movement: the Frederick Douglasses, the Tappan brothers, the Harriet Tubmans. But Ruggles's contributions to the anti-slavery network are largely unknown to many. Before Tubman engineered her first rescue mission, and before Douglass made his daring escape from the shackles of slavery, Ruggles was considered the soul of the Underground Railroad. Ruggles chaired the New York Committee of Vigilance, a group of Black and white abolitionists started in 1835 to help escaped enslaved people through the city, by housing, clothing, and feeding them before using their contacts to send them to safety farther north. He was the most visible member of the committee, boldly publishing his address so any enslaved person in need, or their loved ones, could find him. His home became New York's central stop for the Underground Railroad. In its first year, Ruggles recorded, the committee helped some three hundred enslaved Africans get to freedom. Douglass was one of the many captives Ruggles sheltered and guided through the Underground Railroad. Douglass, then known as Frederick Bailey, made it to New York in September 1838 and was immediately whisked away to Ruggles's home. He lived with Ruggles for several days, and his then-fiancée Anna Murray soon joined him. In front of Ruggles, the famed Reverend James W. C. Pennington officiated Douglass and Murray's wedding. Secondhand accounts of Douglass's escape, and even his life after, rarely mention Ruggles. But Douglass did. He wrote in his autobiography, *My Bondage and My Freedom*, that he knew he was safe with Ruggles, whom he called the "first officer" of the Underground Railroad. Ruggles knew Douglass was a caulker. He arranged for Douglass and Murray to go to New Bedford, Massachusetts, where he could find work. Years after Ruggles's death—and after a very public and expensive libel suit led many of his fellow abolitionists to turn on him—Douglass spoke well of him.

"He was a whole-souled man, fully imbued with a love of his afflicted and hunted people, and took pleasure in being to me, as was his wont, 'Eyes to the blind and legs to the lame,'" Douglass wrote of Ruggles in 1855. Today, Ruggles is credited with helping approximately six hundred to more than a thousand enslaved Africans.

Little is known about Ruggles's bookstore, and what is known comes from advertisements in centuries-old newspapers and small lines in Ruggles's writing. His life was short but powerful. Although he has become something of a forgotten hero, with his name known among only a few, his legacy has lived on in the Black bookstores that have come after his. His influence is seen in the radical literature Black bibliophiles sell and in the community service that defines Black bookstores. When tracing the life and history of Black bookstores in the United States, all roads lead back to Ruggles. It's been almost two hundred years since Ruggles opened his little anti-slavery bookshop in Manhattan, but it hasn't ever really closed. It's existed over and over through the centuries in the Black bookshops that have dared to position themselves as radical spaces, ones dedicated to the uplift and liberation of Black people.

We likely wouldn't know much about his life had it not been for historians like Graham Hodges, who published the only full-length book about Ruggles's life, aptly titled *David Ruggles: A Radical Black Abolitionist and the Underground Railroad in New York City*; Dorothy Porter, the renowned librarian who uncovered the lost details of Ruggles's life in a journal article in 1943; journalist Abiola Sinclair; and the David Ruggles Center, founded in 2008. Without Hodges and Porter, and historians like those who founded the center, Ruggles's story would likely still live in obscurity.

||| ▬▬▬▬▬ |||

Ruggles's reading room was in good company alongside literary societies started by and for Black people. The first of these organizations was Philadelphia's Reading Room Society, created in 1828 for Black men in the city to rent books and read together. But the societies soon spread from Pittsburgh to New York, and they were among the earliest resources for Black people to collectively read, learn, and hone their leadership skills outside of school settings. These literary groups were the result of a period of self-actualization. They were short-lived, though—most lasted no more than twelve years. Before Ruggles, it was these literary societies and book collectors who met community needs for literature. Leading bibliophiles of the nineteenth century, who were usually wealthy and based in New York, Washington, DC, and Philadelphia, were friendly and collaborative, helping one another acquire periodicals, newspapers, pamphlets, and rare books about Black life that were at risk of being lost forever. Many of their massive collections ultimately ended up at major cultural centers, such as HBCUs like Howard University and Clark Atlanta University, as well as the Library of Congress. For example, William H. Dorsey, a wealthy Black Philadelphian, compiled four hundred scrapbooks about Black life. W. E. B. Du Bois would come to rely on Dorsey's scrapbook to write his groundbreaking sociological study, *The Philadelphia Negro*. Dorsey's collection now sits at the Cheyney University of Pennsylvania. Jesse E. Moorland, an esteemed minister from Ohio and early leader in the YMCA, gave his vast personal library to Howard University, forming the foundation for the school's Moorland-Spingarn Research Center. Perhaps most famous, Arturo Schomburg, an Afro–Puerto Rican historian and bibliophile, traveled the world collecting thousands of books that would seed the New York Public Library's Schomburg Center for Research in Black Culture.

Up until then, Black people able to read turned to Black newspapers and periodicals for essays, poems, and articles by Black writers. The country didn't see its first Black commercial book-publishing firm until John W. Leonard and Company of New York City opened in 1855. It ran for two years. Afterward, Thomas Hamilton Sr., who ran *The Anglo-African Magazine*, began publishing, and after his death, his son and brother continued his work, publishing a book by William Wells Brown. Ten years earlier, Brown had become the first Black American person to publish a novel. Black publishing was still new and very slow to advance as the 1800s ended and the twentieth century began. Black bookstores had a similar story. The early 1900s saw a handful of Black bookstores pop up across the country. Because these establishments were few and short-lived, most running only for a couple of years before going out of business, there aren't many historical records reflecting their existence. But, in Mississippi, a man named Granville Carter was proving Black bookselling wasn't a passing fad. By 1908, he'd outlasted a handful of booksellers in Greenville and his store was the sole Black bookstore for several surrounding counties. Booker T. Washington visited Carter's Book Store in 1908 and was astonished to find such a successful Black-owned business.

"Mr. Carter told me that at one time there had been as many

as five book-stores in the town, but he had succeeded, by close attention to business and offering his books at prices more favorable than his rivals, in outliving them all, until at the time I was there, his was the only book-store in the town," Washington wrote.

Carter was a beloved, trusted figure in the town, selling books, stationery, and even children's toys to patrons. He was known to always keep school supplies on hand at his shop so that community kids didn't go without during the school year. Black bookselling began to pick up steam as the twentieth century continued. Young's Book Exchange was perhaps the first massively successful Black bookstore in the United States. George Young, a former Pullman porter, opened the shop in Harlem in 1915. Young began collecting books during his time as a porter visiting "every important city in the United States, never failing to search through the principal bookstores for books concerning the Negro." In its first year of business, Young's Book Exchange, at 135 West 135th Street in central Harlem, was lauded as the "center of information of achievement in this city." There were pamphlets, postcards, and books by W. E. B. Du Bois, Harriet Tubman, famous Black intellectual Kelly Miller, Angelina Grimké, Booker T. Washington, Frederick Douglass, and others. Although he had numerous titles by Black people, Young was sure to include white authors as well—any literature was welcome, as long as it addressed race. The articles written about the Exchange, also called the "Young Book Emporium," marked the first time a Black bookshop received such public recognition and success.

Young was born in Virginia in 1869 and spent a large part of his life collecting books and pamphlets, buying them for as cheap as he could. He started the Exchange with just half a dozen books stacked on a single desk in the store. By 1921, the little shop, which journalists described as "dingy and drab, but atmospheric," had a half dozen desks and a handful of employees. Eventually, Young's Book Exchange stocked up to ten thousand titles by or about Black people and race, and Young described the shop as "the Mecca of Literature Pertaining to Colored People."

||| ▬▬▬▬▬▬▬ |||

One hundred years after Ruggles opened his shop, and shortly after Young's ascent and death, a man named Lewis Michaux would become the architect of modern Black bookselling. Michaux was the first Black person to have a lengthy and prominent career with a brick-and-mortar Black bookstore. He was the first bookseller of the twentieth century to boldly espouse pro-Black ideas and link his shop to a radical Black movement—the Black Nationalist movement. He opened his National Memorial African Book Store in 1933 after arriving in Harlem from Virginia in the early 1930s. He quickly went from selling books from a pushcart along 125th Street to becoming one of the most renowned Black booksellers in history. His charisma and zeal were always on display. He was usually seen in an oversized suit, a hat, and thick-rimmed glasses, with his small stature often overshadowed by his larger-than-life personality. In his early days as a bookseller, Michaux could be found selling periodicals to Harlemites with a bullhorn outside his shop. He'd sleep in the store's cellar and make about $1.25 a day. Once a deacon, Michaux drew on the charm he'd used on his congregation to attract Harlem's Black population. "I left the pulpit for the snake pit," he once said. He wasn't in the book business for money. Like Ruggles, Michaux saw education as the key to Black liberation and opened his store as a vehicle for that knowledge. And he wasn't shy about telling his thoughts on Black culture and advancement to anyone who would listen. One day, Michaux was manning the front desk of his shop when a group of Black boys came in with their fists in the air, yelling, "Black Power!"

"I said, 'Look, son, I'd like to straighten you out,'" he recalled in a 1973 interview. "I said, 'Black is beautiful, but Black isn't power. Knowledge is power! You can be Black as a crow, you can be white as snow, and if you don't know and ain't got no dough, you can't go! And that's fo' sho!'"

Lewis Michaux showing his wares
on 125th Street in Harlem in June 1943.

It was this personality and commitment to learning that helped catapult Michaux and his shop into national notoriety. A sign outside the bookstore read, "The House of Common Sense and Home of Proper Propaganda." Another read, "This House Is Packed with All the Facts About All the Blacks All Over the

World." Michaux was a proud Black Nationalist and Garveyite; in fact, he had a poster of Marcus Garvey hanging in the store alongside other Black leaders. He led a group called the African Nationalists in America to advocate for all the programs he thought would bring about Black advancement. The National Memorial African Book Store became the gathering place for Black Nationalists in Harlem. Nationalists including Malcolm X would deliver their impassioned speeches to crowds of people on the store's doorstep, which had been dubbed "Speakers' Corner." It wasn't just a place of activism, but one of joy. His customers included Eartha Kitt and Langston Hughes, who held autograph parties at the shop, as well as popular activists and scholars like W. E. B. Du Bois, who even met his wife Shirley Graham at the store. The bookshop was a welcome disruption of the anti-Black sentiments that ruled the country in the 1940s. Black Americans were still feeling the disproportionate effects of the Great Depression and were migrating from the South in droves to the North and West. Although Black Americans saw victories over discrimination in the military and with the NAACP's new legal defense fund, the decade did little for social advancement. Michaux's position as a Black bookseller was peculiar at a time when just 5 percent of Black men in the country did nonmanual, white-collar work, and 60 percent of working Black women were domestic servants.

Tension over an influx of Black people in the North erupted in a series of protests in the country in 1943. In New York, a Black woman's violent arrest prompted a rebellion that sent officers flooding into Harlem. Six Black people were killed, and hundreds were injured. Michaux kept his store open through it all and became something of a local leader championing Black causes—

from picketing to keep Black-owned businesses open to protesting the 16th Street Baptist Church bombing. He was eager to address the crowd alongside James Baldwin, Adam Clayton Powell, Dick Gregory, and several others at a 1963 rally sponsored by the Pan-African National Association in response to the bombing. A flyer circulated ahead of the event didn't mince words about the activists' intentions.

"The United States racial pot is boiling! White America's democracy, and Christianity is on trial. Is race hatred, white racism, brutality, murder, lynchings, bombings, rapings, all to go unpunished, forgotten, forgiven, or repaid? Compensated? Justified? Pres. Kennedy said nothing about the six children in Bombingham Alabama, which is an insult to 30 million Black people, but we will!"

When Michaux wasn't working at the bookshop, often lovingly called "Michaux's," he was leading groups of Black people down to the board of elections to register to vote, and telling reporters about the group's plan to open a Black-owned-and-operated bank and launch a political action committee to push for legislation that would help Black people in the city. "Now we are united in Harlem for the good of Harlem and those who love Harlem," he said of the group in 1962. Michaux enjoyed commercial success while positioning himself firmly against the status quo, and his store's influence extended far beyond Harlem. Families ordered books from Michaux's for relatives serving in World War II; universities and colleges ordered so many titles employees could barely keep up. (Decades later, owners of movement bookstores like Drum and Spear would buy titles from Michaux to stock their shelves.) He had set out to provide a resource for Black people to learn and "grow" and ended up doing much more, advancing the Black Nationalist movement, organizing Harlemites around political issues, modeling activist entrepreneurship, and proving to the country that Black people would buy and read books. The National Memorial African Book Store came to be a vital center for civil rights activists on the front lines of the fight for equality, in large part because of its dedicated, radical owner. Entering the 1960s, only a dozen Black bookstores existed in the US. But that number began to skyrocket by the end of the decade, with Michaux's at the center.

When FBI director J. Edgar Hoover launched his surveillance of Black bookstores three decades after Michaux opened his shop, it was no surprise that a spy reported Michaux to be "responsible for about 75 percent of the antiwhite material" distributed in Harlem. Michaux died of cancer in 1976 at the age of ninety-two, two years after closing his store in 1974. He opened his famous bookstore in the 1930s with just eight books and closed it forty-four years later with a reported two hundred thousand volumes. Decades after his death, booksellers would recall driving to New York to buy books from Michaux and sit at his feet for guidance and encouragement. Young activists who turned to bookselling during the Black Power and civil rights movements would rely on Michaux's wisdom. From there, they'd build out their own visions for activist bookselling. Michaux, born in 1884, came of age around the turn of the century, during a small but impactful proliferation of Black bookselling, publishing, and other literature-based advancements. His life was marked by a love for books and Black education that certainly didn't begin with him, but with the bibliophiles, activists, and booksellers who came before. Ruggles's shop is known to be the only Black bookstore to exist in the 1800s. But the early 1900s presented a picture of Black people's fortitude, with Young's Book Exchange and a sprinkling of Black bookshops without records or documents to prove their existence. The 1922 *Negro Year Book* listed "Books" among the two hundred businesses Black people were involved in by 1917. Though New York is the birthplace of Black bookselling and was the home of its most renowned early stores, there are traces of these literary epicenters throughout the nation. By the end of the 1940s, during Chicago's Black Renaissance, there were eleven bookstores in the city's Black Belt, according to the 1947 edition of *Scott's Blue Book*. Less than ten years earlier, in 1939, researchers wrote in *The Negro Year Book* that there were just fifteen bookstores of "Negro proprietorship" in all the country.

The increase in bookstores during the late '40s follows a familiar pattern: when Black writing is popular, so are Black bookstores. *Ebony* magazine's very first issue, in November 1945, had a hopeful headline about the state of Black literature: "Book Boom for Negro Authors."

Veteran writers like Arna Bontemps and Richard Wright were finally seeing large profits and recognition for their work. And publishers were dusting off forgotten manuscripts to get in on the popularity of "race books" that reached "book stores around the nation." One of the many prevailing truths about bookstores is their ability to build on one another's work and move the industry forward with new ideas. I liken the "Black book ecosystem," a term coined by Troy Johnson, creator of the African American Literature Book Club, to a tree in this way. There are branches and leaves of booksellers, writers, publishers, and more that all exist on a single root system grounded in a desire to educate at the very least and mobilize at most. The story of Michaux's National Memorial African Book Store began some thirty years before the United States would have its first Black bookstore boom in the 1960s and 1970s. Before radical bookstores of the mid-twentieth century began popping up en masse and overtly aiding resistance efforts, Michaux modeled a new form of entrepreneurship that brought communities and booksellers together in the fight for social advancement. His name would be remembered and respected among Black booksellers for generations to come.

CHAPTER TWO

A BOOKSTORE UNDER SIEGE

Judy Richardson (left) and Tony Gittens
(right) ran the newly opened Drum and
Spear Bookstore in August 1968.

CHARLIE COBB THOUGHT ABOUT BLACK STRUGGLE AS HE
drifted down Africa's west coast in 1967. He and Courtland Cox,
a fellow activist, spent the summer traveling through Guinea, Liberia, Ivory Coast (now Côte d'Ivoire), and more. Cobb connected
what was happening back home in the United States—the protests, the sit-ins, the police dogs sicced on protesters—to the fights
for liberation and independence happening throughout Africa.

Before he and Cox headed back to continue their own work in the Black Power movement, they decided to stop in Paris and visit the Présence Africaine, a small African bookstore in the heart of the city's Latin Quarter. Visiting the shop was a no-brainer for a young, Black activist like Cobb. After all, the bookstore, founded by Senegalese writer Alioune Diop, was the unofficial headquarters of the Négritude movement. The little shop, filled with works by Black writers, intellectuals, and artists, ignited a fire in Cobb. The books about Black struggle lining the Présence Africaine's shelves, the artists hanging out in the store, and the political figures going to and from the bookshop all intrigued Cobb. Surely, he thought, he and his fellow activists could replicate such a place in the United States. The idea for Drum and Spear was born.

A Black-owned and Black-centered bookstore in Washington's Columbia Heights neighborhood seemed like a natural progression for Cobb. He'd spent years organizing with the Student Nonviolent Coordinating Committee (SNCC), a direct-action civil rights group largely made up of Black college students, including famed organizer Stokely Carmichael (later Kwame Ture) and Congressman John Lewis. The organization began as the student arm of the civil rights movement in the early '60s and took on a more militant position alongside the Black Power movement as the decade went on. Cobb was among the scores of young, Black students in the South who staged sit-ins and led massive voter registration campaigns. Ever the visionary, Cobb was the one who came up with the idea to establish the historic Freedom Schools of 1964. Cobb wanted to interrupt what he called the "sharecropper education" most Black children were getting, a substandard education system with a poor curriculum and underprepared teachers, all in run-down buildings. Thousands of Black students in Mississippi participated in the summer programs, learning about Black history, civil rights, and leadership. With these Freedom Schools, Cobb cemented his passion for Black-centered education in just two years after joining SNCC as a nineteen-year-old. It was this focus on education and Black consciousness, the overall awareness of and concern about Black struggle and oppression, that set the stage for Drum and Spear.

By 1967, Cobb and many of his peers had left SNCC, and Cobb returned to Washington from the South with all he'd learned from the organization—and a new dream. And he wanted to bring his friends along with him in this new venture. He enlisted the help of fellow SNCC veterans Judy Richardson, Cox, Jennifer Lawson, and Curtis Hayes to create a bookstore. With some seed money from the United Church of Christ's Commission for Racial Justice, which his father led, Cobb and his comrades created a nonprofit foundation called Afro-American Resources, Inc. (AAR), to govern all the projects, like Drum and Spear, that he had in mind. Then he found a run-down building in a Black neighborhood, just a few blocks from Howard University, to set up shop. His goal for Drum and Spear was simple: to create a haven for Black people to read books by and about Black people from all over the world.

"What we were about was Black consciousness, and we didn't feel that that was limited to the United States," Cobb said of the group he'd assembled. This Pan-Africanism was reflected in everything from the store's inventory to its name. The drum in Drum and Spear represented a way of communicating information, while the spear symbolized using any tactics and tools necessary for liberation.

The group's mission for the store reflected a national shift among young radicals. Black communities were breaking away from a US-centered view of the world and instead championing a revolution that included Black communities globally. In the '60s, people came to understand that Black oppression in the US was linked to imperialism, colonialism, caste systems, and other injustices against Black and non-Black people everywhere. The Drum and Spear activists were constantly expanding their own politics. They leaned into their Pan-African ideology and promoted the philosophy that Black struggle wasn't confined to America—that it was vital to seek liberation for African communities around the world. They made this clear to customers in word and deed, draping a sign that read, "Africans Home and Abroad," from a wall inside the store. Black Power activists embraced communist Mao Tse-tung's stance that the racially subjugated people of the world should unite against the imperialism wielded by Western countries. This anti-colonial, anti-oppression position appealed to Black people who were already developing similar politics. They were some of the biggest buyers and peddlers of Mao's *Little Red Book*, a collection of his statements and speeches. In 1967, SNCC condemned Zionism in its newsletter and linked Black American oppression to the Palestinian struggle. This was a historic departure from the pro-Israel stance traditional Black leaders had taken in the generations before. This international framework, or internationalism, was important to the Drum and Spear crew, with the activists selling materials—African-liberation based, communist, socialist, Marxist, and more—that communicated ideas that they felt were necessary for Black liberation and freedom for oppressed people everywhere.

◼◼◼▭▭▭▭▭◼◼◼

Columbia Heights was a risky place to start a business. After white flight in the '40s and '50s, Black people transformed the area into a Black business district, with jazz clubs, restaurants, and other businesses, by the 1960s. But this self-determination was no match for the urban renewal, unaffordable and poor housing conditions, underfunded schools, and more that ravaged the neighborhood's Black population. It was only a matter of time before the simmering tensions over years of neglect and injustice reached a boiling point, and Martin Luther King Jr.'s assassination on April 4, 1968, tipped the cauldron over. In just a few days, protests left hundreds of businesses and homes along the Fourteenth Street corridor damaged or destroyed. In the months that followed, businesses that couldn't recover closed for good. The planned site for Drum and Spear, which Cobb had leased that March, sat just blocks away from the epicenter of the rebellion. Risky? Yes. But Columbia Heights was perfect for the activists' vision. It was important to the group of young organizers to make sure the bookstore was in the heart of a Black neighborhood, specifically in a working-class area where people of all classes and with all levels of education could come and feel welcome. While the struggling Columbia Heights may have not been the ideal place for a new business, it was the perfect spot to establish a community hub for Black awareness. It wasn't hard for Cobb to rally his SNCC friends to join such a project. Richardson was immediately in. She'd left SNCC in 1966 and gone back to college but missed organizing with her friends. She and Hayes loaded up a car, put her mattress on top, and moved her from New York to Washington in May 1968. Cobb had tapped Richardson and Tony Gittens to get the business going. He trusted them. Gittens hadn't been a part of SNCC, but he was no stranger to organizing. Just a few months before becoming the manager of Drum and Spear, Gittens had been a major student leader at Howard University, helping to organize the takeover of the school's administration building alongside about a thousand other students.

The March 1968 sit-in was one of several takeovers happening throughout the US as part of the Black Campus Movement. The movement arguably began in 1965 and continued to ramp up as the decade went on. Black students led protests, sit-ins, occupations, sieges, and other demonstrations to push their respective colleges and universities to implement courses and programs that focused on Black life, history, and struggle. They also demanded more Black student enrollment and diverse faculty. By the end of the '60s, nearly a thousand schools had organized Black studies courses, programs, or departments. Gittens and Adrienne Manns Israel led students in a sit-in that would turn into a days-long takeover and briefly shut down Howard University. Among several demands, Gittens and the protesters wanted to see changes in student discipline, as well as Black history and struggle reflected in the university curriculum, which didn't even have a Black history course at the time. And they wanted to be able to play jazz in the fine arts building—not be restricted to European classical music. This moved protesters to declare, despite the school's majority-Black student body, "Howard is not a Black university."

Gittens didn't know much about managing a bookstore, but he

was passionate about education, and Cobb's vision for the store intrigued him. One night, the pair sat in Cobb's apartment and Cobb told Gittens all about his hopes for Drum and Spear, while mentioning that the shop still needed a manager. Gittens, with no plans after graduating from Howard, said he'd do it. Cobb tossed him the keys to the store, and Gittens knew he had his work cut out for him. He and Richardson didn't have much time to get the store ready to open by June 1968. And there was a lot to be done. When Richardson first saw the shop that May, there were a few stained bookshelves, certainly not enough to hold more than a few titles. The shop needed a good cleaning, bookshelves, and, most important, books. Gittens had some accounting experience from his time working as a bank teller in New York, and Richardson had experience as an office administrator, but they both knew they'd have to learn the bookselling business as they went along. They were opening the shop in the Black business district at a time when DC, much like the rest of the country, was still reeling from Martin Luther King Jr.'s assassination. Black residents would clash with police in sporadic protests in the months after his death. Richardson and Gittens caught the tail end of one of these disturbances as they made their way to the shop at 2701 Fourteenth Street Northwest for the first time that May. "They had just tear-gassed Fourteenth Street," Richardson recalled. "I'm walking through tear gas, I'm barely able to breathe, and I go to meet Gittens."

They weren't fazed. The pair got straight to work, collecting books, contacting publishers, and buying titles from a wholesale distributor called Bookazine. The activists wanted Drum and Spear to house a wide range of titles by Black authors. They sought books on Black history and revolution most but picked up a few popular titles like *Pimp* by Iceberg Slim. Richardson and Gittens rented a Volkswagen and drove from Washington to New York to meet with a Bookazine staffer. They walked into the office with a list of books they hoped to buy in bulk, titles on the African diaspora and Black history, culture, and politics. They were pleased to see a Black man at the Bookazine office.

"He was so happy to see we were two young Black people who were doing this bookstore in DC," Richardson recalled. The employee was excited to help, offering backlist books, even Black children's books, and giving the pair free rein over the distributor's inventory. There were titles that major publishers scoffed at and general booksellers wouldn't even consider selling, like C. L. R. James's 1939 book *A History of Pan-African Revolt*, *Great Slave Narratives* by Arna Bontemps, and Zora Neale Hurston's *Their Eyes Were Watching God*. It was music to Gittens and Richardson's ears. They left the city with the Volkswagen van filled from floor to ceiling with books. Despite having little experience, the small team managed to transform the damaged shop into a bona fide bookstore in a matter of weeks. They finished building and staining bookshelves and the shop opened to the public on June 1. By the summer, Drum and Spear had about five thousand volumes in the store. The inventory reflected the activists' commitment to serving the Black community. They stocked books that Black locals could buy and learn from but didn't shy away from popular titles that served solely as a source of entertainment. Just a few shelves over from Iceberg Slim, customers could find Frantz Fanon's *The Wretched of the Earth* and *Enemy of the Sun*, an anthology of Palestinian poetry. This surely set Drum and Spear apart from white-run bookshops that sold books of all genres by white authors and general titles, but seldom anything that reflected radical leftist politics or the experiences of people of color. But it didn't come without controversy. Everybody had an opinion about the store. Members of the Black Panther Party thought Chairman Mao Tse-tung's *Little Red Book* should be front and center in the shop, rather than off to the side. Others objected to the shop carrying books like Chester Himes's Harlem detective series. Cobb had to put his foot down.

"What's the point of having a Black bookstore if you're going to now start to decide who's too Black or not Black enough to be in the shop," he said.

Catering to the diverse tastes of Black communities proved to be the right call. Drum and Spear was an immediate success, and Black Washingtonians could feel the intentionality. Locals came in to read books they'd never heard of, universities and public-school teachers placed large orders, and Black authors found, in Drum and Spear, the perfect shop to talk about their writing. Titles like *The Autobiography of Malcolm X* and *100 Amazing Facts About the Negro with Complete Proof* by J. A. Rogers, as well as children's books like Lucille Clifton's Everett Anderson series and *A Is for Africa* by Jean Carey Bond flew off the shelves. Customers walking into Drum and Spear, including locals who hadn't been interested in politics, got their first taste of radical Black discourse. Inside, people young and old had casual conversations about current events and politics. It was common to see Shirley Graham Du Bois perusing the shelves in a pair of white patent leather boots, Tanzanian leaders thumbing through radical books, or Toni Morrison checking out the fiction section. The activist entrepreneurs lined the walls with posters of Carmichael, SNCC activist H. Rap Brown, Huey P. Newton, and Argentine revolutionary Che Guevara. Everyone from students and activists to local drug dealers turned to Drum and Spear staff as guides along their political education journeys. "What was amazing was that you could see folks readily change," Richardson said. Customers would go from "light" reading to more serious titles. People who had spent time in prison and adults with sixth-grade educations were transforming: reading with ease and learning more about Black history and oppressive systems in the process.

Book parties at Drum and Spear were lively community events. Gwendolyn Brooks and Eloise Greenfield were among countless Black authors who held talks at the store. Greenfield, later a legendary children's book author with dozens of popular titles under her belt, published her very first book with Drum and Spear Press, and in 1972, Drum and Spear's shelves would be the first place she saw one of her titles. Greenfield rushed down to the store with her children and looked incredulously at the dozens of copies of *Bubbles*, a story about a little Black boy learning to read, on the store's shelves. A few days later, she read the story to a bunch of bubbly Black children and their parents. The little ones piled into the store and sat cross-legged and hung on Greenfield's words. She was animated and passionate as she delivered each line, grinning and waving her hands. The children giggled and laughed and left clutching their own copies of the book. It is these types of stories that would come to define Drum and Spear, with its commitment to authors and community. It didn't take long for the store to develop its reputation. In just the first year, what Richardson and Gittens struggled to set up was off to a great start and growing. So much so that they brought in more help, including Daphne Muse, a twenty-three-year-old public school teacher who'd first visited Drum and Spear to buy books for her young Black students.

Drum and Spear's influence was felt throughout the city. "It was doing exactly what we wanted it to do," Gittens said of the store. The young organizers decided to expand. They brought in Juadine Henderson, another SNCC organizer who was fresh off of participating in the Poor People's Campaign.

It was the city's turmoil in the late '60s that attracted Black Washingtonians to the store. Drum and Spear became the perfect place for people to learn about the racial dynamics that colored their everyday lives and the Black political movements working against inequity. Through the store, the activists hosted book exhibits at conferences for Black educators. Founding Drum and Spear Press was an obvious next step in the activists' education-for-liberation strategy. Cobb, Cox, and the rest of the AAR team wanted a hand in creating Black books instead of just selling them. The first book released under the press was its raison d'être: a revised edition of C. L. R. James's classic *A History of Pan-African Revolt*. The group even hosted a pair of weekly radio programs: *Sauti*, a news program for general audiences, and a storytelling hour for children called *Saa Ya Watoto*. The host of the children's show even visited DC classrooms in traditional African dress and read from Black children's books.

The Drum and Spear institution was growing. Alongside the store and press, the activists joined with other local Black community organizers to open the Center for Black Education in the fall of 1969 to offer the city a Pan-African political education and training in technical skills. The center would serve as a place where organizers could equip Black people with the practical skills and historical knowledge necessary to combat white supremacy. The joy of Drum and Spear's successful first year was short-lived. Not long after it opened, Drum and Spear was caught in the middle of one of the many clashes between locals, police, and the National Guard after King's death. Once, troops lined the sidewalk while Gittens tried to make his way into the store. That's when a trooper shot a canister of tear gas directly at him. It missed Gittens but crashed into the store, spreading tear gas that choked Richardson, Gittens, and the store's customers. Drum and Spear was closed for days afterward. It was the closest Gittens had come to being killed. The shop was situated just a few blocks from the FBI headquarters. And although the activists had left SNCC behind, the familiar brushes with law enforcement weren't a problem of the past.

The shop's affiliation with SNCC was enough to make it an unlikely enemy of the US government. And the FBI agents' job was simple: prove Drum and Spear was a threat to national security. The bookshop was under fire months before federal law enforcement expanded its surveillance of Black Power groups to Black bookstores nationwide. In October 1968, FBI director Hoover issued a memo ordering Bureau offices to turn their attention to an especially menacing threat to the status quo: Black-owned bookshops, or "Black extremist bookstores," as he called them. To Hoover, these shops were "propaganda outlets for revolutionary and hate publications" and served as "cultural centers for extremism." Hoover became suspicious of Black-owned bookshops as he worked to quell Black Power efforts through COINTELPRO, a series of covert and sometimes illegal operations to disrupt and destroy political organizations. Black bookstores from New York to California were subject to these operations, but the attack on Drum and Spear was the most severe. One time, Richardson was manning the store when a pair of FBI agents waltzed inside. The shop didn't get many white customers, and thanks to her time in SNCC, Richardson knew how to spot law enforcement.

"They always looked the same," Richardson recalled. "Very buttoned up, standard-issue shoes. They were buying up Mao's [*Little*] *Red Book* and all of the revolutionary literature . . . to 'prove' the case that we were left-wing and to minimize any support we might have in the public sphere. It was an attempt to smear us."

A trio of customers talk inside Drum and Spear Bookstore.

Federal agents had been spying on the shop from the beginning, when they learned that Carmichael visited the store in early June. Agents had strict orders to learn everything they could about Drum and Spear: what kind of books were sold and any political connections its workers had. They spoke with staffers and even dove into the store's business documents, including its application to rent the space. By mid-July, a little more than a month after Drum and Spear opened, the FBI had sent at least three agents to the store to pose as customers. While the bookstore wasn't a front for any militant political group, it did support national radical movements. After all, part of the shop's purpose was to educate and spur Black people to action. As they continued advocating for Black history courses at the university, Howard students were at Drum and Spear from the moment the store opened to the moment it closed buying books for classes. Black students often turned to Black bookstores like Drum and Spear to supplement their formal education through the shops' community programs, educational events, and author talks. These informal lessons, or "dual degrees," meant that Black people found in local Black bookstores the culturally relevant instruction and education they weren't getting from formal higher education. And Drum and Spear was in perfect reach for Howard students, as the university was just a few blocks away from the store. With students visiting, books to sell, and events to put on, the activist entrepreneurs had far too much to do to let the FBI's espionage distract them. They were used to the surveillance and lived with a general awareness that the FBI was watching. This was the case for most Black bookstore owners with connections to political organizations. At a time when Black political groups were using everything from marches to occupations to advocate for equity, targeting from federal and local law enforcement and local racist groups was par for the course. But the team behind Drum and Spear wouldn't learn the extent of the federal surveillance until decades later, when historians uncovered FBI files related to the targeted shops. At the time, all they had to confirm their suspicions of surveillance was their run-ins with agents and local police. Muse worked long hours at Drum and Spear and didn't get home until after dark. One evening, a pair of agents trailed alongside her in a car as she walked to her apartment nearby the bookshop. The car paced slowly beside her. She would take two steps and stop; the driver would move along slowly before stopping, too. Agents following her home was a common occurrence, as were their visits to the store. They'd fling books from the shelves, remarking, "I read that. That ain't shit!"

They were even bold enough to knock on Muse's front door. One day, as Muse was leaving her apartment, she opened the door and saw a pair of agents standing there. "They didn't even get to speak 'good morning'! I slammed that door so hard!" she recalled. But they were persistent. They knocked and knocked for about an hour before slipping a note under her door asking her to call them. She never did.

The FBI went to great lengths to confirm their suspicions that Drum and Spear wasn't really about bookselling but rather a headquarters for Black Power and communist organizations. A supervisor ordered one agent to go to the store to buy a copy of *Little Red Book* to prove the shop was part of a "Communist conspiracy." When the agent went and learned the title had sold out, he went to Brentano's, a popular bookstore chain, and bought the book there. He passed it off as a Drum and Spear purchase to please the supervisor. Agents even lured customers into their investigations, asking them questions about the store. Early on, the agents relied on a Black painter who visited Drum and Spear every day and told them that there were never political meetings or gatherings at the store. With the FBI already on their back, it didn't help that Drum and Spear brought in Ralph Featherstone to replace Gittens as the store's manager in 1969. Agents immediately flagged Featherstone's involvement in the shop when he joined, making sure to document how often they saw him at Drum and Spear and any grants he received to support the store. Featherstone had joined SNCC in the mid-'60s after working as a speech therapist for Black children. He dove headfirst into activism with SNCC, teaching at its Freedom Schools, helping to lead voter drives, and participating in the Selma-to-Montgomery marches — and spending over a week in jail for it. He was more activist than bookseller, though, so he joined Drum and Spear with a single piece of advice for the team: "Never talk to the FBI."

Featherstone's death only increased the government's ire against Drum and Spear.

On a Monday night in March 1970, Featherstone was riding in a 1964 Dodge Dart through Bel Air, Maryland, with fellow SNCC alum William "Che" Payne when a bomb went off in the car, killing them both. They were driving near the courthouse where their friend, SNCC leader H. Rap Brown, was to be tried on riot charges. The explosion was immediately shrouded in suspicion. Authorities told the public the pair was likely transporting the bomb, but Black activists said the explosive was planted to kill Brown. News articles about the explosion painted Featherstone as a "bitter" civil rights activist fed up with white people and cast doubt on claims that law enforcement or racist vigilantes may have planted the bomb in the car. The Drum and Spear team took the death hard. For Muse, who had worked closely with Featherstone in the store, his death turned her world upside down. She spent months operating in a state of dazed confusion as she worked to heal from the loss. She ended up leaving Drum and Spear in the year after Featherstone's death. The explosion led to heightened surveillance of the store. Federal agents knew Featherstone had spent the last year of his life as Drum and Spear's manager. What started with agents posing as customers escalated to their visiting Richardson's home and pressuring her to give them information about Featherstone. She refused to tell them anything and sent them on their way. Protecting the store became a full-time job as COINTELPRO waged on and Featherstone's death drew even more attention to Drum and Spear. The store was burglarized at least twice and set on fire once. Muse recalled a fire marshal coming to the store and telling the staff it looked like arson. The group decided to get a guard dog. "Those were the lengths we went to protect that store because it was about more than a business," Muse said. "It was about a community, and people who had never in their lives read a book came into Drum and Spear and bought a book, read the book, and came back and talked to us about what they read! We had to protect that."

The activists never found out who broke into the store or started the fire, but they suspected that the FBI sent people to do the dirty work the agency couldn't do themselves.

The Drum and Spear activists weren't deterred by misfortune. Despite Featherstone's death, break-ins, and constant threats from law enforcement, the early '70s was a time of accomplishment for the shop. The booksellers had established Drum and Spear as an important fixture in DC's Black communities and a vital resource for Black liberation in the Western world. By the time Drum and Spear published its third catalog, it had reached about 233 pages and boasted about ten thousand titles, which, although they carried much less than major white booksellers in the area, was impressive for such a young, dissident, Black bookstore.

Richardson led the charge to beef up the store's children's section and connect with Black kids in DC. Drum and Spear Press published workbooks and storybooks for Black children and their families in the early '70s. The government had shown a greater investment in education with the Elementary and Secondary Education Act in 1965. This incentivized schools to prioritize literature and other educational materials that focused on the experiences of Black and Latino children. It was a golden opportunity for publishers like Doubleday, Macmillan, T. Y. Crowell, and Whitman Publishing, which published more and more books with Black characters through the 1960s to meet the rising demand. This was Richardson's passion. The radical movements, the Black consciousness, sweeping the country couldn't pass over little Black children. Richardson saw educating and appealing to the youth as equally important as all of Drum and Spear's other community efforts.

It was Richardson who opened Drum and Spear's short-lived second location, in the Health, Education, and Welfare building, called Maelezo, Swahili for "information." Black HEW employees had fallen in love with Drum and Spear, buying books and Christmas gifts there and spreading the word about the Black-centered bookshop. So, they advocated for a second Drum and Spear location in the building. Despite their successes, Drum and Spear members were consistently confronted with the racial disparities they worked to eradicate. One day, a salesman from children's book behemoth Scholastic visited the store to show his children's book catalog. But when Richardson suggested Anne Norris Baldwin's *Sunflowers for Tina*, a story about a young Black girl who explores her love for flowers in New York City, the salesman replied with disgust, "Oh, I didn't know this was a Black bookstore." He left and returned shortly after with a different catalog, of Black children's books, which he evidently didn't share with "white" stores.

The activists were doing everything they set out to do in the community and more. Drum and Spear Press was gaining traction as a serious publisher and the Center for Black Education was becoming an important training institution for the community. The idea for the center came after Cobb, Cox, and other activists like James Garrett and Geri Augusto grew frustrated with working at the local Federal City College, an urban land-grant school created through the District of Columbia Public Education Act of 1966.

The aims of Federal City College were noble: to serve as a higher education option for poor Black people with high school educations or GEDs. Several Drum and Spear and SNCC members were tapped to teach Black-centered courses at the school. But the activist teachers couldn't provide the radical Black education they wanted at a federally funded institution. They didn't want to settle for simply teaching Black Washingtonians Langston Hughes literature; they wanted to ensure Black people would get an education that empowered them to join the fight for liberation in one way or another. The teachers sought more power in the school to create a Black education program that would equip students to use their education for "the redemption and vindication of the race." Higher-ups at the college weren't having it. So the activists decided to create a "black-financed and black-operated" university of their own in the Center for Black Education. It would become the formal educational arm of Drum and Spear, as many bookstore workers contributed to the center in some capacity. The activists and booksellers taught classes on Black history, Pan-Africanism, politics, journalism, law, and more. At the center, Black people from any background could get an education that disrupted the subtle and overt racism of the traditional school system. The activists tied the community and the center together through services and programs like a free clinic. Drum and Spear staffers were developing relationships with schools and universities throughout the country through the Center for Black Education. To this end, Cobb frequently visited Malcolm X Liberation University in North Carolina and built a relationship with Owusu Sadauki (then Howard Fuller), a SNCC associate who led the school. Owusu would visit the center and Drum and Spear as well; the institutions quickly became united in their efforts to educate Black communities.

"We realize that there is no Black education in a white financed institution," Douglass Jones, the director of operations for the center, said just before the school opened. The activists believed in the project so much that they volunteered 10 percent of their incomes to run the school. This center was part of the "Drum and Spear Complex," a strategic plan to build Black institutions that would support and sustain Black communities. Drum and Spear was more than a community and resource center; it actively supported national political groups working for Black people. The booksellers didn't overtly recruit customers into radical organizations at the store, but they made sure to stock leaflets from local political groups advertising their events, meetings, and protests—called leafing. Radical groups, like the Black Panthers, would even go to Drum and Spear to tell customers about their work. There were few rules barring who could "leaf" at the store, but the booksellers wouldn't stock leaflets they believed were "antithetical to what [they] felt was the progress for the community," Richardson said.

Drum and Spear members consistently attended protests and even organized demonstrations of their own to bring attention to the armed struggle in South Africa, anti-colonial efforts in Guyana, US interference in Chile, and opposition to the Vietnam War. Cobb, Lawson, and Cox were back and forth to Tanzania in East Africa, developing relationships with officials in President Julius Nyerere's government. The Drum and Spear organizers wanted to replicate their press in Tanzania. Lawson and Cobb learned Kiswahili and set up a branch of the press in Dar es Salaam. This was part of the Pan-African vision, and the activists adopted the Tanzanian concept of ujamaa, an African socialist ideology articulated by Nyerere that prioritized kinship and communal liberation and rejected capitalism and Western forms of socialism. They believed this ideology could be vital to global Pan-African unity. With that, Drum and Spear activists were on board when Malcolm X Liberation University, along with the Student Organization for Black Unity (SOBU), developed African Liberation Day.

On May 27, 1972, thousands of demonstrators flocked to Washington, DC. They gathered at Malcolm X Park and marched down

Sixteenth Street NW to the foot of the Washington Monument. They gathered outside the Rhodesian Information Office, the South African embassy, and the US State Department with signs that read "Africa For The Africans," "Africa Belongs to Africa Not Portugal," and "Bros. And Sis. In Southern Africa, You Have The Support Of Bros. And Sis. In America." The first African Liberation Day was a mass expression of solidarity, intended to garner support for African liberation globally. It also served as a tribute to Kwame Nkrumah, the former prime minister and president of Ghana who led the Gold Coast's independence movement. Along with Owusu, Angela Davis, Haki Madhubuti (then Don L. Lee), Reverend Ralph David Abernathy, and Amiri Baraka were among the figures who spoke at the massive event. Thousands more gathered at events around the world. It was the culmination of a series of activities and marches held throughout the country beginning on May 25. Today, some fifty years later, people of African descent around the world continue to celebrate African Liberation Day, also called Africa Day or African Freedom Day.

Drum and Spear's success couldn't last forever. Not without the passion for literature brought on by the Black Power movement, and certainly not without the loyalty of patrons who had no money to spend on books. When the '60s ended, the allure of Black liberation movements began to die down. The Black Panther Party was bogged down by attacks from law enforcement and consumed by legal troubles, and SNCC was rapidly losing supporters; many of the militant groups that had gained popularity in the '60s had been dismantled or were in decline by the mid-'70s. Black bookstores felt the effects of this downturn. Any activist booksellers had a decision to make: expand their inventory and compromise the store's political position, or stay true to their convictions and risk the shop's success. The activists behind Drum and Spear chose to close the radical shop rather than give in to the pressure to sell mainly general titles—mainstream bestsellers—and significantly cut down their books on Black history and revolution to make a profit. One board member told the *Washington Afro American* in 1974, the year it closed, "Drum and Spear can survive if it foregoes the political aspect and concentrates on books and materials that are of interest to Black people in light of what is happening today."

The context of the shop changed, too. Thanks to urban renewal and a struggling economy, much of the Columbia Heights neighborhood was in shambles after the 1968 protests over King's assassination. By the mid-'70s, the Fourteenth Street corridor in Washington, DC, was no longer the main drag it had been the decade before. It wasn't just a lack of business prowess that led to the shop's demise. Big bookstore chains saw the appeal of shops like Drum and Spear and began stocking the Black-centered titles that Black people could, at one time, only find at Black-owned bookstores.

"They were also discounting in a way we couldn't afford to do because they're a big chain," Richardson said. "They may not carry the *African Writers Series*, but they carried some of the more popular books at Brentano's because they now know there's an audience for those books. Drum and Spear showed them that." The Black Student Movement, which provided an institutional market for Black bookstores, had gone into decline, too. In 1972, Black studies programs at public institutions suffered under budget and student aid cuts. This served as another financial blow to Drum and Spear, which had already begun losing Howard University's support because of attacks from the FBI and police. University officials warned students to stay away from the embattled bookshop. Even at Maelezo, Richardson saw sales slow rapidly. The pattern followed at Drum and Spear, with the activists constantly confronted by the pressure to sell more of apolitical, entertaining books about pimps and tricks and less of the radical titles they were passionate about selling. They refused. The salacious, popular books were meant to be tangential in Drum and Spear, not the bulk of the store's inventory. Both stores began relying on jewelry, clothing, and children's book sales to make ends meet. That, to them, was better than selling books that they believed crippled Black communities instead of nurturing them. Between refusing to carry popular books and overstocking political books that were no longer selling, Drum and Spear's profits dwindled so much the activists could barely make the store's rent.

Meanwhile, the Internal Revenue Service had a hand in repressing Black bookstores. The IRS repeatedly investigated Drum and Spear for failing to pay its withholding tax. But it's impossible to tell which investigations were genuine and which were simply attempts to shut the shop down. Richardson suspected that the IRS was working to sabotage Drum and Spear, even going so far as to send people to infiltrate the shop as employees and involve the store in illegal tax activities. This wasn't simply paranoia. Activist booksellers had good reason to suspect the IRS was targeting them. In 1974, the nation learned that President Nixon appointed a special unit in the IRS to investigate at least ninety-nine organizations labeled "ideological, militant, subversive, or radical organizations." The unit existed from 1969 to 1973 and targeted groups like SNCC and the Black Panther Party for potential tax audits and collections. Because Drum and Spear had been hampered by repression everywhere from finance to law enforcement, it was only a matter of time before the store shuttered. Drum and Spear was evicted from the building in 1974 after failing to pay rent. One day the store was running—just barely—and the next, people were rescuing its discarded books scattered across the street. In a 1974 article in the *Washington Afro American*, Drum and Spear staffers lamented the numerous cost-cutting measures—everything from doing the store's cleaning themselves to slashing staff salaries—as they struggled to stay afloat. They admitted then that the activists simply "tried to do too much."

"We didn't run it very well as a business," Cobb said. "It was a movement bookstore."

There was constant tension between the demands of the book market and the activists' personal politics. This was a common problem for booksellers who'd opened stores at the height of the Black Power movement. Drum and Spear faltered under the weight of economic hardship, repression, and the activists simply spreading themselves too thin. But it remains one of the most important and influential bookstores of the period. Drum and Spear gave authors their first breaks, introduced Black children to more books about themselves and other people of color, and exposed the city to radical ideas that changed the store's patrons forever. The booksellers laid out these accomplishments, their failures, and their hopes for the future in a statement about the store's closure.

"We hope that, if nothing else, Drum and Spear Bookstore has provided the kind of involved community store on whose foundation future Black-oriented stores can build with success," they wrote. Although DC wouldn't see another Black bookstore like Drum and Spear for several years, Black communities in the Northeast could get their fill of Black books and culture from shops in nearby cities. Una Mulzac's Liberation in Harlem and Dawud Hakim's bookstore in Philadelphia weathered the storm that Drum and Spear fell victim to. But not without struggles of their own.

CHAPTER THREE

LIBERATION COULD GET YOU IN TROUBLE

Una Mulzac (right) with a customer at
the Liberation Bookstore in 1967.

"WHAT ARE YOU TRYING TO LIBERATE?" THE CLERK ASKED
Una Mulzac. It was less of a question and more of a rejection. Mulzac rolled her eyes and shook her head. She'd lost count of how

many phone calls she'd made to large publishing firms like this one, trying to order books for her new store in Harlem. She was in her forties when she opened Liberation, with more experience in bookselling, political organizing, and evading law enforcement than Drum and Spear's young, green radicals. Mulzac had seen more than her fair share of targeting and ridicule from critics. She was used to the sarcasm and concerned questions over the name of her bookstore, Liberation.

The shop was a dusty hole in the wall on Lenox Avenue and 131st Street, just a few blocks from the Apollo Theater and in the same area where George Young once ran his book exchange. It was the end of the 1960s. The Black Power movement was underway and young activists and organizers were opposing the Vietnam War with all kinds of rallies and demonstrations. To Mulzac, these were the perfect circumstances for a revolutionary bookstore. But others didn't quite see her vision. People told her "Liberation" would only invite trouble, and maybe she should name the store after her father or simply call it "Bookstore" instead. But the name held a special meaning to her. More and more African countries were gaining or fighting for their independence at the time, so Mulzac chose the name to support the liberation movements happening all around her.

She knew the store would court controversy and she knew the FBI might even surveil it. But neither fazed her. Mulzac responded to the naysayers with a boisterous grand opening. She lined Liberation's walls with posters of Malcolm X and blasted his speeches through a loudspeaker as she served apple juice to locals. Though major publishers shunned her, Mulzac used her own money to buy titles from a smaller, communist-run publishing house. Karl Marx

shared the shelves with J. A. Rodgers. And as time passed, Liberation's inventory expanded. There were works by poets, authors,
and playwrights, all focusing on Black life and politics. The African history section had rare books on African culture; a political
section had titles about fights for freedom in Asia, Africa, and
Latin America; the children's category held books with covers of
little Black kids; and the "Know Your Enemy" section, which Mulzac always kept up to date, had information on current events like
the Watergate scandal. Banners affixed on both sides of the front
door displayed Liberation's motto: on one side, "If you don't know,
learn," and on the other, "If you know, teach." The slogan aligned
perfectly with Mulzac's mission to "liberate the minds" of Black
communities. And she was dedicated. She spent her first year in
business working ten hours a day, six days a week. She was rarely
away from the store. She opened Liberation at a time when selling
Black, radical books was hot. The civil rights, Black Power, Black
Arts, and Black Student movements were all happening at once,
creating a racial awakening that made people want to read and
learn more about Black justice efforts and history. Liberation was
just one of a swath of stores Black people, many of them activists,
opened to join the moment.

Activism was in Mulzac's blood. Her father was the great Hugh
Mulzac, an officer on Marcus Garvey's Black Star Line who later
became the first African American to command a US merchant
marine ship, with an integrated crew at that. Like his daughter's,
Hugh's politics landed him in hot water on more than one occasion. The FBI kept tabs on him for years in the 1950s, believing

him to be a member of the Communist Party. Hugh Mulzac was blacklisted as a seaman for his affiliation with the socialist American Labor Party at the height of the Cold War and was later called before the House Un-American Activities Committee over his political beliefs. But he wouldn't give the committee the satisfaction of a response. However, he publicly denied being a member of the Communist Party and made it clear that he was dedicated to Black liberation and socialism. Mulzac watched her father's struggles, seeing law enforcement spy on him and his beliefs impact his career. She inherited his persistent spirit.

In her early twenties, Mulzac was speaking at leftist youth events, and by the 1950s, she was known to attend meetings and events for the local Communist Party. As the daughter of a socialist troublemaker, she was the perfect target for the government. In January 1954, a pair of FBI agents watched Mulzac's home and followed her when she left in the morning. They walked two paces behind her, calling her name until she gave them her attention. After she checked their credentials, the men told her they wanted to talk to her about a confidential government matter—the local Communist Party. Mulzac didn't say a word. She turned away from them and kept walking. The feds decided they wouldn't try to interview her again, writing in their files that she had an "uncooperative attitude." Mulzac grew used to seeing out-of-place agents and strange figures from then on; it was a common occurrence, even if the agents knew better than to try to talk to her again. When she wasn't attending Communist Party meetings or local social justice rallies, Mulzac was planning her break into the literary world. She landed a secretary job at Random House, where she learned the ins and outs of publishing, and began to see books as a tool for revolution. She grew bored of her desk job, though. Mulzac had a passionate, a vibrant personality, and simply couldn't stay away from the political advocacy and liberation work she'd grown accustomed to. But she didn't have to trade in her love of books to respond to the revolutionary call. When she got the offer to move to British Guiana and run a bookstore for the People's Progressive Party in 1964, Mulzac couldn't book her flight fast enough. The anti-colonial group, led by Prime Minister Cheddi Jagan, a revolutionary Marxist, was embroiled in a fight for Guianese liberation against its US-backed opposition, the People's National Congress. Mulzac learned all about the Guianese struggle while working briefly as a clerk-typist in the country. It was a turbulent time for British Guiana, and Mulzac saw the people's desperation firsthand. The popular Jagan was promoting socialist ideals, and the Guianese people were working to rid themselves of Britain once and for all. Mulzac wanted in. She hit the ground running as the store's business manager, selling books to local students for cheap and establishing the store as the educational arm of the People's Progressive Party.

"Building up the shop was hard but rewarding work, during a very trying period, which included all the horrors of Wismar," Mulzac said, referring to the violent 1964 riot, "shops and cinemas bombed, and people killed or injured, almost, it seemed, every night."

The horrors made it into the bookstore in July 1964, when a man left a package on the store's counter. Mulzac and Michael Forde, another PPP member who worked at the store, were immediately suspicious. They looked at one another with wary expressions, no doubt skeptical of mysterious packages while racial terrorism plagued the country. Forde went to take the package out of the building but didn't get very far before it exploded. He died instantly. The package was full of dynamite. Mulzac, who was just a few feet away behind an oil drum, was saved. But the explosion sent fragments into her eyes and ruptured her eardrums. She went home to New York for treatment and took weeks to recover from her injuries. From her hospital bed, Mulzac told her fellow PPP members to change the store's name to the Michael Forde Book Shop. She continued working at the store until Guiana gained its independence in 1966. In truth, she was forced back to the US because the PNC wouldn't give her a visa to stay in the country. But when asked about leaving, Mulzac said she simply had a new political endeavor in mind.

"I am deeply sorry to be leaving Guyana, but the barbarous war against the Vietnamese people being waged by Government of my country, has made me decide that my place is with those Americans who are determined to put an end to American imperialism," she told her supporters. Black people and their allies in the US were carrying out "a most courageous and unyielding struggle." She said, "They have risen magnificently against the enslaving policy of the US government, and with them, I would once again join hands."

It took Mulzac just a few months to get her plan for a bookstore off the ground. Back in Harlem, she joined the Progressive Labor Party, a Marxist-Leninist group that vehemently opposed the Vietnam War. The bookstore was initially supposed to be a sort of headquarters for the PLP. And it was just that for a while, until Mulzac's politics began to expand, shifting away from the group's strict Marxist-Leninist views and toward Black nationalism and Black Marxism. Mulzac began selling communist and Black nationalist literature in the store, even when the PLP told her it didn't align with their values. Unfortunately, it wasn't her store to control. But that could easily be remedied, Mulzac resolved. Backed by a group of passionate Black nationalists, Mulzac wrestled control of the store from the PLP, breaking a padlock the PLP used to keep her out. Thus, Liberation was born.

Mulzac's revolutionary lifestyle may have garnered respect in Harlem and may have even seemed cool to young activists. But it was not a glamorous life free of hardship. Just as Mulzac anticipated, law enforcement was on her heels, especially after Hoover sent out his infamous memo targeting Black bookstores. Moore's shop was closed by the time Hoover set his sights on Black bookshops. And after a bit of surveillance, agents turned their attention away from Michaux, writing that he was no longer involved in "Black Nationalist activity as he [was] getting old to be actively involved." Mulzac was another story. They kept hundreds of files on her, dating back to the 1950s, before she'd even conceived of Liberation. Agents called and visited the store posing as customers. They learned that the store brought in only about $1,600 in a three-month span, and she usually ran it with just one employee. They followed Mulzac to and from political meetings and lured people who knew her into their surveillance.

The FBI knew all about Mulzac's feud with the Progressive Labor Party and balked at her persistent, no-nonsense approach to keeping control of the store; she organized a group of Black nationalist poets, some wielding baseball bats, to protect it after she fell out with the PLP. To the agents, Mulzac was a "lying" extremist who sent the store's meager profits to radical causes.

But to Mulzac, she hadn't stolen the PLP's bookstore—she'd liberated it.

Situating Liberation in the heart of Harlem was intentional. Its bustling political scene and rich cultural history made it the unofficial Black capital of America. Pride over neighborhood landmarks like the Apollo and Sylvia's Restaurant conflicted with staggering poverty rates. Harlem was the perfect place for figures like Malcolm X and Queen Mother Moore to launch their attacks on systemic racism. It was the perfect place for Liberation, too, Mulzac reasoned, even after spending much of her life in Queens and Brooklyn. She built Liberation's reputation from the ground up using Black books and her years of local goodwill from being part of radical groups. On Sundays, she lugged books from the store to political meetings and university lectures. She called this her time "in the field," where she developed even more local contacts and relationships. Black bookselling wasn't just about ringing up purchases behind a front desk. Building relationships, staying in touch with the local political happenings, and getting to know customers on a personal level was just as important to Mulzac as keeping her shelves stocked. She made it her business to know the community. That way, she could provide the kind of service it needed. As word of Liberation spread, Mulzac found a committed customer base in prisoners. People behind bars sent dozens of requests for books from Liberation every day. Her most loyal and consistent customers in the late '60s, though, were students. Thanks to the burgeoning Black Campus Movement, leaders of newly minted Black studies courses and programs relied on Black bookstores for resources to fill their curriculums and educate their students.

When New York University founded its first-ever association of Black students, the African-American Student Center, in 1968, professors required their students to go to Liberation and talk to "Sister Una." Teachers at local schools and colleges felt it was their responsibility to place their book orders with Liberation—and professors were known to place particularly large ones. Black students often turned to bookshops like Mulzac's to supplement their formal education through the shops' community programs, educational events, author talks, and debates. People of African descent could go to Black bookstores for the instruction and education they couldn't find in formal higher education. Activists, intellectuals, and curious locals were constantly at the store, talking passionately about Black power, Pan-Africanism, and various forms of socialism. It was the ideal place to be for activists looking to refine their politics and students working to develop their own. Even as Liberation became known and beloved by the community, Mulzac still had run-ins with people put off by the name and its implications in such a tense political climate. A postal clerk delivering a shipment of books to the store confronted her about what she meant by "Liberation" and what she was doing in the shop.

"They often acted like I was shipping guns or something," Mulzac once recalled.

It was common to see respected authors like James Baldwin visit the store one day and political figures like Assata Shakur the next. Mulzac stayed up to date on what was happening in the Black literary world and sold poetry by Black writers published under Detroit's Broadside Press during the burgeoning Black Arts Movement. And even though it was risky, Mulzac wasn't afraid to fashion Liberation as a sort of information and distribution site for local political organizations. She displayed leaflets in the store's windows, on its shelves, and at the front counter announcing upcoming political rallies, protests, study groups, and local services like food programs and shelters. With deep ties to the Black Panthers, she was more than happy to direct her customers to their events and community programs. Liberation fit right in with nearby veteran Black bookstores like National Memorial African Book Store and Richard B. Moore's Frederick Douglass Book Center, both over on 125th Street. Mulzac, Michaux, and Moore were a trio of Black booksellers with Pan-African, Black Nationalist, communist, or socialist backgrounds. Their stores were part of a network of Africa-based information that included the Schomburg Center and local Black clubs and societies. Despite their commonalities, Michaux and Moore's stores were founded some forty years earlier, with Moore's closing in 1968, and the differences in Black culture and political life between their time and Mulzac's time were stark. Michaux's politics focused largely on the US, and he was a devoted Garveyite. But Mulzac had a more Pan-African worldview and tied the oppression of Black people in America to that of Black people around the world. And, with her communist background, she took a more class-based approach when thinking through racial issues. These distinctions couldn't be understated for Mulzac as she watched young radicals push back against capitalism and pursue a liberation that didn't prioritize economic advancement above all else. While Michaux and Moore's stores catered to her predecessors, Mulzac's Liberation became a home for a new generation of radicals and people looking to learn about racism.

Although major activist booksellers at the time shared a similar mission—to combat Black oppression—they varied in their approaches and political beliefs. While Michaux promoted a traditional Black nationalism, Mulzac leaned toward socialism; Bill Crawford, who ran New World Book Fair in Philadelphia, was a longtime member of the Communist Party of the USA. This was a breath of fresh air for Black people. At Crawford's New World Book Fair, customers were most drawn to the "African American material" and the Marxist and socialist titles. Crawford recalled visitors' shocked reactions at his "Marxist library."

"Someone would walk in and they would browse for three or four minutes, and maybe twenty minutes later they would come back and say, 'Man, where the hell did you get all this stuff from?'" Crawford said. "And whether they were Marxists or not, I don't know. I don't think so. I think they just felt that this was—that this should be done. That the store should be here. It should be here. That I got from quite a few people, that I was doing a good job."

But activist booksellers were, and would remain, the minority in the Black book industry. Some Black booksellers didn't consider themselves or their stores to be political at all. They simply wanted to share Black books. That was Dawud Hakim's mission.

Hakim's life as a bookseller began with him selling titles out of the trunk of his car in Philadelphia. He'd read J. A. Rodgers's *100 Amazing Facts About the Negro*—which he called a "revolution" in his mind—and *The Five Negro Presidents* while working at a local

Dawud Hakim stands in front of his namesake bookstore.

post office. The books ignited a fire in Hakim for Black history and a desire to teach others. He was so excited that he reached out to Rogers himself, asking if he could sell the book. Hakim didn't know then that it would be the start of an enduring legacy. He was working as an accountant when he finally opened his namesake brick-and-mortar store in 1959. And business was frustratingly slow. Most days, he and his daughters would sit outside learning from local chess players, and, on a good day, they would sell a greeting card or two.

"I thought they would be busting the doors down to get at these books," Hakim would recall in 1987. "I was wrong."

That all changed as the 1960s went on. Business picked up drastically, and the store moved out of its lean period around 1967 or '68, as Hakim recalled. Hakim became known for selling rare books and periodicals that Philadelphians couldn't find anywhere else. Young Black men who would come into the store with no money would leave with a free book or CD. When they'd return to the store, Hakim would quiz them about the book and ask them what they learned. A devout Muslim, Hakim spoke Arabic and greeted anyone who entered his store with "As-salaam alaikum." His faith played a major part in the books he stocked. The store's inventory was rooted in three subjects: Black history, Islam, and holistic health. Hakim was known for speaking to groups of Black teenagers and young Muslims eager to hear all about his hajj pilgrimage to Mecca. He was much too focused on his mission to pay much attention to the suspicious figures often stalking his store. Pairs of FBI agents would stand across the street from the shop taking pictures and others would walk in and out of the building, rarely buying anything. Hakim would watch them, mumbling under his breath and shaking his head, but never letting the surveillance uproot his gentle demeanor. Hakim knew he was being watched, but he, and the public, wouldn't know the fullness of Hoover's targeting until three years after the infamous memo. A headline in the *Philadelphia Tribune* read, "FBI Documents List Many Black 'Informants': Key Organizations, Book Stores, Bars Were Also Probed." Hakim was infuriated. He ran his shop, originally called Hakim's House of Knowledge Bookstore, in West Philadelphia through the rise of the civil rights and Black Power movements. He wasn't foolish enough to think his bookstore, full of titles on Islam, many written in Arabic, and Black history, would fly under the radar of government officials. To him, Black bookstores shouldn't have been blamed for racial strife but applauded for informing their communities.

"It's a waste of the taxpayers' money," he said in 1971. "We are trying to educate our people about their history and culture. The FBI should be spending their time instead on organized crime and drug peddlers."

Nothing ever came of the targeting, though. In FBI files, agents insisted that Hakim sold "extremist literature" but admitted having no success tying Hakim to any Black Power groups. Though the bookstore wasn't hosting Black Power meetings in its basement, it *was* a gathering place for civil rights activists. It was Hakim who sparked an interest in Black history and Islam in Dr. Muhammad Ahmad—formerly Maxwell Stanford. Ahmad would go on to create the Revolutionary Action Movement, the Black Nationalist and Marxist-Leninist organization that laid the groundwork for the Black Panther Party and SNCC.

Mulzac's and Hakim's journeys are just two defining stories of the 1960s. The turmoil that led to this unprecedented moment in Black history continued through the decade. Just a few years after the Civil Rights Act of 1964, Black America continued to endure poor economic conditions. From 1964 through 1968, Black people responded to police violence and economic, educational, and housing inequities with uprisings in several cities across the country. They were desperate for change. The Black book ecosystem, made up of booksellers, publishers, and authors, continued going strong as the '60s came to an end. But clashes with police dealt a blow to activist booksellers who ran their stores through uprisings and protests. Ed Vaughn and Martin Sostre are two booksellers whose reputations and community efforts led them to war with police. While many bookstores contended with federal surveillance and espionage, Sostre and Vaughn battled with local cops who knew them by name and did all they could to destroy their businesses.

CHAPTER FOUR

BOOKS THROUGH THE REBELLION

Ed Vaughn

BEFORE HOOVER FORMALLY SICCED THE FBI ON BLACK bookstores, there was the long, hot summer of 1967. From June to August, the poverty, discrimination, and almost constant violence from police resulted in uprisings in more than one hundred Black neighborhoods. Detroit and Newark, New Jersey, saw the deadliest riots, but the rebellion stretched across nearly a dozen cities, including Buffalo, New York, where Martin Sostre ran the Afro-Asian Bookshop. Local business owners, both Black and white, locked down their shops and put up Closed signs as young, fed-up Black locals clashed with police and set fires in the city. But Sostre kept his bookstore open through the night. It was a refuge for the Black "freedom fighters" enduring tear gas and police brutality in the streets. With police seething outside, Sostre read writings by Malcolm X and other Black leaders loudly inside the store.

"The shop stayed packed and the cops outside didn't like it, but there was nothing they could do. I had the right to stay open as long as I wanted to," Sostre would write later in a letter from prison. "Needless to mention, I made political hay in denouncing the police brutality going on outside to large crowds in the store . . . With interest stimulated, I would make several sales and create several new freedom fighters."

Sostre was a charismatic man, often wearing a smile and eager to talk radical politics with anyone. He sold Black nationalist books and other leftist material like Malcolm X's writings and communist literature. He blasted jazz music on loudspeakers from the store to attract customers and taught locals about Black history, Black nationalism, and socialism. Sostre watched as familiar faces returned to the store each day to finish a single book, and he gave free pamphlets to those with no money. Young people would start by reading popular works from Malcolm X and move on to works by Pan-African organizer and then prime minister of Ghana Kwame Nkrumah. Sostre would reflect on these moments in his later letters from prison, calling them a dream come true in his mission to teach the youth about Black political efforts. Sostre wasn't shy about spreading his intentions for his bookstore: he wanted to create "freedom fighters," and he wanted the Afro-Asian Bookshop to serve as a place where young people could learn, then join Black radical movements themselves. Sostre was well acquainted with Buffalo police; he was used to being a prime target for law enforcement. The Afro-Asian Bookshop came after his twelve-year stint in a string of prisons, including Attica Correctional Facility. He'd spent his time behind bars organizing his fellow prisoners and filing lawsuits to challenge harsh prison conditions. This made him an international symbol for and monumental figure of the prisoner's rights movement. Sostre's activism inspired countless prisoners to demand rights and better prison conditions, too. And his reputation preceded him in Buffalo. Police began preying on Sostre and his new bookstore the moment he opened the shop in 1965 on Jefferson Avenue. Federal agents approached Sostre at the store, accused him of being part of communist groups, and called the shop a front for a radical organization. On another occasion, police broke into the store and tore posters from the walls. Just a few months before the summer's revolt, a detective came into the store and warned Sostre to stop selling "commie literature." He didn't listen, of course. And he wasn't surprised when firefighters deliberately flooded his bookshop while putting out a fire at a tavern next door. This, Sostre could handle. But the attacks on him and the store were too harsh to rebuff during the 1967 rebellion. Officers accused Sostre of having Molotov cocktails made at the bookstore and urging people to loot. They barged into his shop amid the unrest on July 14, arrested Sostre, and charged him with inciting to riot, arson, and possession and sale of narcotics. Police portrayed Sostre as a drug peddler who'd instigated the riots. He was ultimately sent back to prison on the narcotics charge—although the primary witness in the case later admitted to lying about any drug sale—and the Afro-Asian Bookshop closed for good.

Some 250 miles away in Detroit, Ed Vaughn was getting his own taste of police attacks during the summer's rebellion. Forty-three people died during the five-day uprising in the city and hundreds more were injured; businesses and other buildings across the city were damaged or burned. Vaughn wasn't in town when the rebellion began. He'd locked up his shop, Vaughn's Bookstore, and headed to New Jersey for a Black Power conference, where he planned to meet with Lewis Michaux. On the way back, he and his friends heard radio reports of fires and protests on Detroit's west side.

"We were quite concerned, worried. We could not call our families. The back-up was about three miles on the highway, and all we could hear on the radio was that they were not allowing cars to come into Detroit," Vaughn recalled.

Ultimately, the group snuck into the city through a series of back roads. After making sure his family was safe, Vaughn went to his eponymous bookstore. He was relieved to find that protesters had spared his shop as they set fire to white-owned businesses nearby. But they did leave a message in spray paint on the front door: "Long live the Black revolution." Vaughn's good fortune seemed to take a turn two nights later, though, when he went to the shop and found the windows smashed in; posters of Stokely Carmichael, Martin Luther King Jr., and Malcolm X damaged; and a fire burning in part of the store. Enraged, Vaughn called Detroit mayor Jerome Cavanagh, who told him to call the police. He didn't believe the Black locals who frequented his store would damage the beloved shop, especially during a strict, citywide curfew. Neighbors told him that they saw cops drive up in cruisers around 4 a.m. and smash in the store's windows with the butts of their rifles before setting the fire. Vaughn reluctantly agreed to call the cops, and, to his shock, a sergeant admitted to the break-in after blaming Vaughn for starting the Detroit rebellion, he recalled.

The sergeant said, "We did it and we'll do it again." By Vaughn's account, the police kept their word. "He wasn't lying, 'cause the next night they came back, they broke in again . . . plugged up the sink, turned on the water, and knocked all the books off the wall and waterlogged all of my books in about eight inches of water. That's what I found the next day I came into the bookstore."

His suspicions that police damaged his store were never proved. And when Black community leaders held a public tribunal at the Black Nationalist Rev. Albert Cleage's Shrine of the Black Madonna church, only a single witness was willing to testify about what she saw that night. Others recanted their story under pressure from law enforcement. After the break-in, Vaughn took his damaged inventory out onto the sidewalk, where residents proudly purchased the burned, water-damaged books. Despite the apparent effort to shut down Vaughn's Bookstore, business boomed after the uprising. Word spread across the country, and around the world, about the burned books, and publishers from all over began sending book donations to replenish Vaughn's shelves. As a result, Vaughn's Bookstore was able to survive the attack, even as businesses around his store failed to recover from the rebellion. But amid this good fortune, the FBI and local law enforcement would become a constant fixture in Vaughn's life and his store. It was a struggle he knew all too well. The sergeant's assertion that Vaughn and his political partners started the rebellion wasn't confined to white leaders. Black journalist and fierce Black nationalist critic Louis Lomax wrote in a syndicated article that Vaughn was one of the radical activists who instigated the uprising. Vaughn had a reputation as a disruptor, but he and his activist peers didn't talk about burning the city down. They wanted to build up Black communities and support Black people around the world.

||| ▰▰▰▰▰▰ |||

Vaughn established his eponymous bookshop in 1963 on Dexter Avenue, once an enclave of Black, Muslim, and Jewish communities with a thriving commercial area. Vaughn's life in the book business began simply: he was just a man looking for a book. It was the late 1950s and Vaughn had his head buried in Ralph Ginzburg's *100 Years of Lynchings* as he trudged through his workdays at a local post office. His coworkers were intrigued by the obscure book about anti-Black racial violence and wanted their own copies. Vaughn returned to the local Doubleday Bookstore, where he bought the store's lone copy of the book and asked for more. A clerk told him there were no more, and that the title was no longer in print. Store after store downtown had the same response.

"I said to myself, 'I know they're telling a damn lie!'" Vaughn recalled.

He decided to reach out to the publisher of the book himself and learned the book was, indeed, still in print. He bought several copies to give to his coworkers and anyone else who wanted to read it. But post office officials soon told him he couldn't distribute the book on the property anymore. Vaughn began selling the book out of his car. Vaughn's Bookstore was born. He soon opened a brick-and-mortar store at 12123 Dexter Avenue. The shop was considered the only Black bookstore in Detroit at a time when liberation movements and rebellions were forcing the country to reckon with systemic racism. The significance of this wasn't lost on Vaughn, who witnessed the national rise in Black consciousness transform the city. Black Detroiters knew its reputation as a liberal stronghold with progressive race relations couldn't have been further from the truth. In reality, Black communities were being crushed under the weight of urban renewal and highway projects that displaced Black families and changed the city's racial and geographic makeup. Residents viewed the Detroit Police Department as a white occupying army that relied on profiling and deadly violence to exert and maintain power. Vaughn's Bookstore opened in the aftermath of the Cynthia Scott police killing in 1963. Hundreds of protesters gathered in demonstrations for weeks calling for justice after authorities exonerated the cop who killed the twenty-four-year-old woman. Vaughn himself was part of the group that led the fervent push for justice in Scott's murder, the Group on Advanced Leadership, or GOAL. It was these circumstances that pushed Black Detroiters into his shop. Vaughn's Bookstore was a quick success. People, young and old, filled the store to buy books and ask questions.

"There was a consciousness that was being raised throughout the community," Vaughn recalled. "We were a game-changer. People in the community had a place where they could buy books in their neighborhood and didn't have to order them by mail."

Vaughn continued working at the post office, and then as a social worker, while running the store, but he wasn't short on help. He paid neighborhood kids to sweep the store and the sidewalks. It was important for him to include the community in the bookstore as much as possible. For years, Vaughn's Bookstore was the only place in Detroit to buy Black literature, and it became a place for locals to discuss pressing political issues. On Thursday nights, everyone from local customers to activists from out of town packed the shop from wall to wall for lively discussion and debates in what Vaughn came to call "Forums." Black people in the city finally had easy access to popular radical Black periodicals of the time like *The Liberator* and *Muhammad Speaks*. The shop developed a reputation as not only the place to buy Black books, but as a community center and resource. Popular Garveyite and Nation of Islam activists like Henry Wells and Leroy Mitchell would speak to crowds at Vaughn's Bookstore. Although the store was mainly oriented to Pan-Africanists and Black Nationalists, everyone was welcome, with schoolteachers and children frequenting it to read and buy children's books, too. Vaughn didn't initially set out to make such a change in the city, but he couldn't deny that, through his bookstore, "the consciousness was being developed." A Black Nationalist himself, Vaughn emerged as a major Black Power leader in the city alongside Cleage and organizers Milton and Richard B. Henry, who founded the Republic of New Afrika. Vaughn largely surrounded himself with Pan-Africanists and "old Garveyites," like militant activists from Harlem's Black nationalist scene, and joined Cleage's church by 1965. Cleage was already well-known throughout the country for his radical politics and emphasis on Black economic and political power. Vaughn's public association with the separatist activist only made him more suspicious to white leaders in Detroit. And it didn't help that his activism extended far beyond the bookstore and throughout the city; Vaughn had his hand in a little of everything. He and his fellow GOAL members, including Cleage and the Henry brothers, formed the Michigan arm of the Freedom Now political party to advocate for more Black people in political office and attention to racist inequity just in time for the 1964 state elections. The all-Black party was a short-lived political action against the state's Republicans and Democrats, but the group managed to get 2 percent of the state's Black votes that year with candidates up for offices like governor and in the state board of education.

"It scared the daylights out of the Democratic Party, and it probably scared everybody else to death," Vaughn recalled of the party. "Because we raised hell!"

This militant, separatist posture sometimes placed Vaughn at odds with major civil rights leaders like Martin Luther King Jr., who bluntly declared that year that he did not "now or ever favor an all-colored party." But no opposition was as fierce as that of the local police, who considered Vaughn's quest to spread Black consciousness throughout the city a serious threat, especially after the rebellion. As white leaders placed blame and declared the uprising a "riot," Black Detroiters felt a sense of camaraderie after the summer of 1967. The effects of systemic racism weren't uprooted, but the revolt served as a relief, however slight, of Black residents' pent-up anger. Black community members walked around with a sense of pride and respect as if, as Vaughn recalled, they had "won a battle." This stood in stark contrast to the broader picture of the Motor City after the uprising. Rebellion-torn areas fell into disrepair, white people continued fleeing Detroit in droves, and the police department increased its weaponry with the shift in the city's racial makeup. But amid the downturn, the already-fierce Black radicalism ramped up in the city. And Vaughn was among the swath of Black activists who immersed themselves in community actions to both help residents and take advantage of the renewed racial pride. He became executive director of Cleage's City-Wide Citizens Action Committee (CCAC), a militant group formed after the rebellion to promote Black economic power and Black-run services and rebuild the city. The CCAC was made up of several committees, with activists and residents working together to brainstorm solutions and actions for dealing with housing, labor, employment, and education discrimination in Detroit. The group hired out-of-work locals to provide them with stable jobs. It became a vehicle for a Black-owned grocery store, a Black-owned clothing store, and a Black-owned gas station, all while rallying Black Detroiters to protest police brutality and poor education funding. To Vaughn, the CCAC was a way for Black communities in Detroit to sustain themselves.

"The work we have begun marks a new era in the history of the Black community," he told the *Michigan Chronicle* after being appointed executive director of the CCAC. "It becomes the duty of all organizations to seek effective ways to make the community self-sufficient as well as choose its course of action."

This emphasis on self-reliance was a perfect look into Vaughn's personal politics, which aligned closely with old-school Garveyism—in fact, the Pan-African leader was his hero. Vaughn held fast to the separatism that had drawn criticism from King Jr. and even caused distance between Vaughn and activists like Grace Lee Boggs. Vaughn didn't mince words in his speeches across the city. "I would say, 'Stop begging someone else to do for you what you should be doing for yourself,'" he recalled. This was the principle Vaughn spread to anyone who visited his bookstore.

People would attend his weekly Forums, buy books, and return to the shop asking how they could join the movement. Like Drum and Spear, Vaughn's Bookstore was growing into a network indistinguishable from its owner's political life. On an average day, customers would visit Vaughn's Bookstore and look at the books with intrigue, usually remarking that they had heard about Black radical groups on television. They'd often ask for recommendations, and Vaughn was happy to oblige, fully aware of the ways a single book could expand a person's consciousness. He and his business partner, his aunt Polly Rawls, who joined the shop a few years after it opened, would attend local book fairs and speak at public schools. Vaughn was happy to take on the role of mentor for Black boys in the area. One day a local high schooler wandered into the bookstore looking for books by Bruce Lee. Lee's star was on the rise then, with martial arts seeping into pop culture. But Vaughn could tell the boy didn't know much about Black history, so he handed the teen a different book instead, *The Autobiography of Malcolm X*. Vaughn told him, "You read this book and then you come back and tell me everything you know." And the boy did. He came back to the shop and spent time with Vaughn for about six months, learning all he could about Malcolm X. It was these interactions with customers that affirmed for Vaughn that his bookshop was a place where Black people could cultivate racial pride and a sense of identity.

The 1960s was the most profitable decade for the bookstore, and by Vaughn's account, the store was amassing six figures in yearly revenue. Vaughn relied on his usual bestsellers, like *The Autobiography of Malcolm X* and *100 Years of Lynchings*, but also found success in stocking poetry from Broadside Press, the unofficial publisher of the Black Arts Movement, run by Dudley Randall. Broadside Press was considered the "the poetry hub of the late sixties and seventies" and served as a platform for poets like Nikki Giovanni and Sonia Sanchez. The Black Arts Movement, with Black artists and writers, emerged as the cultural arm of the Black Power era. This artistic surge of political activism and racial pride grew to a sort of "New Black Renaissance." Poets and authors like Giovanni, Sanchez, Amiri Baraka, Haki Madhubuti, Gaston Neal, Jayne Cortez, Gwendolyn Brooks, and many others served as prominent figures in this artistic movement. The works, including plays, music, poetry, novels, choreography, and art, explored struggles for liberation and encouraged Black people to define the world in their own terms, and, as a result, were inherently political. The movement garnered national attention, spread across college campuses alongside student protest movements, and prompted the proliferation of hundreds of Black studies programs in the US.

Hoyt Fuller, editor of the Black-centered magazine *Negro Digest*, founded in the 1940s, spoke of this revolution in 1969, declaring, "We are in the middle of a literary renaissance. Black Americans have glimpsed new possibilities in the world, and there is excitement everywhere. The new Black writers do not have to court the critical establishment; they have their own publications . . . and when the publishing establishment beckons, it must—more often than not—take the Black writer on the Black writer's terms. That is revolutionary."

Vaughn's Bookstore was among the first Black bookshops to carry works from Broadside Press. He was happy to support Randall, who would sometimes personally drop off literature at the store for Vaughn to sell. Vaughn made the shop a hub for authors by hosting autograph parties and poetry sessions, and selling books by lesser-known Black writers. As Vaughn focused on serving the community through his bookshop, the FBI set its sights on his work with the CCAC. But the CCAC was about restoration. Black locals would flock to the Shrine of the Black Madonna church by the hundreds for the committee's meetings, where they talked about ways to combat police brutality and redevelopment plans and gain control of underfunded schools. But the government saw these efforts as nothing more than an attempt to "inflame the Negro community" and "establish a new black nation." FBI agents infiltrated CCAC meetings, taking information about the committee's plans back to their supervisors. Agents submitted several files on the organization, alleging that the CCAC was an extremist organization continuously harassing the Detroit Police Department. In their memos, agents repeatedly identified the CCAC as the perfect target for a counterintelligence attack. Vaughn and other CCAC members didn't know the FBI had invaded their meetings, but they weren't naïve enough to think their businesses would be safe from local and federal law enforcement—especially when protests broke out over King's assassination. Vaughn worried that police would target the CCAC's newly opened, Black-owned grocery store, the Black Star Co-Op, which they launched with just $8,000 in 1968. He was concerned that law enforcement would hassle the grocery just as they had done his bookstore less than a year earlier. And that was exactly what happened.

"When they came to bust the windows out of the Black Star Co-op, we had about five guys in there, reached over the meat counter with shotguns, and said, 'Don't you come in here!'" Vaughn recalled of a run-in with police at the time. "And they didn't come in! They didn't break a single windowpane!"

The government and local police attacked the grocery store from all sides. When the shop wasn't warring with officers, CCAC members were working to fend off the Internal Revenue Service. It was common for radical businesses, like Black-owned bookstores, to run into trouble with the IRS, as the shops admittedly weren't run well as businesses. But activists, like Vaughn, understood the IRS to be a threat for radical organizations whether they'd paid their taxes or not. The IRS hounded Vaughn about the market, even though he wasn't the only one running the co-op at the time. Vaughn believed he'd been betrayed, that the people he'd started the co-op with pinned the store's financial woes on him when the IRS came around: "Some of the other people had already served me up," he said. He turned to his old friend Cleage, who had founded the CCAC, for help even though the activists had grown distant over the years. Vaughn was willing to battle with the IRS over any back taxes owed, but Cleage, who was already under fierce targeting from local and federal police, decided he didn't want to add the IRS to his long list of foes.

"He paid them whatever they charged," Vaughn recalled. "I

still don't know to this day what happened. But I know one thing: they never bothered me again on the Black Star Co-op."

III ▬▬▬ III

This period of influence and book sales went as quickly as it came. As the '70s began and progressed, young Black people were putting down their copies of *The Autobiography of Malcolm X* and *100 Years of Lynchings* to watch new Blaxploitation films like *Sweet Sweetback's Baadasssss Song* and *Super Fly*. And books on astrology and spiritualism were becoming more popular than books on race. Thanks to these cultural changes and economic hardship, more and more Black bookstores began to close as the '70s went on. Vaughn's Bookstore was one of the few that survived, but not without downsizing. The shop ran into financial troubles in the '70s, going from hundreds of thousands of dollars in annual sales to just $10,000. "When the oil embargo came in the seventies, we started feeling the pinch, and people stopped buying our books," Vaughn said.

The number of patrons in the shop daily began to dwindle. Vaughn tried selling a few astrology books to keep up, but he couldn't compete with large book chains that could stock more titles at discounted prices. To Vaughn, the Black revolution was over. The New Age movement, which began in the '60s and ramped up in the '70s, spread through communities and across college campuses. In 1968, there were roughly 169 paperback books on the occult in print. That number jumped to 569 by the next year. A Black bookstore in Harlem, the Tree of Life, specialized in books on numerology, astrology, and herbology. It opened in 1969 at 1010 West 125th Street, near the National Memorial African Book Store's original location. Locals who went to the store for lectures on the subjects considered the Tree of Life an educational institution as much as it was a bookstore. But even this Black, New Age store couldn't make it out of the '70s.

Customers, locals, and celebrities like Dick Gregory and Ruby Dee showed up to public hearings, wrote op-eds, mounted picket lines, and held rallies to save the bookstore when the Harlem Urban Development Corporation wanted to level the store to make way for the parking lot of a multimillion-dollar trade center. In the end, none of it mattered. The Tree of Life joined the list of Black bookstores crushed by repression, money woes, or cultural shifts.

As for Vaughn, his plan to cater to the New Age crowd didn't work. He shut down the shop on Dexter by the late 1970s and began selling his remaining books out of the Langston Hughes Theatre, a run-down theater he'd purchased and restored. Alongside the New Age movement, Vaughn credited the rise of Black exploitation films, which began in the aftermath of the 1964 Civil Rights Act, for the original store's demise. These movies represented both a shift away from reading to more passive entertainment and a change in racial attitudes from prioritizing Black liberation to praising Black representation in media. The cultural significance of Blaxploitation—its impact and its harm—was certainly a topic of discussion during its height in the '70s. But for Vaughn, the effect of its popularity was simple: "All of my customer base was gone," he said.

Across the country, Black bookstores were closing left and right. W. Paul Coates, the father of writer Ta-Nehisi Coates, left the Black Panthers and opened a short-lived bookstore in the 1970s called the Black Book. He partnered with a group of activists, some communists, some Black Nationalists, and some former Panthers, to form the George Jackson Prison Movement, or GJPM, in the spring of 1972. George Jackson was a revolutionary and prisoners' rights advocate who was shot to death at San Quentin prison in 1971, a death activists and Jackson's family deemed an assassination. The GJPM began as an effort to provide prisoners with books and information, and Coates decided a bookstore would be the best vehicle to begin such a project. He held fast to the Panthers' emphasis on spreading information and promoting consciousness. "We'd be getting books into the jails," Coates said of the plan. "When people came out of prison they could work in the bookstore and work to redeem our community and redeem themselves. That's what we envisioned." The Black Book sat near a Panthers headquarters in Baltimore. Six or seven activists started the project, but participation dwindled to Coates and a handful of former Panthers largely running the political organization. The Black Book was open for just five years, bouncing to three other locations before closing for good in 1978. Coates decided to turn his attention to publishing instead. The Black Book was a casualty in the years of Black bookstore decline.

In 1977, a headline in the *New York Amsterdam News* asked an important question: "Is the Black bookstore an endangered species?" This stood in stark contrast to a 1969 *New York Times* article where famed Black journalist Earl Caldwell declared, "A surge of book-buying is sweeping through Black communities across the country." Less than ten years later, the *New York Amsterdam News* seemed to eulogize the businesses, with a journalist writing, "The urban revolutionary literature of the sixties is now historic but also in the context of the seventies, impractical." The heyday was over.

Clara Villarosa poses with a book inside the
Hue-Man Experience Bookstore.

CHAPTER FIVE

BLACK BOOKS WITHOUT BLACK POWER

IT WAS 1983 AND CLARA VILLAROSA WALKED ALONG
Cherry Creek North, past the string of shops, boutiques, and restaurants that had come to define a day out in Denver, Colorado.
Along the stretch of businesses near downtown Denver sat the
beloved Tattered Cover on Second Avenue, an independent bookstore full of new and old books and furniture fashioned into cozy
hideaways, perfect for Denverites to spend hours lost in a book or
talk to staff about what they'd read. Villarosa watched customers
cycle in and out, like relatives shuffling through a family home
during the holidays. And she thought to herself, "I want to start a
Black Tattered Cover."

Villarosa lived just a few miles away in a condo in the city
known more for skiing than for Black businesses. She had no experience running a bookshop, but she'd always been a high
achiever, working her way up to vice president of human resources
at the United Bank of Denver. Less than ten years earlier, the city's
some sixty thousand Black people had lost the beloved Sundiata
bookshop, believed to be the first Black bookstore in Colorado.
During her travels over the years, Villarosa made a point of finding

a Black-owned bookstore in every city she'd visit, like Drum and Spear in Washington, DC, and Shrine of the Black Madonna in Atlanta, which sold books and other cultural items in addition to being a place of worship. Their stories stuck with her. She lived through the allure of the Black Power movement, which catapulted these bookstores into success, no matter how short-lived. And she watched their influence fade as Black America shifted away from rebellion and toward reform in the '80s.

Estimates at the time put the number of Black bookstores in the country at about ten, but the reality wasn't so bleak. At least two dozen Black-run bookshops specializing in Black literature existed in the country during the decade. The activist-backed stores that came and went through the 1960s and 1970s were only a single brushstroke in the larger picture of Black bookstores. Like any other business in the country, Black bookshops were continuously opening and closing no matter the economic environment. The early '80s didn't mark an end for Black bookstores, but a shift. And Villarosa's life was shifting, too. In 1983, she was in her fifties and going through a divorce when she decided she would open a bookshop after losing her job. She was pushed out of her human resources position at the bank for being too ambitious. Word across the company was that the Black woman had been too assertive, talked too much, and offended white higher-ups when she dared an attempt at moving to a higher position in the company. In short, she'd "bumped hard against the glass ceiling," she later reflected. This, to her, was not an omen of more loss to come, but an opportunity to chart new territory in her life. Soon she began dating Louis Freeman, a passionate man with the ability to command a room and an entrepreneurial spirit that Villarosa admired. She shared with him her vision of opening a bookstore and he was quickly on board. Villarosa contributed her business acumen and Freeman his people skills. They rented a space in a two-story row house, where Freeman hoped to open a card store. But Villarosa had bigger dreams. The stroll past Tattered Cover had only watered a seed planted by her years visiting Black bookstores. She resolved to fill the void left by Sundiata and open a new shop just a block or so from Five Points, Denver's historically Black neighborhood. She would avoid the pitfalls of Black booksellers before her by prioritizing business and innovation over a political mission. Villarosa shared with Freeman her vision of a collection of Black books in a social spot that felt like home for Black Denverites. She dreamed of endless expansion and lifelong relationships with customers through books that highlighted Black history and cultural experience. The name for the shop came to Villarosa one night in her sleep. She jolted awake and began thinking about her years in human resources.

"I went to the dictionary and looked up the word 'hue.' It said 'shades and colors,'" Villarosa recalled. "I thought, 'Human resources. Human. Hue. Hue-Man. It's perfect.'"

She opened the Hue-Man Experience bookstore in February 1984.

◼◼◼▰▰▰◼◼◼

The converted row house on the corner of Park Avenue West and Champa Street bordered Five Points. Paintings and Afrocentric murals lined the halls leading to reading rooms with comfy, inviting chairs and slippers meant for staying awhile. Before they could hire employees, Villarosa, Freeman, and a third partner, Mary Beth Mitchell, worked the floors themselves, talking to customers and helping them find the perfect book. Growth was slow those first few years; the store gained a customer at a time. But Villarosa was intentional about building community and relationships with Hue-Man's customers, no matter how long it took. Across from shelves of books sat T-shirts, dolls, board games, stationery, and cards featuring Black motifs or created by Black artists. The expansive inventory explained the shop's slogan, "A Bookstore and More."

Villarosa may not have had any bookselling experience, but she knew business. She'd been a social worker and, while working at the bank, started a consulting firm in 1981 to help Black people move up the corporate ladder. These skills set her apart from her predecessors who ran their bookstores more as movement centers than as businesses. Villarosa used her severance from her bank job, her savings, and help from her partners to scrape together $35,000 to start the store. People scoffed at the idea of Villarosa starting a Black bookstore in a predominately white city, but she knew the power of books. She'd been immersed in them as a child in Chicago, where she watched her father devour title after title. Black books were the perfect tangible item to sell to Black Denverites, to enrich the community, she resolved; community members would feel the covers on their palms and the edges of the paper as they turned the pages. This was, indeed, ambitious in the Mile High City, where Black people ran just a fraction of Denver businesses. Fewer than 150 Black-owned businesses could afford employees who weren't family, and most were barely able to pay their workers at all. Denver's Black business growth inched along, often lagging other minority groups. The odds were certainly stacked against Villarosa, who dreamed of attracting Denver's affluent Black residents to the store. She confronted stereotypes that condemned Black businesses as unprofessional. To her, Hue-Man wasn't simply a bookshop, but a chance to combat stereotypes by proving that Black people do business well.

"A lot of people think that an African American business can't be clean, well-lighted, and well-run," she said back then. "If young Blacks don't see other Blacks running successful businesses, they start to think the only thing they can ever do is work for somebody else."

The biggest barriers to Black business growth at the time were much like those of today; Black people often lacked technical financial knowledge, and racist lending practices made it nearly impossible for them to get the capital they needed to get a business off the ground. Villarosa knew all this, and she prepared herself. She didn't bother going to a bank. She knew none would approve a loan for someone like her, a Black woman with no bookstore experience and no collateral. She set out visiting bookstores in the country to learn on her own and took classes from the Small Business Administration on marketing and managing cashflow. She was meticulous with her business plan, carefully laying out the financial and marketing requirements for making such a project work. She was determined. Even with all Villarosa's preparation and resolve, Hue-Man's first few years were slow. The three business partners knew better than to expect a profit right away, though. From the outside, the oft-debunked stereotypes about Black people—"They don't read," "They don't support Black business"—may have appeared true. But Villarosa never fed into those beliefs, never blaming Black people for lackluster business trends. Instead, she focused on turning Hue-Man into a store worth visiting, a business that knew its market and catered to it strategically. She connected with the Ingram Book Co., a wholesale distributor with staff as interested in selling Black literature as she was.

In the beginning, Villarosa would scrape together what little money she could to print flyers or run ads in local, Black-centered newspapers. She traded books for radio spots and shared press releases to get the word out about Hue-Man, to very little effect. A valiant effort, but Villarosa soon realized that if she wanted to attract Denver's Black middle class, she'd need to do things differently. She'd need to establish both herself and Hue-Man as premier resources for Black literature.

"I began promoting the store as the largest African American bookstore in the country," she said. It may not have been true, but it was the perfect way to brand the store in the Denver media. Villarosa took her on-the-job learning even further. She took courses on bookselling and learned all she could about the new tech invention sweeping the nation: the home computer. And she did it while working part-time as a therapist to pour all the money she could into Hue-Man. Over time, Villarosa's growth both personally and as a bookseller cast a dark shadow over her personal relationships with her partners. The business-minded Villarosa had been resigned to taking a back seat to Freeman's boisterous, all-consuming personality in meetings with sales representatives for publishers and distributors—until one day in 1986.

"The sales reps said, 'You are very good at this. But he overshadows you and you allow it,'" Villarosa recalled. She let the words sink in.

Over the next two years, Villarosa bought out her partners and replaced them with a swath of investors and shareholders. Things began to turn around almost immediately. The store wouldn't see a profit until 1989, but Villarosa's word-of-mouth approach was working. Hue-Man developed the prestige of being the largest Black bookstore in the country, even though it wasn't in terms of square footage. To do this, Villarosa had to build her own status in Denver. She joined the governor's Small Business Council and became a prominent figure in bookseller groups like the national American Booksellers Association and the Mountains and Plains Independent Booksellers Association.

Soon, author book signings were commonplace at Hue-Man, and publishers who had once never heard of the shop were eager to send authors to the "largest African American bookstore in the country." James Baldwin, Maya Angelou, and Ruby Dee are just a few celebrities who visited the store. And Hue-Man found a long-time supporter in Denver Nuggets legend Alex English. By the end of the decade, everyone wanted to know what Hue-Man had going on; a calendar of events circulated through the city like Hue-Man was the hottest ticket in town.

Villarosa joined forces with the owner of the Tattered Cover, Joyce Meskis. "Instead of feeling competitive," Villarosa recalled of Meskis, "she was kind and helpful."

Meskis and Villarosa teamed up to offer publishers two book signings for an author, one at Tattered Cover and another at Hue-Man. The stores often held joint events and donated free books throughout the community. Villarosa's collaboration with the white-run shop didn't deter Black customers, though. Instead, customers praised her for her efforts to "enhance the Black community."

As the end of the decade neared, Hue-Man had expanded from just a few hundred books in a two-story row house to more than four thousand titles in four houses.

Black bookstores weren't deeply impacted by book bans, in comparison to public entities like libraries and schools. They sold the books they wanted, whether banned, challenged, or not. Black booksellers were, however, beholden to their customers. That's why Villarosa was overwhelmed with anxiety over a decision to host Ralph Abernathy at Hue-Man for a talk about his 1989 autobiography *And the Walls Came Tumbling Down*. In the book, Abernathy, once a close friend and confidante of Martin Luther King Jr., detailed the civil rights leader's extramarital affairs—even up until the night before his assassination. This didn't go over well with peers like John Lewis and Jesse Jackson, as well as the Black public. Denver's Black population was up in arms. A local newspaper publisher even burned a copy of the book. But Abernathy was on Hue-Man's schedule, and Villarosa had a decision to make.

She said then that she didn't like book burnings, and added, "I don't pull books off the shelf. But I feel this is too sensitive, and it was best to cancel." The decision may have been the right one, as Villarosa had only sold three of the one hundred copies of the book she'd ordered, and Abernathy's tour came to a halt. Besides, Villarosa wasn't one to court controversy, and business continued as usual at the store.

Villarosa would never consider herself an activist or her bookstore a political space with a radical mission. But it may have appeared to be the case when she started a book club at the Colorado State Penitentiary in Cañon City in Hue-Man's early years. She figured that if general bookstores paid so little attention to Black books on the outside, surely a prison library would be lacking. Villarosa visited the prison once to set up the reading group and again not long after. The prisoners immersed themselves in the books and found in the reading group an escape, and a chance at enrichment through literature. When Villarosa visited again to check in on the group, one of the members stopped her.

"I'm getting out," he told Villarosa. "Would you consider me for a job?" Villarosa agreed. He began working at the store soon after, starting a new practice for Villarosa. In the first six years of Hue-Man, at least two of the store's six core, full-time employees had spent time behind bars. This established Hue-Man not only as a thriving Black business in Denver, but as a vehicle for incarcerated people to safely reenter society. Villarosa didn't set out to hire formerly incarcerated people, but launching the prison book club opened her eyes to the lack of opportunities and resources that came with being locked up. Hue-Man needed employees, and the men needed jobs. They'd developed a passion for Black books while behind bars and brought that fervor to their work at the store.

In less than ten years' time, Hue-Man became the picture of a successful Black bookstore. Some booksellers, both Black and non-Black, historically blamed poor sales at Black bookstores on the belief that Black people weren't interested in books. Hue-Man told a different story. Villarosa watched as customers trickled into the store each day, planting themselves in the chairs or excitedly browsing the latest titles. Black men would make a beeline for the Black history titles, while Black women would usually come in and ask for the fiction. Alice Walker had published *The Color Purple* just a few years earlier, and the literary market became inundated with Black women's stories. Walker and Toni Morrison wrote about the brutality and particularly vile racism oft endured by Black women, Ntozake Shange explored Black coming-of-age experiences, and Shahrazad Ali unpacked the complicated relationship between Black men and women. Black-women-centered fiction increased in popularity as the '80s went on, and Villarosa leaned into it. Black women were leading the charge in a new trend, stories about interpersonal relationships and community that you'd usually only tell your best friend.

"African American women developed an appetite for stories that represented them in society," Villarosa said of the trend. "Once fed, they craved for more."

Villarosa recognized this pattern early and formed book clubs both at Hue-Man and throughout the city to match customers with the books they loved to read and establish Hue-Man as the place to read them. She crafted book discussion groups for men, which she called "male-bonding groups," one dedicated to religious and spiritual books, and another for men who gathered at a local barbershop. Hue-Man's earliest and longest-lasting group, though, was Imani-Nia. "Imani" means "faith" and "nia" means "purpose" or "intention" in Swahili. The twelve members formed friendships and lifelong connections over books of every genre, like Octavia Butler's *Wild Seed* and Derrick Bell's *And We Are Not*

Saved, a book of short stories exploring systemic and social racism through fables. Rickey Riddick, an engineer, joined Imani-Nia desperate to read something other than engineering books. Reading with the group inspired him to write book reviews and send them to the National Society of Black Engineers. The national organization distributed his reviews to high school students. Villarosa's plan to enrich was working. Her intentionality endeared not only customers to the store, but Black writers, too. Word had spread about Hue-Man throughout the city and the publishing industry. Soon, it was a must for Black authors to stop at the store to promote their books. Getting in with Villarosa meant connections with other Black bookstores; she wasn't shy about praising writers to other booksellers after a successful visit. Villarosa recalled getting a letter in 1987 from a writer she'd never heard of—but the woman certainly knew Villarosa.

The author asked if she could come to the store for a reading to promote her debut novel, called *Mama*, about a Black mother of five working to build a life after surviving a violent relationship.

The writer was Terry McMillan.

"She said, 'I've written this book,'" Villarosa recalled. "'I'm trying to promote by going to Black bookstores. I heard about you. Could you help me? Would you tell me where they are in different cities?'"

McMillan's letter was part of a gutsy effort to spread the word about her first novel. And it worked: she sold out *Mama*'s first hardcover printing of five thousand copies. Villarosa recognized that same ambitious spirit in herself, a commonality that would spark a years-long relationship between the women. Hue-Man became a regular tour stop for McMillan as she published book after book. She'd routinely make the two-hour drive to Denver to give author talks at Hue-Man when she taught at the University of Wyoming in the late '80s. She sat at Hue-Man for hours signing copies of her 1989 novel *Disappearing Acts* and had breakfast with groups of Black women from Hue-Man's reading groups, discussing fiction and sociology books over eggs and coffee. The eighties were the time of McMillan, Morrison, Walker, Shange, Gloria Naylor, Audre Lorde, Maya Angelou, Nikki Giovanni, and others who were telling deeply personal stories that reflected the realities of everyday Black women. For the first time, a massive literary movement unveiled the experiences of Black women holistically, through stories of love, death, relationships, violence, and community. The decade saw what's believed to be the first mainstream romance novel by a Black author about Black characters. Just a shelf or two away from Walker's tale of brutality in *The Color Purple*, customers could find *Entwined Destinies*, a romance novel following the love story of a young journalist and a handsome oil executive.

Publishers recognized instantly that these Black-oriented love stories would be profitable. Major romance publisher Harlequin poached *Entwined Destinies*' editor Vivian Stephens, a Black woman, and relied on Stephens to acquire the publisher's first novel by a Black author, Sandra Kitt's *Adam and Eva*, in 1984. Another white publisher, Holloway House, put out its own Black romance series to tap into the budding market. By the early 1990s, Leticia Peoples's small publishing house Odyssey Books had emerged, with the sole purpose of producing Black romances. The Black romance genre wouldn't see its heyday until the 1990s, but that didn't stop Villarosa from paying attention. Hue-Man stocked

Black history, Black romance, and the Black children's books that media outlets declared weren't being written. Journalists would reminisce in articles about the proliferation of Black children's books in the 1960s, and lament their disappearance in the '80s, even going so far as to call Black children's books "almost non-existent." It became the place for every Black reader, whether they sought out new Black fiction or older Black titles.

Villarosa weighed whether to join the American Booksellers Association. On one hand, it was the nationally recognized organization of the independent book trade. But, on the other, it was overwhelmingly white and had a reputation for ignoring Black booksellers.

"I asked Black booksellers about it, and they said, 'Oh yeah, that's a white group!'" Villarosa recalled of Hue-Man's early days. "'They don't relate to us.'"

Freeman was against the organization, too, in the beginning. He didn't want to associate with a group that had a reputation for prioritizing white booksellers and excluding Black ones. And he wasn't wrong. Before the late '80s, Black-owned bookstores had little if any presence at the ABA's annual conventions since it was founded in 1900. Still, Villarosa decided to become a member. She hung on to Freeman's and the booksellers' words, though. Even though she joined the association, she was reluctant to attend its annual convention. She saw little value in it, since the ABA's catalogs featured very little Black literature. Besides, as a new bookseller, she couldn't afford to go to many conferences at all. It remained this way for years, until 1987, when sales reps and her local booksellers' association encouraged Villarosa to go. That year, Villarosa was among a record twenty thousand booksellers, publishers, authors, agents, and middlemen at the ABA convention, where Bill Cosby promoted a new book and Otis Williams and Chuck Berry performed. She certainly stuck out as one of few Black people at the convention who wasn't a celebrity. She put her shoulders back and her chin up and worked the crowds of industry bigwigs, connecting with publishers, booksellers, and distributors. The days-long event turned out to have some value for Villarosa after all; she met publishers and developed relationships with sales reps. Villarosa began going to the conferences regularly. In the next two years, she'd be appointed to the ABA's Small Store Task Force, a group responsible for tending to the needs of small booksellers. She encouraged more Black booksellers to join the ABA and attend its conventions to network with industry higher-ups and talk to authors.

Villarosa knew better than to simply urge Black booksellers to get in with the predominately white space through gritted teeth. She set out to hold the ABA to account and push the organization to meet Black booksellers where they were. She worked her way into a spot on the ABA's board of directors and convinced the organization to form a Black-centered segment, with her as its leader. The story of Hue-Man's success is a tale of sharp business acumen, hard work, and an entrepreneurial passion. It fit well into the Black American climate of the 1980s, one seemingly marked by upward mobility and integration. The revolutionary passion of the Black Power movement was long gone, and many Black people had traded in their megaphones and soapboxes for business suits.

Just decades earlier, Black activists had decried political corruption, but the '80s marked a level of Black political activity never seen before—Black people were elected as mayors of some of the largest cities, and civil rights leader Jesse Jackson garnered millions of votes in his bids to become the Democratic nominee for president. The nation collectively shifted from prioritizing social issues to prioritizing economic ones. And civil rights demands of the '60s were drowned out by white people's belief that racial inequities were a problem of the past. The narrative of the decade rested on a paradox: the existence of a Black middle class was, to some, proof that civil rights gains had worked and advancements were no longer necessary, while Black people unable to break into the middle class only had themselves to blame for their own oppression.

Media images promoted this Black middle class, brought on by access to more education and socioeconomic opportunities, while ignoring those left behind. *The Cosby Show*'s popularity only bolstered these beliefs. A situation comedy starring a Black middle-class family with a doctor father and lawyer mother served as the perfect excuse for racists to overlook systemic inequality. In reality, oppression through systemic racism was alive and well. Black people still endured violence and racist harassment, and Ronald Reagan was strategically undoing civil rights advances of the previous decades. A swath of Black Reaganites emerged and urged Black people to fall in line with the reactionary political realities of the time and pushed white criticisms of policies like affirmative action. At the same time, mass incarceration had begun in earnest, and the number of men and women in prison more than doubled from 1977 to 1989. All while Black people endured racist violence. Racists burned crosses on Black people's properties across the East Coast in a single summer in 1985. The next year, Black people protested in New York after a white mob chased three Black men out of the majority-white Howard Beach, Queens, neighborhood, forcing one, Michael Griffith, to his death in oncoming traffic and severely beating Cedric Sandiford. The contradictions of the decade were glaring, as were the misconceptions of the time. Controversial journalist Tony Brown didn't mince words in 1986 when he disparaged Black people over an apparent lack of Black-owned businesses.

"You can talk about the other problems of our community, but the real cause is that we have simply failed to get into business," he said then. This was a common refrain among many Black leaders, but the facts didn't bear the idea out. Not only did Black people start businesses at twice the national rate through the '80s, but they also maintained sales growth on par with white entrepreneurs. In several cities where Black bookstores popular during the Black Power era had closed, booksellers took up the mantle, starting new shops in their place. And stores like Una Mulzac's Liberation, Vaughn's Bookstore, the Aquarian Bookshop, and others founded during the '60s or earlier managed to hang on through the decade. Ed Vaughn continued running his eponymous bookstore in Detroit even while pursuing local government positions and helping other booksellers start stores of their own. In Harlem, Una Mulzac held true to her political posture at Liberation, prioritizing books on Black history and radical politics—even as the city sent her summons after summons for refusing to sweep the sidewalk in front of her bookstore.

Book publishing in the United States has been overwhelmingly white since its inception; between 1950 and 2018, 95 percent of books published with major companies like Simon & Schuster and Penguin Random House were written by white authors. Only every few decades, beginning in the twentieth century, has some form of racial reckoning—like the Harlem Renaissance or the civil rights movement—prompted major publishers to work with more Black authors and hire more Black editors. The '60s and '70s were one of those times. Black writers were rising in demand, and hiring Black editors became a popular move for major publishing houses looking to court Black talent. Toni Morrison and Marie Dutton Brown snagged editor roles at two major publishers, Random House and Doubleday, respectively. But they were exceptions to the rule. Morrison joined Random House as an editor in 1967 and immediately got to work. Random House published more than two dozen books by Black authors during Morrison's sixteen years with the company. After she left, that number dwindled, with Random House publishing just two books by Black authors between 1984 and 1990 — one of which was Morrison's own book *Beloved*. In 1981, just a few years before Morrison left Random House, she lamented the state of Black books among mainstream publishers.

"That situation is devastating to all writers, so you can imagine its practical annihilation of third-world writers," Morrison said then. But she predicted a coming savior for the shunned Black writer: Black publishers. "Small publishers are publishing quality, elegant books. Somewhere along the way, they will become the 'in' books, and they'll start selling."

The 1980s served as a time of both growth, however slow, and modest sustainability for the handful of Black bookstores that existed. For Black-owned publishing houses, it would best be described as a time of maturation. Many booksellers who tried their hand at publishing in the 1970s were finally seeing growth, and other Black entrepreneurs, dissatisfied with the publishing industry, founded their own presses. Before, Black presses would open, sell one or two books, then promptly shut down. But others put up a more valiant fight and held on as long as they could before financial struggles did them in.

Haki Madhubuti cemented himself as a major player in the publishing industry and was, by the '80s, a sort of sage. Madhubuti started out as an author, publishing his first book, *Think Black*, at the DuSable Black History Museum and Education Center in 1967. He championed connections to Africa and held fast to a message of self-reliance. Although he'd found success with his books and poetry, he decided that a press would be the best vehicle for his message of Black ownership and self-determination. Madhubuti started Third World Press in 1967 out of his basement apartment. Without a reliable distributor for Black publishers at the time, Madhubuti and his employees doled out the books themselves. The small group of workers would publish about twelve titles in the first decade, and Third World wouldn't turn a profit until 1988. But Madhubuti wasn't in it for the money. He ran the press with a single mission: "Whatever we created, whatever we needed, we needed to sell to ourselves," he said.

He launched the short-lived African-American Publishers and Booksellers Association while Villarosa worked within the ABA. Villarosa was supportive of Madhubuti's effort, once calling his association her "critical mass." But there was some tension between the two. Madhubuti believed Black business owners should support and rely on one another rather than seeking out white people's help and funding. And Villarosa believed joining the ABA was the best way to get Black booksellers the same funding and resources as white ones. They did share some common ground, though. Villarosa bought books from Third World Press, and she and Madhubuti used the same distributor, Ingram; Villarosa purchased books for Hue-Man from Ingram, and Madhubuti sold books to them from his press.

Alongside growth for Black publishers, the '80s brought strides in Black distribution. Once, distribution had crippled Black booksellers looking for a way to get their titles to the masses. But the 1980s saw a rise in Black entrepreneurs doing the work themselves. Alfred—whom his friends and students affectionately called "Doc"—and Bernice Ligon, who ran the Aquarian Bookshop in Los Angeles, and Raye and Julian Richardson of Marcus

Books in Oakland and San Francisco, both had presses in their respective shops. These bookstore owners worked together to keep George G. M. James's *Stolen Legacy*, a 1954 book connecting the origins of Greek philosophy to Egypt, in print. On the other side of the country, in New Jersey, Kassahun Checole was building his Red Sea Press into the largest Black distributor in the country. Checole established Red Sea in 1985 as the distribution arm of his Africa World Press, created in 1983. After launching Africa World, he ran into a familiar problem: how to distribute his books. Mainstream distributors refused to work with him, saying there wasn't a market for Africa-centered titles. By the end of the decade, Checole disproved that notion and even lured mainstream powerhouses Macmillan and HarperCollins onto his list of clients.

"I don't understand how he does it," W. Paul Coates would later recall of Checole to *The New York Times*. "When he first started, there were a few Black publishers, but no distributors. He has made his mark in both areas. He is an entrepreneur who is not afraid to take risks. He dreams, and then he executes."

Checole, no doubt, broke barriers in the industry, but he wasn't the first Black person to tackle distribution on a major scale. Hodari Ali was already a major player in the distribution industry by 1980. He founded the Liberation Information Distributing Co. in the late '70s and went from distributing one periodical to twenty-five in just four years' time. He was one of the few Black distributors in the country at the time and landed deals to sell the periodicals at a handful of 7-Elevens, Giant grocery stores, and Peoples Drug stores. It was this cohesive market that, Coates holds, allowed Black publishers to see a period of profit and influence. As the '80s ended, the group of Black distributors—about six—was small but mighty.

"The '80s was really a beginning for us," Coates said. "In the early '80s, we were beginning to learn the ropes. Particularly by the late '80s, we were all engaged with each other."

Some Black publishers of the decade would ultimately partner with mainstream publishers, with their presses becoming imprints within larger publishing houses. Founded in 1986, Charles F. Harris's Amistad Press is considered the oldest Black-centered imprint of any New York–based publishing house. Harris sold the press to HarperCollins in 1999, thirteen years after creating it with the goal of publishing books by Black authors. Harris was a veteran in the industry. He worked his way up to an acquiring editor role at Doubleday & Co., starting its Zenith Books imprint for young readers along the way. He devoted himself to shepherding young Black people into the book industry, founding Howard University Press in the '70s and establishing the Howard University Book Publishing Institute. Harris couldn't have imagined what Amistad would become when he left Howard to launch the press in 1986. Amistad scored wins with books from athlete Arthur Ashe and late *Ebony* publisher John Johnson. Harris's years of experience and connections proved beneficial—and they weren't common for Black publishers, who usually started with only a few resources and a passion for Black books to carry them through. Black publishers who didn't have the power of mainstream publishing houses behind them tapped into Black folks' interests. They understood that Black communities have varying interests that impact the books they buy. There is, perhaps, no better example of this fortitude than Just Us Books, founded by Wade and Cheryl Hudson in the late '80s, specifically to bring more Black books for children to the public.

|||▬▬▬▬|||

The complaints from Black communities—and Black booksellers— were resounding by the time the Hudsons founded Just Us in New Jersey in 1988. *Where are all the Black children's books? Why aren't there many titles exclusively for Black kids anymore?* The flood of Black children's books brought on by government funding in the 1960s had reduced to a trickle. Just Us Books was a welcome intervention. The seed for the press was planted in the late '70s, when Cheryl couldn't find Black images to decorate her daughter's nursery. She began drawing the figures for her daughter and her friends who wanted them for their own children. She and Wade decided that Black children's images and stories should be available on every bookstore shelf. The couple started the press with about $7,000 in savings and worked nights and weekends to get Just Us off the ground. By the end of the decade, they'd published thousands of copies of a half dozen titles.

Over in Texas, the Black Images Book Bazaar likely wouldn't have been born if it weren't for Emma Rodgers's desire for Black children's books. She drove all over Dallas looking for titles with positive images of Black children to add to party favors for her son's birthday in the late 1970s. Rodgers ultimately found them, but not without great frustration. She opened her retail store in 1986 after launching it as a home-based mail-order business alongside Ashira Tosihwe in 1977.

"We knew if we had that need, other parents had the same

need to provide literature for their children and for their families," Rodgers told *Dallas Weekly* in 2023.

Initially, the Ligons didn't stock many books by Black authors about Black children at their store in Los Angeles. They catered to an older market with a specific interest in spiritualism. But Just Us Books inspired the Ligons to expand the store's inventory. S. Pearl Sharp was head of Aquarian's children's department; she fashioned a small section in the store where children and their families could read all the titles they'd bought. They'd sit, wide-eyed and enthralled, as authors Mildred Pitts Walter and Camille Yarbrough read from their children's titles. Walter was a good friend of the Ligons', so she made a point of reading at the Aquarian whenever she released a new book. When mainstream publishers sidelined children's books without government incentives, small, Black-owned presses like Just Us proved that there was still a market for them. Three years into business, Just Us was seeing orders from independent bookstores, schools, and libraries, and by direct mail.

In Denver, Villarosa stocked about six hundred titles for Black youngsters at Hue-Man within just five years of opening the store. The American Black Book Writers Association in 1989 placed Hue-Man among the stores with the largest Black children's and youth selections in the country. Much like everything else at the store, Villarosa put great effort and care into curating these titles. She spent a lot of her time scouring publishing houses, wholesalers, and literary conferences to find books for Black children. The mainstream children's market had shifted toward multiculturalism, with Black characters often sidelined and relegated to the margins of popular books.

"There are quite a few integrated or cross-cultural children books out there where the Black child is only a face in the crowd, but we don't buy them," Villarosa said in 1989. "These integrated books might be okay for the white community, I suppose, but the Black community needs something more. Black children need to read stories where they are the main characters."

Her efforts paid off. Villarosa filled the store with "happy, positive" books about Black childhood relationships at home or at school. A large portion of Hue-Man's customers were parents with children in tow. Villarosa would greet the parents and talk to them and the children about the value of owning books. Soon, little Black children were letting go of their parents' hands and exploring the bookshelves on their own.

||| ▬▬▬▬▬ |||

Although it may not have been the most successful decade for Black bookstores, the 1980s signified a more cohesive market for the Black book industry. Black book peddlers and presses worked together and confronted mainstream bookstores, publishers, and distributors side by side. Black booksellers worked together to push the larger book industry to prioritize and consider them after shutting them out for so long. Villarosa and Rodgers became good friends and were both on the ABA board. They relied on this communal character to promote the ABA among Black booksellers. If the ABA was going to remedy its long-standing reputation of being by and for white booksellers, it would need to genuinely tap into the Black book industry's ecosystem, which meant thinking holistically. Villarosa and Rodgers knew that any effort to support Black booksellers would have to include Black publishers and distributors, too. This community was key. By the end of the '80s, Villarosa had carved out a space at the association's annual conference for Black people in the book industry. In the beginning, the segment's presence was a simple booth tucked in a corner of the conference's massive venue. Villarosa expected these humble beginnings, and continued courting members until the segment hosted luncheons, workshops, and author talks for the hundreds of Black book industry members who had come around to joining the ABA. It was at one of these meetings that Villarosa made a lifelong friend in a beloved poet and author.

One year, Villarosa was irritable and anxious as she set up tables for an author talk at the conference. People were already shuffling in. The stress of the day had gotten to her, and it showed in how she commanded the members into the space and the staffers helping with setup. It didn't occur to Villarosa that someone might have been watching, until she heard a familiar low and even voice ask, "Do you know any sweet words?"

Villarosa, in the middle of unfolding a chair, stopped in her tracks and looked up to see Maya Angelou.

"Everybody knows you're in charge. You don't have to act like it."

Stunned, Villarosa stared in shock before letting out a "Yes, ma'am."

When the shock wore off, Villarosa was back to her snappy, quick-witted ways. "What are sweet words?" she asked Angelou matter-of-factly.

And the poet told her, "'Honey,' 'sugar,' 'baby.'"

The two became fast friends, and Angelou even invited Villarosa to her home that Christmas.

As Villarosa went full steam ahead in her bookselling career, Alfred and Bernice Ligon were settling into more than forty years in the business. Alfred opened the Aquarian Bookshop and the accompanying Aquarian Spiritual Center—named after a book by Levi Dowling called *The Aquarian Gospel of Jesus Christ*—in 1941 in Los Angeles at a time when the city was less than 5 percent Black. He'd started the business with $100 from his salary working on the Southern Pacific Railroad, and he and his sister Jeni LeGon stocked its shelves with used fiction, nonfiction, and metaphysics books from a store nearby. Ligon wanted to share his deep love of metaphysics and philosophy with Black communities through books. He convinced Bernice to work with him at the store, and the two were married by 1948. They shared a love of metaphysics and Bernice fit right into the shop, starting a brief book-of-the-month club.

The idea was ahead of its time, though, and the couple was left with several books originally intended for the now-defunct club collecting dust. In the early days, white people made up a lot of the Aquarian's clientele. It wasn't until the Black political movements of the '60s that Black communities saw the store in a different light. The Ligons began adding titles from Langston Hughes, J. A. Rodgers, W. E. B. Du Bois, and other famed Black authors. Black Angelenos headed to the Aquarian for books about Blackness. Political groups began using the Aquarian Bookshop and Spiritual Center as a meeting place after the Watts rebellion of 1965. Alfred wasn't a Black Nationalist, nor was he involved with any Black Power organization, but that didn't stop him from letting leaders like Maulana Karenga use the Aquarian Spiritual Center to meet with members of his Black Nationalist group US Organization. The radical group believed that Black people must reassert their cultural heritage and embrace African aesthetics and rituals if they want to see true liberation. They protested the Vietnam War, organized Black Power conferences, and created Kwanzaa—a seven-day celebration fashioned after African harvest festivals—all from the Aquarian. The Aquarian was among the several bookshops universities relied on during the Black studies movement. Black students and their professors ran to the Aquarian Bookshop in 1969 when the University of California, Los Angeles, launched its Center for Afro-American Studies, now the Ralph J. Bunche Center for African American Studies.

The university staffers were among the last to tap into the store's influence, though. Even before the Black studies movement began in earnest, Black students saw the Aquarian as the perfect place to supplement their usually whitewashed education from the major universities and colleges they attended. Earl Ofari Hutchinson was one of those students. He first met the Ligons in 1963 when he was a student at Los Angeles City College. Hutchinson would spend hours at the store, buying books to stock his personal library, and talking to Bernice and other patrons there about current issues and events. Hutchinson saw that the Aquarian was nurturing the growth of the Black consciousness movement in Los Angeles, and he wanted in. Today, Hutchinson is an author, political analyst, and cultural commentator, a career in advocacy he said he owes to his time at the Aquarian.

The Ligons' shop surely felt the economic pressure as the '80s rolled in. By the time Sharp began volunteering at Aquarian in

1977, business was coming to a lull. The Ligons saw about fifteen to twenty customers a day. That didn't deter the couple from using the bookstore for classes on Black history, lectures, and theatrical performances for the city's Black population. By the 1980s, the Aquarian had moved four times. Los Angeles's Black population had grown and changed several times, and Alfred moved the shop to follow the ever-changing Black center in the city. Sharp was often there managing inventory, working on press releases, or helping customers. She watched as locals marched into the store and up the stairs.

"They'd have books in their arms," Sharp recalled. "They'd nod 'Hi' and they'd go upstairs. That's how I found out the spiritual center was on the second floor."

Stories about popular New Age beliefs, spiritualism, and mysticism had faded from headlines by the '80s, but they were very much alive at the Aquarian. After spending years studying metaphysics and philosophy, Alfred Ligon put together his own program called Black Gnostic Studies. At least one hundred people cycled in and out of the shop to attend Ligon's esoteric lectures, which rested on learning what he called a "hidden knowledge" about oneself and the world around them. Ligon's program was fundamentally different from the mainstream New Age movement that had swept the nation. Ligon discussed race and related the metaphysical to Black communities. He relied on *Stolen Legacy* to introduce members to the idea that philosophy wasn't by and for white people but led by Black people and ancient African cultures. The Aquarian was one of a kind: one of very few shops in the nation's history where books like *Stolen Legacy* and the Egyptian Book of the Dead were stocked just steps away from titles by

Maya Angelou and W. E. B. Du Bois. The Ligons were different from Villarosa. There was no grand marketing plan or trips across states to take classes on bookselling. Even when Alfred called bookselling a "starvation business" in 1982, he was content with the store's modest profits and steady patronage. The shop saw annual sales of about $100,000 to $125,000 at the time. The Aquarian was more an institution than a business, Ligon reasoned, saying then, "Even just a trickle of people who want these books justifies our existence." He was used to the ups and downs of the book industry; he'd been at it since he was a teenager.

Born in 1906, Ligon was about thirteen when he took up printing. He was an errand boy and later apprentice at the printing shop where his older sister, Mary Bell, worked in Chicago. Ida B. Wells's sister, Annie—sometimes called Anna—Fitts, owned the press. He learned the ins and outs of printing and got to see Wells at work. The journalist and crusader would sit in the front office of the small press, talking with politicians and local leaders. As a young boy, Ligon didn't understand the significance of what he witnessed, but it moved him to learn all he could about Chicago's political scene at the time. Ligon would use those printing skills decades later at the Aquarian. He didn't publish many books but devoted his press mainly to his own journal, *Uraeus*. *Uraeus* was Ligon's vehicle for spreading Black-centered metaphysical philosophies to the public. If books like *Stolen Legacy* and the Book of the Dead were too heavy for the general public, *Uraeus* was an easily accessible way into metaphysics. Ligon tapped into an interest that seemed to withstand market trends and popular culture; astrology and philosophy were sustainable. In the '80s, the Aquarian was considered the oldest consistently operating Black bookstore in the country. It had become a cultural staple in the community and a must-visit for stars and authors. Michael Jackson, Maya Angelou, Alex Haley, Dick Gregory, and Malcolm X's wife Betty Shabazz had all visited the Aquarian by the end of the '80s. Although both their stores were successful in their own ways, Villarosa and the Ligons had different approaches to bookselling. Villarosa was concerned with growth and expansion, while the Ligons were content to sustain their shop as a small but mighty community service. Still, both confronted common enemies in racist stereotypes, economic struggles, and, ultimately, mall bookstore chains.

Franchises had threatened small, Black independent bookshops for at least ten years, and in the '80s, this trend only continued backing Black booksellers into a corner. Chains like Waldenbooks, B. Dalton, and Crown Books were swallowing up small booksellers; Waldenbooks was rumored to have opened a store a week at one point. The three brands were relatively new, but all had managed to become the biggest names in book retail by the mid-'80s. They took advantage of the mass migration away from cities, setting up shop in malls for suburban populations. The stores offered discounts and focused on bestsellers to make money. Most Black booksellers couldn't afford to do the former, though, and didn't want to do the latter. The chains ramped up their Black literature selections, ultimately poaching customers from the bookstores that seemed to have a monopoly on the Black market. David Lemaire, a manager at a B. Dalton in Los Angeles, told the *Los Angeles Times* then that Black literature was the store's third-best-selling category. Eileen Watts Welch's Book Art Ltd., a small

Black bookstore in Reston, Virginia, was among independent bookshops feeling this pressure in the early 1980s.

"Crown, a Washington-area discount bookstore, has taken some of the market," Welch told the *Washington Informer*. "But we are hanging in by also discounting and offering special features." These efforts weren't enough to compete with Crown, and Book Art Ltd. closed in 1982.

The competition from chain stores that Black booksellers were seeing in the '80s was just a glimpse of what was to come. Independent bookstores accounted for 60 percent of all titles sold since the '70s, but the chains were beginning to chip away at this domination. The publishing industry had changed, too, and the '80s saw several mainstream titles from Black authors. This proved to be both a blessing and a curse for Black booksellers. On one hand, popular authors were stopping at their shops for author talks to promote their new titles, and on the other, chain bookstores were taking advantage of this shift in the literary market by selling the books that, years earlier, could only be found in Black bookshops. But these booksellers still had something their chain competitors didn't. They were stocking obscure books, including titles that wouldn't appeal to big chain stores, and they had the lasting appeal of small bookstores. Owners and their staff loved their small shops and could relate to their communities and customers in ways stuffy, corporate-feeling chain stores couldn't. At Hue-Man and the Aquarian, Villarosa and the Ligons would greet customers and help them find their next read. They knew some of the customers by name and would ask about their lives. Neither Dalton, Waldenbooks, nor Crown could know their communities so intimately. This would remain the case even as chain stores began to cover more ground, and Black booksellers would see perhaps the fiercest fight for their livelihoods.

III▬▬▬III

Black booksellers of the '80s forged ahead, with some sticking to the political missions of the '60s and '70s and others adapting to the current political climate. They were all making the best out of the cultural shifts that made Black books less popular than in the decades before. Hue-Man was perhaps the highest-earning Black bookshop of the decade, thanks to Villarosa's sheer determination. And the Ligons' commitment to community and niche literature allowed the Aquarian to see its forty-eighth year in 1989, despite modest overall sales. The two stores are proof that Black bookselling has never looked just one way. Their resilience allowed them to make it through a decade marked by conservative backlash to the civil rights advances of the years before. Black people were contending with mass incarceration and familiar racist violence.

These political and social conditions were a stark reminder of the systemic racism and oppression Black people were already accustomed to. Along with protest and demands for equality, Black people responded to these stressors with creativity.

In 1988, Public Enemy released their second album, *It Takes a Nation of Millions to Hold Us Back*. It was a boisterous rap offering, full of Black Nationalist politics and visuals at a time when Black America seemed removed from the radical movements of the '60s. Chuck D and Flavor Flav rapped about power, equality, mass incarceration, and, it seemed, all the frustrations and pent-up anger young Black people were feeling. While mainstream news outlets described the radical moment in hip-hop history as extreme and aggressive, it was a breath of fresh air for most of Black America's youth. Groups like Public Enemy, Boogie Down Productions, and Stetsasonic were conjuring Black Power and Black Nationalist imagery and using Malcolm X's words in their music. Black youngsters began wearing Africa-centric clothes and red, green, and black medallions—the colors of the Pan-African flag. The mixture of systemic oppression, the cultural expression of hip-hop's golden age, and movies highlighting Black life all pushed the nation into yet another period of Black radicalism and renewed Black pride. Hakim's Bookstore in Philadelphia and Una Mulzac's Liberation in Harlem were suddenly inundated with requests for Malcolm X's books and speeches. The end of the '80s was the start of a reawakening, one that would last through the 1990s and bring about a new period of influence for Black bookstores.

One day, an eighteen-year-old wandered through Liberation and asked Mulzac if his uncle was right, if he indeed looked like Malcolm X. "He was thrilled when I told him he did," Mulzac said.

CHAPTER SIX

THE GOLDEN AGE OF BOOKSELLING

Thomas Hamilton (left) and James Fugate (right) inside
Eso Won Books in Inglewood, California, in 1996.

PROTESTERS MADE THEIR WAY THROUGH SOUTH CENTRAL
Los Angeles on Thursday, April 30, 1992. They burned buildings
and broke into stores; they made sure the country felt their frustration and pent-up anger over rampant police violence in the city.
The day before, a jury had acquitted four Los Angeles police

officers in the brutal beating of Rodney King. Gunfire rang out and smoke billowed from fires set throughout the city. This was the breaking point for Black Angelenos. Protesters marched to Martin Luther King Jr. Boulevard and Western Avenue, delivering their wrath on a mini-mall and torching the Aquarian Bookshop in the process.

Alfred and Bernice Ligon were at home at the time, wondering how their beloved shop would fare in the chaos. Members of a local protest group called Alfred the night before, cautioning him that destruction was on the way and warning him to protect the store however he could. But Alfred, a spiritual man, resolved to leave the store to fate. When they got the call that the Aquarian was on fire, Alfred turned to his wife with acceptance. "There's no need to go down there now. There's nothing we can do," he said. When the smoke cleared and citywide curfews were lifted, Alfred went to what was left of the Aquarian. He shuffled past debris in the street. His eyes wandered over the burned-out businesses and shattered windows of the mini-mall. Only three walls of the Aquarian were left standing. He looked over the charred façade and the remains of some five thousand volumes. He waded through the ashes, searching for anything he could salvage. From a shelf he pulled a socialist magazine, water damaged, but its words still legible. He'd never cared to read it before, but its significance as the last of thousands of books, magazines, periodicals, and more sparked Alfred's intrigue. He took the magazine away with him. A lone memento from the bookshop he'd founded half a century ago.

Just one year earlier, Black Angelenos, authors, artists, and Alfred's students had gathered at the Aquarian for a weekend of celebrations to ring in the store's fiftieth year. The shop buzzed with loyal customers and friends reflecting on their time at the store and the ways the Ligons and the Aquarian impacted their lives. The couple had experienced more than their fair share of ups and downs as booksellers. But the anniversary was a sweet reminder of the store's longevity, and encouragement that the shop could continue through almost anything. In the weeks before the Aquarian burned, Rosa Parks was at the shop signing books and sharing life stories with wide-eyed customers. The loss of such a literary landmark was great. Alfred didn't dwell on the tragedy for long, though. He tapped into his spiritualism and his own teachings to make sense of the blaze. He was sure that the uprising and the demise of his shop served a larger purpose. The Ligons were almost poetic about the $300,000 uninsured loss, relying on their metaphysical philosophy to cope. The burning wasn't just some careless destruction, he reasoned, but a sacrifice to a new astrological age.

Alfred saw the end of his store as part of a five-hundred-year cosmic cycle that would allow a phoenix to rise from its ashes. He published his beliefs about the blaze in a newsletter called *Aquarian Phoenix Fire*.

"I realized that these things had to be destroyed to give one an opportunity to move to a higher stage," he resolved. Bernice agreed. "This is the birthing of the Aquarian Age. And birthing ain't easy," she said then.

Those who had studied under Alfred for years and loved the shop understood his approach, but they wouldn't let go of the store so easily. The burned books prompted a response from the community, much like the global support Ed Vaughn's bookstore received during the 1967 summer rebellion. Just two days after the fire, on May 2, Earl Hutchinson, a longtime Aquarian customer and student of Alfred's, met with other Black folks who loved the store to form the Friends of the Aquarian. They set out to raise the hundreds of thousands of dollars needed to rebuild the store, all while the Ligons continued providing books from their home. Alfred converted a room into a lecture hall so he could continue teaching courses on the metaphysical. The city and the book industry came together to reconstruct the Aquarian. Donations poured in from locals, while mainstream publishers Macmillan and Random House agreed to cancel the Aquarian's debts and donate books to the store. City council members pledged their support for the repair and the American Booksellers Association was among a string of organizations that put up thousands of dollars for the store's reconstruction. Everyone did their part.

It was enough to reopen the store in 1994, but the Aquarian never managed to regain its footing. It closed for good the same year it reopened after Bernice was diagnosed with liver cancer. It was a devastating loss for all who loved the Aquarian, and for Black people in Los Angeles in general. Times had changed since the Ligons first opened the store in the '40s, though. The Aquarian may have been the only bookstore of its kind in the city when it opened in 1941, but, in the '90s, the Los Angeles area had more Black bookstores to meet the community's literary needs. The Aquarian shuttered just as another bookstore boom was sweeping through the US, one that would rival the Black Power era and bring the rise of Eso Won Books.

|||▬▬▬▬|||

The '90s marked a time of influence and popularity that Black bookstores hadn't seen since the 1960s and '70s. From 1988 to

1991, the number of books purchased by Black households rose by 26 percent, and Black people spent an estimated $175 million on books a year. The American Booksellers Association held special sessions on Black bookselling and even started the *African-American Bookselling* newsletter. These changes didn't come out of nowhere. Cultural moments of the era coincided with political ones to make for what headlines called a "boom in books for Blacks." Black people, newly released from Ronald Reagan's clutches, were reacting to the conservative climate and embracing the culture of rebellion that the Reagan era set out to squash. Rap music with Black Power imagery dominated media and gave many young Black people their first taste of figures like Malcolm X and Huey P. Newton. And Spike Lee's 1992 movie *Malcolm X* only fueled the budding political moment. The cultural impact of rap music and Black-centered movies combined with frustrations over policing, efforts to end affirmative action, and injustices in the criminal legal system coalesced to create a decade of influence for Black bookstores. The King verdict and Latasha Harlins's death sparked an already-brewing moment of racial consciousness, and cultural spectacles like the O. J. Simpson trial only added to it all. These social and political movements influenced Black writing and drew the masses to Black bookstores as both resource and education centers and places of escape to find joy during the social and political turbulence.

Romance novels and other Black-centered fiction, like Terry McMillan's *Waiting to Exhale*, were becoming huge hits, and publishers were again considering Black books a lucrative source of revenue. The Shrine of the Black Madonna's Atlanta location reported seeing a 30 percent increase in sales in a year's time. While the previous surge in Black bookstores saw the shops go from a meager dozen to an estimated seventy-five, book industry veterans put the number of Black bookstores in the 1990s at two hundred at least. There's no way to know the truth of these figures. The ABA didn't track the number of Black bookstores in America. But Villarosa said that the increase in Black ABA members in the early 1990s likely meant there were more Black bookstores opening. This literary boom made space for both popular Black authors and lesser-known writers working to make a name for themselves. It was the latter group that Faye Childs had in mind when she created the BlackBoard: African American Bestsellers list in 1991. Childs surveyed more than forty bookstores to determine which Black titles were flying off the shelves. The list became a de facto buying guide, featuring expected names like Toni Morrison and Terry McMillan while also introducing readers to lesser-known authors like Tina McElroy Ansa and Bebe Moore Campbell. The list not only proved that Black books were worth celebrating but disproved long-held notions that they didn't account for many in-store sales.

In 1996, Oprah Winfrey got in on the literary action. That September, Winfrey, on her daytime talk show, invited the public in on her love of literature with her eponymous book club, featuring picks of her own that everyone could buy and then discuss. Winfrey selected at least a dozen books by Black authors in the first five years of the book club. It was a cultural and commercial success. Authors like Toni Morrison were seeing hundreds of thousands of sales for forgotten earlier works. Lesser-known writers like Breena Clarke were also receiving their due. Clarke's publisher Little, Brown initially published just twelve thousand hardcover copies of her debut novel, *River, Cross My Heart*, but after receiving Winfrey's stamp of approval, they moved to print eight hundred thousand paperback copies. Making it onto Winfrey's list was like hitting the lottery for writers. Winfrey's blessing could send a book that once saw modest sales straight to bestseller lists. It was a cultural phenomenon so impactful that it's been dubbed the "the Oprah Effect." With her book club, Winfrey not only invited countless people to join in a larger reading effort, but she influenced the literary world commercially and culturally.

The national phenomenon of Winfrey's book club meant Black booksellers could count on customers to buy her picks, boosting the store's profits. But Winfrey's book club didn't prioritize or even cater to Black communities—it was mainstream. Even with Black titles made popular through Winfrey's book club, it was Black booksellers, publishers, and readers who created and supported this era of Black literary success. Fiction by Black women and celebrity books dominated Black book sales, but scholars like Cornel West, bell hooks, and Henry Louis Gates Jr. were shifting from university presses to mainstream publishers. It was the perfect time to make such a change. While avid readers were awaiting Walter Mosley's *Gone Fishin'*, budding literary giants were beginning their ascent in the book industry. Paul Beatty published his first US novel, *White Boy Shuffle*, in 1996, and Jacqueline Woodson's *Autobiography of a Family Photo* came out in 1995. The Black book ecosystem was growing and expanding. In 1992, Max Rodriguez founded the *Quarterly Black Review* literary journal and followed it up six years later with the Harlem Book

Fair, a sprawling literary festival where Black writers spoke in libraries, churches, hospitals, and vending booths lining Harlem's streets.

There were a lot of firsts for the Black book industry in the '90s, from the bestseller list to sessions at the ABA, and 1994 saw the first ever National Black Bookstore Week, though the proposed annual event only lasted a few years. From June 14 to June 21 that year, Black bookstores held community activities and author readings, and donated books to the ABA to send to children in South Africa. Maya Angelou served as the face of the first NBBW, and the theme, "Keeping Us Connected," represented recognition of Juneteenth.

"Thoughts by African-American thinkers have helped us to survive," she said then. "Poetry by African-American poets has helped us to thrive. Bookstores owned by African-American merchants have helped us to survive and thrive with some passion, some compassion, some humor and style."

In Los Angeles, the burning of the Aquarian didn't cripple Southern California's flourishing Black literary scene. Black Angelenos found solace in other Black-owned shops like Eso Won in Inglewood at La Brea Avenue and Plymouth Street. Eso Won was a small but dense store with African décor and jazz music regularly filling the space. Its neatly stocked shelves had everything from self-help books and children's titles to fiction and Black history works. In just a few years after the store's opening in 1988, Eso Won had become the spot for Black literature and education. It didn't start this way, though. James Fugate and Thomas Hamilton began by selling books out of a car, calling the project Eso Won on Wheels, and later sold books out of the second floor of a converted home. They regularly put in sixteen-hour days, with Hamilton often sleeping there overnight on a worn sofa. Fugate's bookselling career began with managing college bookstores, first at Florida A&M University in Tallahassee and later at Compton College in California. In Florida, the owner of the college shop lamented to Fugate that he couldn't get people to buy their general titles. A young Fugate knew exactly what the problem was: "You don't have anything these students are interested in. You need more Black books," he said. Fugate convinced the owner to stock titles from authors like James Baldwin and Malcolm X, which transformed people's perception of the bookstore. "It led to Florida A&M becoming more than a college bookstore—it became a very important Black resource in the community," Fugate recalled. With years managing college bookshops under his belt, Fugate was well prepared to run Eso Won after moving to Los Angeles in the '80s. Fugate and Hamilton were friends first before launching the business together. Fugate was the more vocal of the bookselling duo. He was the owner who spoke in media interviews and volunteered to be Eso Won's public spokesperson, while Hamilton enjoyed a quieter life as a bookseller. Eso Won wasn't political in the sense that it propped up a radical organization or the owners were activists, but the store's inventory—centered on Black history and titles by Black authors—made it a haven for Black dissidents and the books they liked to read. Even in Eso Won's earliest days, Fugate and Hamilton squeezed Black youth into their small store for discussion groups. They figured that if they could sell Black books and get the community talking about them, this would fill educational gaps and promote racial pride. The store was a subversive project that grew out of a love for Black books and community education, and into one of the most popular bookstores in the country.

Eso Won remained open through the 1992 uprising. Fugate was at the store when he learned that the Aquarian had been burned. Sadness swept over him. *Maybe the vandals didn't know the bookshop was part of the mini-mall*, Fugate reasoned to make sense of what happened. Before, Eso Won had struggled to attract authors for book events. Publishers usually sent writers only to the Aquarian before whisking them away to book signings at bigger, white bookstores. But, with the Aquarian gone, Eso Won would become known for hosting readings and signings with authors from every corner of the book industry. It was in the months after the uprising that Eso Won saw one of its first big signings. Former Black Panther Elaine Brown stopped at the shop during the book tour for her memoir, *A Taste of Power.* Former gang members and Black Panthers were among the dozens who filled the store, hanging on her words. Brown's rhetoric was right at home in the political Eso Won. She called police "pigs," called poor Black neighborhoods "internment camps," and questioned Clarence Thomas's Blackness, which drew laughter from the crowd. Fugate and Hamilton couldn't believe their eyes. The store was packed wall-to-wall on a Thursday afternoon. Major publishers couldn't believe it either. They began to pay attention to the small store, sparking a decades-long tradition of notable author talks and signings. Eso Won had come a long way from its humble beginnings. Fugate and Hamilton made modest sales and salaries their first few years in business.

They paid to bring authors to their stores in events that would end up paying for themselves, In 1990, controversy pushed the store from obscurity into the limelight. Shahrazad Ali had just published *The Blackman's Guide to Understanding the Blackwoman*, and Black America debated whether it was a self-hating diatribe against Black women or an accurate critique of romantic relationships. In it, Ali condemns "disobedient" Black women and boldly blames them for the problems of Black communities. The book had been burned and banned, and an angry crowd chased Ali out of the Apollo Theater during an appearance. Fugate and Hamilton sold the book anyway.

"It's selling as fast as romance novels do," Fugate told the *Los Angeles Times* in 1990.

Like Black booksellers in general, Fugate and Hamilton weren't too concerned with national book bans. They sold Angelou's *I Know Why the Caged Bird Sings* and Walker's *The Color Purple*, despite the two being among the most challenged books of the 1990s. Fugate "evaluated" the books Eso Won sold, making sure they didn't sell anything the owners deemed too extreme. They were okay with books that courted controversy but rejected titles that they believed could promote dangerous and violent ideologies. As for their decision to sell Ali's controversial book, the booksellers thought the work was foolish and even ridiculous but essentially harmless in the grand scheme of things. Perhaps Fugate underestimated the social impact of such a book. But he figured no one would take Ali's directives seriously. He saw the book simply as an interesting, hyperbolic diatribe that would sustain sales but have no real, material effect on the Black community. Though the controversy and fanfare over the book faded, Eso Won's new-found notoriety continued thanks to Fugate and Hamilton's communal approach to bookselling.

Alongside sponsored author talks, locals constantly stuffed themselves into the store for impromptu, passionate discussions about Elijah Muhammad, Malcolm X, and Martin Luther King Jr., sorting out their legacies and connecting their missions to movements of the '90s. It was through this community engagement that Eso Won gained its reputation as an educational center. Fugate and Hamilton appealed to young readers by sponsoring book signings at local high schools and colleges. Soon, Eso Won's name was routinely mentioned in local newspapers, with journalists citing it alongside the Aquarian for its impact. The *Los Angeles Times* declared in a 1993 article that the store "adds to life in this city." Eso Won's vast inventory set it apart from shops like the Aquarian and specialty bookstores that sold only certain genres. Along with works by Langston Hughes and James Baldwin, customers could find audiotapes from historian Yosef Ben-Jochannan and titles by Paula Giddings.

The booksellers were also being inundated with books from publishing houses and self-published authors, so much so that they certainly couldn't stock everything that came their way. Being overwhelmed with Black books was a good problem to have after slow periods in the late '70s through the mid-'80s. The literary boom stretched across states, to small towns where Black people had little access to books about themselves. Akbar Watson never imagined that starting a small bookstore in Boynton Beach, Florida, would turn into a community service. He and his friends had a reading group but even with the apparent "boom in books for

Blacks," there were some obscure Black titles they couldn't get their hands on.

"One time, one book was retailing at fifty dollars and this guy was selling it to us for a hundred dollars!" Watson recalled. "So, the guys, we all made a pact. They told me if I'd buy the book wholesale, they'd buy it from me at retail price. And voilà! That launched the book business!"

Watson's plan was to sell books at or below their retail price. He began selling them from his car, and even his bedroom, until community members began to ask about the store's physical location. So, Watson took his $10,000 life savings and opened Pyramid Books in 1993 in Boynton Beach. He didn't initially view opening a bookstore as a political statement. After all, he just wanted a place for Black Floridians to read. Soon, he was facilitating lectures, holding book talks, and gathering the community to talk about Black life, culture, and social issues.

"I was housing [books] with universal issues that catered toward Black people," Watson said. "It was a vehicle for people looking for new ideas and thoughts from a Black- or African-centered perspective. It quickly became political because it was part of the business. It's what people wanted. Reading was hot."

⦚▬▬▬⦚

While Black booksellers were settling into a profitable era, Black publishers were organizing themselves. W. Paul Coates brought together seven of the country's leading Black presses to serve as an official entity for promoting and supporting Black publishers. The group announced the creation of the National Association of Black Book Publishers at the 1994 ABA conference. A trade association that prioritized the needs and concerns of Black publishers, Coates held, was necessary during a period when Black books were seeing unprecedented popularity. The association tripled in size by the end of the year, growing from the seven founding publishers to nearly twenty-five members. If anyone knew the ins and outs of publishing and what presses needed to survive, it was the founders. By then, Coates had been running Black Classic Press for sixteen years, and other founding members, like Haki Madhubuti, who had launched Third World Press nearly thirty years earlier, and Kassahun Checole, with his ten years in the business, had established themselves as sages in the industry. In 1996, Mosley offered *Gone Fishin'* to Coates's Black Classic Press. It sold more than a hundred thousand copies, becoming one of the biggest books the press ever published. Once totally absent from ABA conferences, Black publishers waltzed into the association's 1996 convention on a high. Business was booming. Meanwhile, some major, white-run publishers were absent from the convention that year thanks to the ABA's lawsuits accusing them of colluding with chain bookstores. Gone were the days of Black presses operating for just a few years before shutting down. The '90s brought sustainability for Black publishers. This, Checole believed, was thanks to both trial and error and the publishers' connections to their communities.

"We've grown, matured, and we know what we're doing," Checole told the *Chicago Defender* then. It was a common sentiment throughout the Black publishing industry.

The Hudsons, of Just Us Books, were among the most successful Black publishers by the mid-'90s. To Wade Hudson, mainstream publishers just didn't understand the Black market. He associated Black presses' success with their deep knowledge of

Black communities. Black publishers knew the culturally relevant local radio stations, organizations, and newspapers, while mainstream houses "just sort of throw the books out there," Hudson said then. More general-interest stores were increasingly stocking Just Us's titles, and Ingram had recently begun distributing its books. But despite their expansion, Just Us kept Black bookstores as the core of their customer base. Major publishing houses were getting in on the popularity of Black books, too. More Black people had editorial jobs at mainstream publishers, and although the Black authors on bestseller lists were primarily big names like Maya Angelou, Toni Morrison, and Bill Cosby, publishers were finally looking into lesser-known writers like Bebe Moore Campbell and Connie Briscoe. It was these names that Cheryl Woodruff prioritized when she helped create a Random House imprint called One World in 1991, one of the first multicultural imprints at a major New York house. Authors, both renowned and obscure, like Queen Afua, Johnnie Cochran Jr., Nikki Turner, and Donald Bogle, found a haven in the imprint, which quickly became known for its focus on works by Black people.

Chris Jackson would revive the imprint years later, in 2017, with the publication of Ta-Nehisi Coates's *We Were Eight Years in Power: An American Tragedy*. Coates and Jackson released the book through Présence Africaine Editions, the press of Paris's historic Black bookshop Présence Africaine — the same bookshop that inspired Charlie Cobb to open Drum and Spear fifty years earlier. While leaders of Black presses continued pouring into Black communities and supporting the Black book industry, mainstream publishing editors like Woodruff worked to carve out a space that prioritized Black people in the broader book industry. Leaders like

Coates, the Hudsons, and Woodruff mentored the young writers, editors, and publishers around them.

||| ▬▬▬▬▬ |||

Eso Won was bursting at the seams. By the middle of the decade, it was a famous cultural center for customers and a profitable tour stop for Black authors. Lines stretched down the block for packed author talks from the likes of Berry Gordy and Terry McMillian. This was the case when Sapphire visited the store in 1996 to read from her new book, *Push*. Customers and journalists filled the store to hear Sapphire talk about the controversial novel shaking up the industry. This, Fugate thought, was the perfect time to break some special news.

"I announced that day that we were moving to a new location!" he recalled.

The audience cheered. The small shop that had become a third place for so many Black Angelenos was moving to a larger, busier area just a few miles away in Ladera Heights. The booksellers were happy to have snagged a slot in the new Ladera Center. That is, until Magic Johnson and a group of investment companies bought the center. The companies billed the $20 million purchase as part of an effort to develop retail centers in poor neighborhoods. But when the previous owners handed the building over to the Johnson Development Co., Eso Won's new lease was gone. This kicked off a flurry of local news articles, a David-and-Goliath tale. Fugate and Hamilton had heard rumors that the group was looking to bring in a big chain bookstore, Barnes & Noble, instead. Ken Lombard, then president of the Johnson Development Co., denied the rumors. Still, the rejection stung. Fugate and Hamilton thought with Johnson, a Black man, coming to town, Black businesses would be celebrated and amplified. Instead, strapped for time and with no lease, Eso Won moved to a smaller shopping center near their previous location.

Fugate and Hamilton weren't crazy about the new spot, a strip mall away from where they had built their customer base. But they were determined to make do. It was a bigger space, after all, which they'd need as Eso Won continued to gain popularity. As it turned out, it didn't matter where Eso Won was located: customers and authors continued to come from far and wide. More than a hundred people attended signings with well-known figures like Cochran, Patti LaBelle, and Muhammad Ali. There were some lesser-known faces, too. The booksellers invited an obscure civil rights lawyer from Illinois to read from and sign copies of his new book, *Dreams from My Father.* Only five people showed up to see Barack Obama. Years later, the former president would remember that Fugate and Hamilton invited him to Eso Won "back when nobody knew who [he] was or could pronounce [his] name."

As if business couldn't get better, the inaugural Los Angeles Times Festival of Books drew UCLA students, staff, and faculty to the Black-centered shop. Some thirty-five thousand people attended the first day of the festival. Attendees rushed to Eso Won's booth and gushed over the store they'd heard so much about, bolstering Eso Won's influence and customer base.

"Our events were really big," Fugate said of the period. "There was rarely an author, by the mid-nineties, that if we wanted them we didn't get them."

The success of California stores in Los Angeles and Oakland wasn't the only story defining Black bookstores of the era. Black bookstores both flourished and faltered in the '90s, much like in the decades before. While bookshops like Eso Won, Marcus, and the Hue-Man Experience continued to see massive sales through the years, other shops, like Austin's Just for Us, closed for good—along with a handful of other Black shops in Texas.

"We wanted our life back," Juanita Stephens, who ran Just for Us, told the *Austin American-Statesman* of the store's closure. "A small business is very tough."

The idea of a shuttered Black bookstore may have seemed paradoxical at a time when Black books and Black authors were more popular than they'd been in decades. But this spoke to the consistent precariousness of bookselling. Running a Black bookstore was hard work. Many shops simply couldn't compete with chain stores like Barnes & Noble and Borders. To be successful, Black bookshops had to be exceptional. There was a precise and important recipe for staying afloat and competing with chains: a vast inventory, investment in both new and established authors, innovative advertising, communal programming like book clubs, and customer loyalty. More than the book clubs and the allure of countless titles, it was perhaps the author talks that won many booksellers popularity and reliable customers. Kareem Abdul-Jabbar and B. B. King drew hundreds to Marcus Books in Oakland, and Joann and Feron Roberts became known for their innovative proposals to get celebrities, both literary and otherwise, to their small store, the Phenix Information Center, in San Bernardino, California.

In 1995, the Roberts managed to snag a coveted book-signing with Colin Powell during the twenty-city tour for his book *My American Journey*. The pair set up a speaking event for Powell, distinguishing themselves from other bookstores who had simply settled for a signing. The next year, they held a barbecue in the town square for George Foreman's *Knock-Out-the-Fat Barbecue and Grilling Cookbook*. In 1997, it was the Robertses' own idea, rather than the publisher's promotions, that brought Coretta Scott King to the shop as part of her speaking tour. The booksellers convinced the City of San Bernardino, a local credit union, and other leadership entities in the city to help them put on the event. And it was a grand affair. Only a baseball stadium could hold the thousands of people who turned out. The mayor welcomed King and a choir sang "His Eye Is on the Sparrow" before she delivered a rousing speech. The Robertses topped off the event with a $65-a-ticket reception where King would hand out autographed copies of her 1969 book *My Life with Martin Luther King, Jr.* This marketing flair, this self-reliance, was Phenix's stock-in-trade, a clever strategy to build a name for the store and endear the shop to city officials and influential community groups. A sustainable bookstore would require nothing less.

It wasn't only bookstores vying for authors; literary celebrities often recognized just how much they owed Black bookstores for their successes. Lonnice Brittenum Bonner went from peddling her book *Good Hair: For Colored Girls Who've Considered Weaves When the Chemicals Became Too Ruff* on her own to signing copies for dozens at Nkiru Books in Brooklyn. No one in the publishing industry would bite, so she sold the book from her California home. Nkiru's manager C. J. Pose heard about the book and called Bonner for twelve copies. When those sold out, Pose asked for twenty-four more. Before long, Bonner was in the shop signing books for about sixty customers. Walter Mosley and E. Lynn Harris were among top authors who supported Black bookstores even as they reached successful heights. In a 1997 interview with *Publishers Weekly*, Glenderlyn Johnson, the owner of Black Books Plus in New York City, lauded Mosley as an author "committed to going to Black-owned bookstores." Emma Rodgers cited Harris as the perfect example of a faithful friend of Black bookstores. "E. Lynn is on the *New York Times* bestseller list, but in every city he goes to an African American store," she told the publication. These bookstore-author relationships have long characterized Black-owned bookshops. And publishers noticed. A Simon & Schuster publicist knew Dallas's Black Images Book Bazaar had a stellar track record of handling Iyanla Vanzant's books (Black Images had sold "thousands of copies" of one of her earlier titles, *Acts of Faith*). So the publicist consulted the owner, Rodgers, to make sure she had no objection to Simon & Schuster sending Vanzant to Barnes & Noble after her stop at Black Images to promote her book *In the Meantime: Finding Yourself and the Love You Want*.

"S&S did its homework," Rodgers said, praising the publisher. Rodgers was familiar with the ins and outs of the publishing industry. Black Images began as a tent at an Oak Cliff flea market, and Rodgers and co-owner Ashira Tosihwe moved the store into a neighborhood building in 1992. They courted customers with poster-size book covers of Michael Baisden, Tavis Smiley, and Bebe Moore Campbell in the store's windows. Vanzant was among the big names Black Images either hosted or worked closely with, including Patti LaBelle, Rosa Parks, and Maya Angelou. So they knew a thing or two about building relationships with authors and publishers.

That same year, in 1997, Marcus Books celebrated its thirty-fifth anniversary at Geoffrey's Inner Circle event hall in Oakland. Friends and customers packed the room, and even more formed a line around the block to see the literary royalty in attendance. Founders Raye and Julian Richardson told stories of knowing Maya Angelou when she was a teenager, and Terry McMillan recalled the Richardsons' daughter Blanche picking her up in a station wagon during one of her early book tours. Ishmael Reed, Pulitzer Prize–winning playwright August Wilson, Angelou, Walker, and *Essence* magazine's then–editor in chief Susan L. Taylor were just a few of the literati who made a point of celebrating with the Richardsons. Novelist and critic Nelson George called it a "book groupie's paradise." "Outside of a Black literary conference, I can't imagine where you would ever see this many writers in one place," George said then. Other bookstores were marking milestone years, too. Hakim's Bookstore in Philadelphia rang in forty years that decade, a bittersweet anniversary as its founder, Dawud Hakim, died in 1997 of cancer. Hue-Man in Denver turned ten, and Una Mulzac's Liberation saw thirty years.

॥ ▭ ॥

As Black booksellers enjoyed business from loyal customers and long-awaited attention from publishers, a familiar foe lurked at their back doors. The struggles that came with '80s bookstore chains like Walden and Crown followed Black bookstores into the '90s. This time, it was Barnes & Noble and Borders threatening the shops with price wars and competition. The big-box retailers adopted familiar strategies once they learned that Black books were becoming increasingly popular. They beefed up their Black book sections, discounted books, put on community events, and tapped authors they knew Black people would venture to their stores to see. This was enough to cripple any independent bookstore, let alone a Black one. On one hand, Black booksellers were pleased to see more books by Black writers and more notoriety for the authors. On the other, Black authors' commercial clout meant that big bookstore franchises began gobbling up the Black book market. In turn, the franchises stripped Black bookstores of one of the things that made them special: the exclusivity of their inventory.

Before, a customer would have to venture to a Black bookstore to find the latest fiction from an obscure Black writer. But as time passed, chain bookstores made it so anyone could access the books easily at their conveniently placed locations, and often at a lower price than the mom-and-pop Black bookstores could offer.

In 1993, Glenderlyn Johnson watched with dread as a new Barnes & Noble superstore went up just twelve blocks away from her store, Black Books Plus, on New York's Upper West Side. She'd already been losing customers to the retailer. She knew there would be more loss to come thanks to the new store. A year later, in 1994, she lamented the decrease in both book sales and attendance at author events. Some customers would buy books from local chains for cheap and bring them in to get signed at one of her author events. Johnson held an author event for J. California Cooper that year, who was promoting her book *In Search of Satisfaction*, and the turnout was devastating. Cooper had already appeared at the nearby Barnes & Noble earlier in the day, and everyone had already had their fill of the writer. Black Books Plus didn't stand a chance.

"I'll never do that again," Johnson told *The Network Journal*, a monthly business magazine. "Everybody went to see Cooper at Barnes and Noble and only a few people came to my store. I got their crumbs."

Before 1993, Johnson had no problem booking authors like McMillan. But she soon learned the hard way that if she wanted a chance to host an author and turn a profit, she'd have to request the author visit her store before appearing at the large chain store.

Authors noticed the dangers of big-box stores, too. Shahrazad Ali declared that white-owned chains were waging "war on Black bookstores." To Ali, the chains were exploiting the industry and underselling Black books. It was about more than profit, in Ali's view; they were "invading our communities nationwide opening 'Superstore' book chains designed to abolish neighborhood competition, eliminate the need for Black bookstores, and destroy our cultural economic base," she speculated. Meanwhile, distributor Hodari Ali was accepting a harsh truth about his small chain of independent bookstores. He'd opened the first Pyramid shop in 1981 in Washington, DC, and had four more in the area, plus Dar es Salaam in Maryland, by 1995. His sales once exceeded $1 million, he said. But even his successful, groundbreaking chain was no match for the big franchises. Pyramid's Baltimore location was struggling so much in 1993 that Ali began looking for a buyer. By 1998, competition had ground the chain down to just two stores. This was a familiar pattern in Black America: when an aspect of Black culture became popular, large companies would capitalize on the market. With few resources to fight back, Black small business owners faltered under the disadvantage. As independent bookstores shuttered under pressure from big chains, ABA membership began to decline by the thousands through the middle of the decade. But booksellers put up a fierce fight when they learned that Barnes & Noble was poised to purchase Ingram Book Group, the beloved wholesaler that had supported Black bookstores for years. They wrote letters, made phone calls, and did all they could to let the companies know they weren't in favor of the merger. In the end, they were successful. Barnes & Noble walked away from the deal amid allegations that such a merger would give the already-powerful chain even more of an unfair advantage.

The accusations were bolstered by booksellers' beliefs that chains were involved in shady deals with publishers for illegal discounts and preferential treatment that further disadvantaged independents. The ABA responded with lawsuits. In 1994, the ABA sued Penguin USA and four other publishers for the alleged under-the-table deals. Penguin ultimately agreed to pay the ABA $25 million, and about half went to ABA members in payouts ranging from $1,000 to $100,000 or more. The ABA would go on to sue Barnes & Noble and Borders before the end of the decade. Major publishers denied claims of back-door dealings with the big bookstores, but they couldn't shake the rumors completely. In 1997, Black booksellers wondered why an Iyanla Vanzant title, *The Big Book of Faith*, published by Simon & Schuster, was being sold at Barnes & Noble weeks before the booksellers even learned of its release.

The publisher was silent about the book, a repackaged combination of two of Vanzant's works, and it was listed as out of stock to independent booksellers. This led booksellers to believe Barnes & Noble and the publishing house had inked a secret deal. Simon & Schuster officials admitted then that Barnes & Noble did suggest selling the book exclusively, but the publisher decided against it. This excuse didn't hold water to booksellers like Fugate.

"It really bothered me. We created this demand," Fugate told *Publishers Weekly*. "Three or four years ago I don't think you would have found Vanzant in Barnes & Noble."

As if competition from chains weren't enough, Amazon.com launched as an online bookseller in 1995. In two months' time, Amazon.com sold books in every US state and forty-five countries. If chain stores offered the comforts of home and cheap books, Amazon took it a step further, cutting out the middleman and making books available for cheap with delivery directly to customers' homes. The ABA knew it had to act. By 1999, hundreds of its members supported its effort to create an online retailer of its own, BookSense.com, where readers could order books online from their local bookstores. It was a valiant effort, one that would last, but it was still no match for a Goliath like Amazon. Bookstores' struggle against Amazon would continue indefinitely, painting a bleak future for the brick-and-mortar shops. Through this all, Eso Won maintained a privileged position. Eso Won had a devoted customer base, nationwide notoriety, relationships with publishers, and beloved community events all working in its favor. While the owners planned a signing with Chris Rock, other Black bookstores complained that they couldn't get Black authors to speak at their shops anymore. Shops like Afrocentric Books and Café, run by Antoine Coffer in St. Louis, and Johnson's Black Books Plus warred with publishers to send writers and fought chains looking to snag the authors before the smaller, Black bookshops could. Coffer decided he'd had enough when the Library Ltd., a general bookstore in Clayton, landed McMillan during her hardcover tour of *How Stella Got Her Groove Back*, and he was subsequently told it was too late to add his shop as a tour stop. Coffer criticized Penguin, accusing the publisher of discriminating against Black bookstores; urged Black booksellers to boycott McMillan's books; and threatened to picket the Library Ltd. The controversy made headlines and prompted a response from Mc-Millan herself. "[Coffer has] made money off of selling my books, and now he wants to boycott and picket my book signing. I pay his mortgage!" she said then.

In the end, McMillan canceled her lone appearance in the city, much to the dismay of fans who were looking forward to seeing her. Coffer said he and his wife received countless calls from people cursing them out and even sending them death threats over the cancellation. McMillan demanded an apology, but Coffer held that his qualm was never with her, but with the publisher. He simply wanted to come to an agreement with Penguin.

"The only thing we were hoping to accomplish was a compromise," Coffer told the *St. Louis Post-Dispatch*. "We were looking for a win-win situation. As it is now, it's a loss-loss situation. No one gets to see her because of Penguin's inability to share her with any Black bookstores."

If you asked longtime book industry leaders like Fugate and Coates, they'd say the author problem didn't fall solely on publishers' shoulders. Shops like Eso Won and Phenix had invested time and energy into developing a strategy and marketing flair that cemented them as must-stops for author tours. Of course, the larger book industry didn't support Black bookshops as they should, but booksellers had to do their part too, Fugate reasoned.

"Some booksellers who don't even do $100,000 in sales per year are complaining, 'These white people don't want to send me authors.' But there is a commitment to independent stores on the part of publishers," he told *Publishers Weekly* in 1997. That was easy for him to say. Fugate and Hamilton, with the store's popularity and reputation, had fought off big chains and managed to maintain a lucrative business while other booksellers were constantly threatened with closure. While the booksellers supported the booksellers and bookstores around them, Fugate wasn't shy about calling out what he considered to be poor business practices on the part of some of them.

||| ▬▬▬▬ |||

Times had surely changed between the Black bookstore booms of the '60s and '70s and the '90s. The Black Power and civil rights eras made for about seven years of influence and success for Black bookstores, which largely rested on the power of the political movements themselves. But Black booksellers in the '90s thrived for at least ten years, thanks to an amalgam of cultural, political, and even commercial forces. Although the political climate awakened interest in Black books, there was a major difference between the types of books that dominated during the Black Power era and those that dominated in the '90s. "In the past, you would almost be chastised as an Uncle Tom or an Aunt Jemima if your work wasn't relevant to the struggle of Black people," Hodari Ali said in 1991, speaking about the Black Power era. "You don't find that today. It runs the gamut from militant homosexual to books that reflect middle class values."

The protests and small movements that did exist in the '90s focused on criminalization, poverty, and sporadic incidents of injustice. Though there were still Black-led efforts to combat these inequities, time and social changes shifted the ways Black communities went about them. Radical, nationwide organizations were few and short-lived. There were no well-laid plans by the federal government to target and repress Black bookstores during the

'90s, but booksellers still endured racialized threats to their existence. Rent hikes, squabbles with local leaders and landlords, and the hardships of operating in underresourced and overpoliced neighborhoods all contributed to a challenging environment. Through the '80s and into the '90s, the New York City Department of Sanitation gave Mulzac up to fifty summonses for refusing to sweep a foot and a half in front of Liberation. She was convinced that the trash in front of her bookstore wasn't the issue, but the city simply wanted to control her. And she wouldn't have it.

"I'm not paying anybody off and I'm not becoming a street sweeper," Mulzac told the *New York Amsterdam News* in 1995. "There's nothing wrong with being a street sweeper; it's simply not the profession I have chosen."

The city was trying to punish her by freezing her bank accounts and destroying her credit, she accused. She adamantly refused to sweep or pay any of the summonses, and instead spent her time enjoying the business the new literary moment brought to Liberation. The previous literary and Black bookstore boom was, at its core, more about the political movements of the time. In the '90s, renewed conversations about systemic racism and Black pride were part of the boom, but popular fiction titles by Black authors, representation in media, and better business practices held a greater weight for Black booksellers. The scales of political influence and commerce were tipped, however slightly, toward commerce. Black bookstores were no longer connected to cultural political organizations, even though their commitments were to the Black communities they served. When asked in the late '90s about any affiliations with such groups, Emma Rodgers said she'd love to support such an effort but "there was currently a lack of activism within the Black community." When confronted with the same question, Desiree Sanders, who ran the Afro-Centric Bookstore in Chicago, said she didn't even know linking her store to activist groups and efforts was a possibility.

But just like in the '60s and '70s, Black people, young and old, continued to see Black bookstores as safe spaces. Even without direct links to radical groups, customers simply valued walking into a store where their culture was prioritized above all else. For example, when a jury in 1995 handed down a not-guilty verdict in the O. J. Simpson trial, Black Chicagoans knew Afrocentric was the perfect place to celebrate. Sanders said that groups of people would come into the store to talk about the verdict and "just holler and do whatever." This sense of safety and community has proved consistent no matter how the Black bookselling industry changes. By the late 1990s, the time of success and profits for Black booksellers was coming to an end. Soon, there would be a new millennium, and new challenges would come with it. Some of the Black bookstores that opened in the '90s wouldn't make it through the early aughts, others would downsize, and a lucky—and determined—few would survive. The impending economic devastation of the 2000s would overshadow the subtle, but ever-present, racial disparities prevalent in the country. But much like in the '90s, Black booksellers would prove themselves resilient. The '90s was a decade of ups and downs, for sure, but it was certainly one of the most profitable eras for Black bookstores. And Black booksellers would need to remember the lessons and marketing savvy they'd learned and hold on to this period of growth for the rough decades ahead.

THE EARLY AUGHTS AND THE KARIBU BOOKSTORE CHAIN

Novelist Walter Mosley gives a reading at
Karibu Books at the Iverson Mall in Maryland's
Hillcrest Heights neighborhood in 2001.

ESO WON WAS ONE OF THE FEW BLACK BOOKSTORES STILL
standing as the decades progressed. Owners Fugate and Hamilton
didn't keep their business and marketing prowess to themselves,
though. Even as they worked to build up Eso Won's reputation,

Fugate and Hamilton took under their wing a pair of young booksellers with similar humble beginnings.

Simba Sana and Yao Glover began selling their books at street fairs and conventions on a rickety table alongside oils, incense, and cheap jewelry. They got into bookselling at just the right time. With Black books selling rapidly and bookstores benefiting from the attention, Sana and Glover's table was popular at a Howard University Black Friday event in 1992. They made $464 that day. Thus, Karibu Books was born. "Karibu" means "welcome" in Swahili. Sana and Glover were eager to get the business off the ground. Sana met Fugate and Hamilton when Eso Won was still in Inglewood, before it landed at its final location in Leimert Park; their friendship began with casual conversations. As the pair planned to open Karibu, they'd sit on the phone with Fugate and Hamilton, hanging on their every word, jotting down their advice. *This is how you get authors to your store for events. Here's how to talk to sales reps. Make sure you join the American Booksellers Association. Make sure you get to know Paul Coates and Kassahun Checole.* Sana and Glover had become friends with the bookselling veterans, but this didn't preclude them from having to learn hard lessons about developing their own business. During one of his many visits to Eso Won, Sana strolled through the aisles, looking at all the titles. When he found one that seemed interesting, he'd pull it off the shelf, sit on the floor, and write down the title, author, and international book number. Hamilton watched Sana from the store's front desk. After seeing Sana pluck book after book from the shelves, he knew he had to speak up.

"You should not go into a Black bookstore and just start writing down titles," Hamilton told him, polite but firm.

Sana flushed with embarrassment. But he understood, as

Hamilton told him that Black booksellers often do vigorous research, pouring time and money into rediscovering obscure titles, finding books by little-known authors, and determining what should go on their shelves. To waltz into a Black shop and write down the titles they'd worked hard to find and acquire was a form of disrespect. Hamilton told Sana that if he wanted to run a meaningful, successful business, he'd have to put in the work that other booksellers did. Sana should buy the books he'd been looking at, Hamilton said. Sana was angry. He hadn't planned to spend much money on books that day. But he decided to purchase them anyway. The embarrassment soon turned to humility, and Hamilton noticed. From that day on, both Hamilton and Fugate had a deeper respect for the young bookseller. The phone calls for advice turned into trips to conventions and dinners together. Sana and Glover had found serious mentors in Hamilton and Fugate. The young booksellers opened a pair of outlets, a kiosk in Hyattsville, Maryland, and a cart a few miles away in a mall in Landover. They were able to swap the Hyattsville kiosk for a brick-and-mortar store in 1994. That shop led to another, and another. Karibu Books had three stores in Maryland and Washington, DC, by 1999.

The stores' shelves featured the usual suspects, including Toni Morrison, Walter Mosley, and Connie Briscoe. Sana and Glover shirked a lot of the characteristics of traditional Black bookstores, though. Although Karibu was born out of Sana and Glover's affiliation with a Black liberation group, they were determined to be more business-minded than their predecessors. They didn't want to be strictly political centers. Sana told *Publishers Weekly* in 1998 that Black bookstores' community focus had "actually made them worse businesses." He held that booksellers of the past were more focused on activism and community than on building their businesses. An apparent mistake in Sana's eyes—and one he was determined that he and Glover wouldn't make with Karibu. Instead, they wanted their inventory to be their activism; the books would be what fed the community. They'd run a successful business while promoting Black literature. The duo decided that they wouldn't choose between promoting Black books and longevity in such a volatile business. They could do both, they resolved. This mindset wasn't surprising, considering the shift of Black bookstores from political centers in the '60s and '70s to more profit-focused businesses in the '80s, '90s, and beyond. This trend would continue for the next twenty years.

▏▏▏▋▋▋▋▋▋▋▏▏▏

Sana, whose given name is Bernard Sutton, considered himself a "street guy" before being swept up in the Black consciousness movement of the late 1980s and early 1990s. He was looking for a way to put his Black Nationalist and Pan-African ideologies into practice and soon found the African Development Organization, a DC-based Black Nationalist and Pan-African collective. Its twenty members were determined to carry on the work of the radical activists and organizers of the 1960s. It was just what Sana had been looking for. The weekly study groups, food programs, prison reading groups, and lectures on African history at local schools seemed to be the perfect political home for his burgeoning Pan-African worldview. Sana followed along in the tradition of other notable Pan-Africanists and Black Nationalists and changed his name. He put Sutton to bed and became "Simba," a Kiswahili word meaning "lion." A passionate speaker, Sana would address rooms of people hoping to learn about Pan-Africanism and the struggle against white supremacy. But after a few years with the ADO, Sana wanted to do more. He enjoyed giving speeches to small crowds on behalf of the ADO, but he believed that in order to make real change in Black communities, he'd have to go beyond just stringing together some inspiring words. Sana, impressed with Glover's poetry, introduced Glover to the ADO in the early 1990s, and the pair bonded over their shared love of reading and commitment to Black empowerment.

The small group began to falter in the mid-'90s, but by then Glover and Sana had something more substantial. Something that would last. They seemed to encompass the new posture of Black bookselling along with the traditional ways of activist entrepreneurs.

Sana had big ideas, and Glover was a businessman. They were determined to build a lucrative, well-run business that supported their political ideologies and avoided the pitfalls of their predecessors. Karibu first emerged from a small street vending operation that Glover started with his wife, Karla, after the birth of their first child in 1992. The couple purchased a vending license in Washington, DC, and spent about $500 on incense, T-shirts, hats, and a few books to sell in hopes of caring for their daughter and keeping some money in their pockets. It was an unforgiving business that sometimes sent them home with as little as a dollar in profits. But within a few months, they'd hit a comfortable stride. The Glovers built relationships with vendors who were glad to share tips on retailing, and one vending stand in the area eventually became three. Sana got a glimpse of Glover's vending operation at that fateful event at Howard University on Black Friday. Sana, already frustrated with his job as an accountant, decided to quit and focus on street vending with Glover. His passion was the perfect complement to Glover's retail experience and business prowess.

They intended for Karibu to be a vehicle for African American freedom through literature. In that regard, Glover considered the bookstore chain a "free Black space." A place where all definitions and forms of Blackness could exist, and those differences could be freely exchanged in a safe, intentional environment. Despite Glover and Sana's differences, in both personality and approach to the business, their political commonality was enough to usher Karibu into its years of success. While some of the more radical booksellers of the industry took an anti-capitalist approach to their entrepreneurship, the Karibu duo saw pursuing profit and capital as an extension of their need for independence. The men fashioned their business format to address both the financial and the conceptual problems the chain would run into. For Sana, Karibu allowed him to use his accounting skills in service to Black people, and for Glover, Karibu was a way to engage his activist tendencies while providing for his family. When the two began Karibu, they knew the shop would be the perfect vehicle for making the substantial change they had hoped to make through the ADO.

⫶▬⫶

Many of the activist entrepreneurs who ran bookstores in the '60s and '70s had died or left the business by the early 2000s. In addition to Hakim's passing, Marcus Books lost its founder Julian

Richardson to heart failure in 2000. Both were massive losses for the Black bookselling community and a reminder of just how long it had been since Black bookstores' heyday in the 1960s and early 1970s. Una Mulzac was feeling this shift on a personal level. There was much fanfare over the Hue-Man Experience moving to Harlem in 2002. Clara Villarosa sold her Denver bookstore and moved to New York in 2000 to be closer to her daughters and grandchildren. That year, the Upper Manhattan Empowerment Zone offered Villarosa a nearly half-million-dollar loan to open a Hue-Man Experience Bookstore in Harlem. She brought on Rita Ewing and Celeste Johnson as business partners and they ran the shop with a coveted spot inside the Harlem USA shopping center at 125th Street and Frederick Douglass Boulevard. It was lauded as the first bookstore in the area to offer Black books. It was almost offensive to Mulzac.

"They are calling it Hue-Man to perhaps suggest it will be a store offering books by people of all colors, but our specialty over the years is a wide assortment of books by Black authors covering the Africa, Caribbean, and African American experience," Mulzac told the *New York Amsterdam News* in 2001. "People have been supporting my bookstore for 34 years. The public should know that major chain stores were not interested in African American writers until a profit could be made."

Mulzac was just one existing representation of the radical Black bookselling tradition of decades past, following in the steps of Michaux and even David Ruggles. But as the nature of political demonstrations changed, so too did the Black book industry. Stores like Drum and Spear and other small, short-lived shops that overtly supported political groups and radical ideologies represent only a small portion of Black bookstores throughout American history. But even if booksellers weren't planning rallies or housing targeted political groups, they were operating with a purpose: to empower and educate Black communities. As time went on, booksellers began to learn that they could accomplish this goal without exposing themselves to the ire of law enforcement and government pressure.

Activist entrepreneurs who joined radical organizations and propped up dissident groups have always been the minority of Black booksellers, but the latest iteration of subversive booksellers considered their inventory to be their activism. Shops like Marcus Books, Eso Won, Liberation, and Karibu were among a handful of Black bookstores carrying what activist booksellers like W. Paul Coates called "core books," such as *Stolen Legacy* by George G. M. James and titles by Carter G. Woodson and Frantz Fanon. Although several bookstores carried popular Black books, the latest fiction, and titles by celebrities, many made sure to sell books with political messages or those they felt were vital for Black people to develop a politic rooted in Black consciousness and liberation. Sana and Glover were among these booksellers. They weren't convinced they had to choose between a flourishing business and activism. For Sana especially, Karibu was part of his political mission rooted in Black Nationalist and Pan-African ideologies. Many of Karibu's stores were fashioned after the big chains, like Barnes & Noble or B. Dalton, with fancy frills and fixtures. But the categories marking their bookshelves illustrated their worldviews. "Race/Culture," "Revolutionary," "Caribbean Studies," "Conspiracy," and "Street Life." The stock was proof of a commitment to both lucrative business and Black consciousness.

Princess Sister by Sheila Copeland and Tavis Smiley's *Keeping the Faith* lured readers into Karibu's stores in the early 2000s, when fiction and familiar famous faces dominated Black book purchases. Titles in the "Core Books" section, like *The Mis-Education of the Negro* by Carter G. Woodson and *The Autobiography of Malcolm X*, weren't selling as much, but the booksellers considered them too important not to have on their shelves. These core books were the titles they believed every Black household should have. Sana and Glover promoted *The Mis-Education of the Negro* vigorously, often relying on the hand-selling skills they developed in their early years as hustling vendors. "Buy it as a gift," they'd tell their customers. "Buy it for a friend."

Like Sana's, Glover's politics and worldview developed during his college years in the late 1980s. He aligned with the Black Consciousness movement, drawing inspiration from Malcolm X and Black Power ideologies. He quit his job at Shell after learning the company's operations in South Africa supported apartheid policies. This period of Black consciousness, more than a decade after the Black Power movement dissipated, served as the foundation for Karibu. In the years to come, Glover's time as an activist bookseller would help him to understand the words he'd heard from a college professor as a young, impressionable student: "Each generation must exhaust the prior generation's means of struggle." Karibu would be part of a long tradition of struggle, one that stretched back to the slave trade. In the past, enslaved Africans were barred from reading, and the danger and radicalism of the act imbued it with a special kind of power. And Glover believed that more than a century later, in Karibu's years, reading was charged with that same power.

The end of the '90s, with its fierce online and chain store competition, didn't foreshadow great things to come for bookstores in the new millennium. Popular Black bookstores were experiencing flat or declining sales. The outlook for independent bookstores in general was unrelentingly grim. One reason large bookstore chains were able to dominate about 25 percent of the market was that their wide inventory and appealing prices led to loyalty from customers. But this allegiance was born out of necessity and convenience, not necessarily devotion to the chains. The indies had loyal customers, too. A research group found in 2001 that customers of small bookstores bought four out of ten of their books at the same shop. And these stores' book clubs and events for readers only helped to nurture that loyalty and establish them as an almost familial part of the communities they served. Along with the uncertainty prompted by the competition, the new decade brought an air of possibility for Black booksellers. Online retailers hadn't defeated the independent shops yet, and Black booksellers continued to put up a valiant fight. Amazon could offer quick, contactless book deliveries and Barnes & Noble had a large, discounted inventory. But Black bookstores could lean into what they knew best: their unique connection with their communities. Many beefed up their in-store reading groups, some took books straight to customers with a van service, and others added an online ordering service to their in-person offerings. This was necessary at a time of insecurity; Black bookstores no longer had a virtual monopoly on Black books.

Nkiru Books in Brooklyn was the place to go for Black-centered community events and to support authors since the mid-1970s. Writers like E. Lynn Harris, Gloria Naylor, and Michael Eric Dyson made stops at Nkiru for various readings and literary events. But neither its longevity nor its beloved reputation in the community could protect it from skyrocketing rent, high overhead costs, and major bookselling competition. By the early 2000s, owner Adelaide Miller had sold the store to a young employee, rapper Talib Kweli. He, along with fellow rapper Mos Def (now known as Yasiin Bey), tried to breathe new life into the cultural staple by running it as an educational center, the Nkiru Center for Education and Culture. They moved the store from its longtime Park Slope location to another in nearby Prospect Heights as competition and neighborhood restructuring altered the area. Things looked brighter, and the rappers brought in Kweli's mother, Brenda Greene, to fashion the new iteration of Nkiru as a place for education and empowerment in the neighborhood. But not long after, Nkiru was unable to hold off the competition or recover from its dire financial straits and closed its brick-and-mortar store in 2002.

Black booksellers got a brief reprieve when the dot-com bubble burst. The resulting recession didn't last long, but struggling Black booksellers managed to hang on as Amazon's stock tumbled month after month in the two years after the crash. The September 11 attacks prompted mainstream publishers to halt releasing new titles with sensitive subjects and many authors put their tours on hold. Despite the financial and political turmoil, the old publishing belief that books are recession-proof seemed to hold true, and the first three years of the decade looked promising. A Washington, DC, couple, Derrick and Ramunda Young, took advantage of the new technological shift and opened MahoganyBooks as an online bookstore run out of a one-bedroom apartment in Virginia in 2007. Both Derrick and Ramunda worked at Karibu before launching their online store. They started Mahogany, named after their daughter, as the Internet was gaining momentum and evoking fear in the hearts of booksellers everywhere. Their website was more than a way to provide books by and about people of African descent; the Youngs saw MahoganyBooks as a way to bring people together from far and wide. MahoganyBooks sold titles ignored by traditional publishers, everything from philosophy to cookbooks, all written by Black people from around the world. They were community oriented and tech savvy, the perfect combination for success. The Youngs spent years developing a committed base of customers and relationships with others in the bookselling industry. Naturally, they called on their former boss, Glover, to help them as they stumbled through the bookselling business in the early years. The couple established the Lit Lounge, an online forum for both writers and readers to watch videos from literary events and talk about what was going on in the literary world. Meanwhile, the Youngs cemented a physical identity for MahoganyBooks by hosting community events in the DC and Maryland areas. This strategy was a unique, refreshing way to run a bookstore and build a community connection even without a brick-and-mortar shop.

Meanwhile, Black booksellers had tapped into a subculture of self-published Black books, from romance to general fiction. Sometimes the titles had cheesy book jackets and bad prose, but customers flocked to the fiction that exaggerated and romanticized everyday Black life. Kristina Laferne Roberts, who wrote

Black erotica under the name Zane, was perhaps the biggest self-published name in the genre. Her 1998 book, *Addicted*, sold almost sixty thousand copies before agents and publishers caught wind of her. Roberts had initially tried to get an agent and appeal to publishers, but like many authors before her, she was told by industry leaders that no one would buy her writing. So, she peddled her books herself, often relying on small Black bookstores, before her popularity landed her a deal with Simon & Schuster.

This was proving to be a common tale for Black self-published writers. After they sold thousands of their books on their own through Black bookstores, mainstream publishers would sign the authors and reissue the popular books. Writers like Omar Tyree and Karen E. Quinones Miller regularly sold their books at stores like Basic Black Books and Liguorius Bookstore before being signed by Simon & Schuster. In August 2007, forty Black authors descended on the third annual Los Angeles Black Book Expo. Three-quarters of them were self-published writers, and prospective authors saw it as the perfect place to network and learn the ropes. An Adelanto housewife promoted her memoir chronicling her abusive childhood and time in foster care, a former gang member peddled his novel about his twelve years in prison, and a mother shared her self-published book about accomplished women of color. The popularity of self-published authors amounted to a mini movement partly born out of the rise of the Internet. Supporting self-published authors wasn't simply an innovative way for Black bookstores to compete in the volatile book industry; it was a natural progression of the Black bookselling tradition. Karibu Books had four locations by the time the early 2000s rolled around, and the shop had become known for supporting self-published writers and young poets. The authors were regularly at the stores, promoting their books and engaging with readers. Karibu held book signings and spoken-word sessions as well as other literary events for writers to gain exposure and even experience promoting their books. This support wasn't simply about profit.

"We came up together, right," Sana said of booksellers and authors. "We were on the bookselling side, but we're basically doing the same thing. We were both selling books. They needed a place where people could come and buy their books. And we wanted to carry them, especially if they were popular."

These relationships were foundational to Karibu. In the chain's early years, Sana and Glover didn't focus much on marketing, instead setting out to build and develop relationships with other Black people in the industry, from publishers and distributors to authors and poets. By the time Karibu reached its tenth year in 2003, self-published authors like Tyree were celebrating at the store's anniversary events alongside veterans like Eloise Greenfield. Ten years in, Sana and Glover still considered themselves servants to Black communities. After all, Karibu was, in part, an extension of their political ideologies. The duo saw Karibu as a tangible way to promote Black liberation even outside of a political organization. Karibu's mission was simple: to increase awareness of African and African American culture in their communities and grow a successful business in the process. Glover would sometimes refer to Karibu as an organization, too. It was, to him, an extension of the Black Power resurgence of the time. Glover and Sana immersed themselves in books by Assata Shakur, Chancellor Williams, Amiri Baraka, and others, not just to learn, but for inspiration to run their stores. They were committed to infusing their mission into every aspect of the chain. Their logo designs featured Adinkra symbols, and they had African priests and African American Christian ministers bless every store they opened.

If you asked Sana, the more vocal of the two at the time, to describe the perfect Black bookstore, he'd say it would be a mixture of Eso Won and the Black Images Book Bazaar. Fugate and Hamilton were well-read, knowledgeable educators, and Emma Rodgers was a community treasure. Black Images had become a destination in Dallas and a mainstay in Oak Cliff's Wynnewood Village, in part because of the store's author talks, cozy ambiance, and longevity, but largely due to Rodgers's charisma.

"I've never seen somebody hold court like her," Sana said. "The way she interacted with people, the things she did in the community, the way customers responded to her and loved her. I've never seen a bookseller with that kind of presence."

Rodgers was a sort of community outreach person for Black Images. When she wasn't working as a board member for the ABA, Rodgers was planning and facilitating programs for the Dallas community. She arranged selling events at a local convention center and, alongside co-owner Ashira Tosihwe, helped guide customers in everything from what to read to personal life choices. Customers would pile into the shop and sit on stained yellow folding chairs to take part in Black Images' workshops on writing, finance, and nutrition. The store found a friend in the local school district, selling thousands of books to the school system each year. At its most successful, Black Images was what Rodgers called a "destination store," akin to a sort of tourist attraction thanks to years of community outreach and word of mouth. Alongside author talks and educational workshops, the owners held voter registration drives at the store and sometimes hosted local politicians. Like the activists behind Drum and Spear in the 1960s, Rodgers and Tosihwe encouraged locals to display information about happenings in the community, like college tours and elections. Rodgers and Tosihwe didn't initially plan for Black Images to become the community resource center it had grown into, but their outreach was simply an extension of their work as social workers before they became booksellers.

In one of the store's most memorable events, Rodgers and Tosihwe arranged to have an American Sign Language interpreter accompany Connie Briscoe, who is hard of hearing, when she visited the store for an author talk. Briscoe usually provided her own interpreter, but Rodgers and Tosihwe were adamant that they wanted to do the work of making the event accessible themselves and employ someone from the community. Between eighty and one hundred people were packed in the store that day, and Rodgers watched as the community hung on Briscoe's words and learned about the ways people who are deaf or hard of hearing communicate. Black Images became known for these communal, informative events. Since the 1980s, the store was a consistent fixture in Oak Cliff. Rodgers and Tosihwe gave comfort and hope to amateur writers who had been turned away from publishers and general bookstores, and self-published authors praised the owners for their investment.

"Emma is an anchor because I can't do a book signing in Barnes & Noble," said Susan Perez, who often promoted her titles at Black Images. The beloved Dallas bookstore was celebrating its seventeenth year in its brick-and-mortar shop when its money woes began in 2001. High rents and a poor economy were suffocating the already meager sales by the mid-aughts.

Although industry leaders had once touted their optimism about the state of Black bookselling in the new millennium, Black booksellers' experiences stood in stark contrast. Black shops that once appeared able to withstand the economic downturn were now relying on community fundraisers and rallies to stay open. Black Images was among a swath of Black bookstores that experienced a sharp decline in sales following the September 11 attack and the economic turmoil that ensued. Media began eulogizing independent bookstores yet again and questioning their place in a world of eBays, Walmarts, and book superstores. It was a tiring pattern, another iteration of a dilemma plaguing bookstores for the last century. At the beginning of the nineteenth century, drugstores, discount stores, and newsstands poached customers from independent bookstores by appealing to working-class readers intimidated by the affluent, elite patrons of bookstores. This commercialization continued with the chain stores that proliferated beginning in the 1960s. Over time, independent bookstores, especially those run by Black booksellers, cultivated a sort of literary culture, one marked by community and shared cultural experience regardless of class status. But the repeated periods of downturn over the century made it clear that sometimes economic pressure can overpower cultural and even communal interests.

When rents are high and wages are low, buying a discounted Black book at Barnes & Noble or Walmart can be more appealing than spending dollars more at a Black independent bookstore simply for the sake of supporting the business and, in turn, the community. It was chain stores and retail giants that finally did Black Images in. A Barnes & Noble and a Walmart had opened just miles away from the store. Rodgers and Tosihwe watched anxiously as the independent bookshops around them began closing one by one. They began to suffer a fate like that of the Black booksellers before them: big, general stores nearby began selling the Black literature titles customers used to only find at Black Images.

"The handwriting was on the wall. People would say, 'Well I can go here and get this discount.' Then gas was going up, the desire to get books two dollars and three dollars cheaper someplace else. Those were the kinds of economic factors," Rodgers said. "We had to deal with reality. We couldn't sustain ourselves."

By 2004, Rodgers and Tosihwe were coming to terms with the decline and considering closing the store. Beloved Black bookshops across the country like the Apple Book Center in Detroit and Brooklyn's Nkiru Books had shuttered or were on the ropes. But Black Images' struggle was shocking proof that a once massively successful bookstore perhaps didn't stand a chance amid the perils of independent bookselling. It was enough to disappoint and worry other Black booksellers. Rodgers and Tosihwe announced in 2004 that they'd be closing the store in the next year when their lease expired. Sales were down, they could barely scrape together the shop's $3,500 rent, and keeping old customers was becoming a challenge, let alone drawing in new ones. Community members, local leaders, and authors all bemoaned the impending closure. Customers would rush to Rodgers with sadness, saying, "Please, please tell me it's not true." It seemed Rodgers and Tosihwe had accepted the store's fate by the time Cheryl Robinson, a self-published author, heard the news. The booksellers hadn't marketed or promoted her books much, but Robinson still valued what the store meant to the community and to other self-published authors who'd found a home at Black Images.

She rallied the community in a valiant effort to save Black Images. She sold shirts featuring the store's logo, and local organizations and residents vowed to step up however they could. A local literary review club, Ebony Dimensions, held a book-a-thon where authors like Robinson and Victor McGlothin read from their books and encouraged the audience to buy from Black Images. Meanwhile, customers signed pledges to buy a book a month. The community effort made Rodgers and Tosihwe hopeful. It seemed their work in the Dallas community over the decades was paying off in support, pledges, and donations. But in the end, it wasn't enough to keep the store afloat. After the shock of the impending closure and the excitement of working to save the store in the spring, the dust settled, and Black Images faced the same problems. Business over the summer was devastatingly slow, and closure seemed inevitable yet again. As they licked their wounds, Rodgers and Tosihwe continued running the store as usual, providing books and conversation and holding author talks. The next summer, customers crammed into Black Images, stuffing themselves between bookshelves and standing in whatever space they could, to catch a glimpse of Terry McMillan, who was at the store promoting her book *The Interruption of Everything*. One customer cheered, "Terry! Terry! Terry!" and another remarked how beautiful McMillan was while standing on her toes to take a picture of the author.

If optics told a story, it would be hard to believe that a store with enough respect to book McMillan and enough popularity to fill its space wall-to-wall with people would hold nothing but bare walls just months later. McMillan appeared at the store in August 2005. By September, a "Clearance" sign led to the store's entrance, indicating slow business. Black Images closed for good at the end of 2006. Yet again, customers, local organizations, and leaders mourned the store's end. Rodgers was adamant that nothing could save Black Images, not another push from the community or a short-lived surge in sales. One headline read, "Oak Cliff Loses an Anchor," and authors, customers, and local leaders spoke about how much Black Images meant to them. Rodgers and Tosihwe appreciated the outpouring of support and knew that Black Images' end didn't have to mean their commitment to providing Black literature was over. As locals mourned the store that had been a resource center, a gathering place, and a haven for little-known authors, Rodgers and Tosihwe said the closure felt less like a funeral and more like a transition. They vowed to continue to serve the community, provide books, and promote reading however they could. Even decades after the closing, booksellers would speak fondly of Black Images' owners and go to them for advice and guidance. Black Images' end seemed to be a warning for the already-struggling bookstores across the country. And if its demise sent a chill across the Black book industry, what happened to Eso Won would certainly constitute a death knell.

For the first time in its history, Eso Won was contending with stubbornly declining sales. There was a point in the '90s when business was so good that Fugate and Hamilton's accountant encouraged them to take a $95,000 yearly salary, which they declined. But by 2007, they were facing closure themselves. Like Black Images', Eso Won's woes began after September 11. Slow sales and mounting debt led Fugate to the Small Business Administration, hat in hand. He explained Eso Won's struggles and officials recommended Fugate appeal to the public for support. So, that's what he and Hamilton did. Fugate mentioned Eso Won's woes to a friend, Linda Watts, who worked with the Los Angeles Unified School District. Unbeknownst to him, Watts sent out word to thousands of people in the school community in October 2007: "Eso Won is in trouble. They're talking about closing. We have to save our bookstore!"

Shortly after, the *Los Angeles Sentinel* published Fugate's plea with a rousing headline: "Only the Community Can Save Black Bookstore: After 20 Years, Eso Won Books May Be Closing Its Doors in December." Fugate acknowledged the common problems: chain stores gobbling up the Black book market, and the economy suffocating Black bookstores. He and Hamilton were prepared to confront the end of Eso Won, but they mourned the overall decline of Black bookstores in the nation. Even in the face of the store's bankruptcy, Fugate stressed the importance of "core books." Although Barnes & Noble and Dalton were selling popular Black titles, they weren't carrying the books that were crucial to mission-driven stores like Eso Won. And if there were no Black bookstores around, where would Black communities find obscure titles rooted in Black liberation and history?

"You might go in and find a new book, but if you want a book like *Destruction of Black Civilization*, which is a classic book for us, or *The Mis-Education of the Negro*, you may not find that book or it may be very hard to find where you have to do a special order for it," Fugate explained then. "That's going to lessen those books' impact, it's going to lessen them being available."

Fugate and Hamilton watched the Internet, online shops, and chains usurp Eso Won's business. But the booksellers valued their connection with customers. The Internet couldn't provide knowledgeable and charming staff who could sit with customers and help them pick the perfect book. That uniqueness seemed to be losing its appeal, as customers chose discounted prices and convenience over what indie stores could offer. Outcomes didn't look promising when Eso Won began to falter. Fugate and Hamilton were forced to ponder the reality of closing their shop, marking the end of their dream and vision. Unlike Black Images, though, Eso Won was saved. The *Sentinel* article led to others. Writers penned op-eds sharing their experiences with the store, and even Earl Ofari Hutchinson, who had been openly critical of Fugate's and Hamilton's celebrity and complained that they did not carry one of his books, encouraged the public to shop at the bookstore.

Local leaders, politicians, and pastors took up the cause, with Pastor John J. Hunter of the First African Methodist Episcopal Church urging his some nineteen-thousand-member congregation to buy from Eso Won. The efforts worked. "It was like Christmas in October," Fugate said of the store's sales. Meanwhile, Fugate and Hamilton set their minds on paying off the store's debts to banks and vendors. It would be years before Eso Won would be debt-free and back in a profitable position. However, the community efforts let Fugate and Hamilton know that the city not only wanted Eso Won but would support the store as Eso Won had done the community. Sana and Glover watched solemnly as the booksellers they admired most struggled and scraped to get by, while they saw unprecedented success. This was largely due to having their stores in malls where there was high foot traffic. By

2005, Karibu had six locations and nearly fifty employees, and was closing in on $4 million in sales annually. About a decade earlier, they had been the new kids on the block, seeking guidance from more experienced booksellers. Now young booksellers were coming to them for advice. Karibu had become the darling of the country's Black bookselling community, and Sana and Glover had become book industry leaders themselves. The chain was growing fast, and the bookselling duo saw a bright future for Karibu: thirty more stores across the region or country in the next five years.

From the outside, all looked well with Karibu. But a storm brewed behind closed doors. As Karibu grew stronger, Sana and Glover's relationship weakened. Years of butting heads led to resentment between the two, and whatever friendship they had grew into disdain. They couldn't be called friends. In fact, much of their relationship revolved around Karibu; it was all that kept them tolerating one another. Running a successful chain store meant putting out small fires often. Glover was vocal about the problems the chain faced and would have to tackle as Karibu expanded. And he felt he was doing more of the work than he was being paid for — and enduring disrespectful rumors while he did it. He managed accounting and human resources, orientated employees, and handled buying inventory, while Sana was the public-facing representation of Karibu. There was a constant, thick tension between the former friends. Sana was, by then, the face of Karibu, speaking in most interviews about the store, while Glover worked behind the scenes, managing the business intently. Employees could sense a rift in the cofounders' partnership, even if they didn't know the exact cause. Frustration over seemingly preventable money woes were only bolstered by anger-induced cheap shots. And the accusations were many. There were threats of violence, severe salary gaps, poor business decisions, and insults, according to both of the men. All this, Glover said, "made it impossible to manage effectively."

Glover said he wasn't compensated for his work during his last two years with Karibu. Sales dropped dramatically and Karibu lost more than one million dollars over those two years, Glover said. (Sana has denied Glover's claims of withholding pay.) The dysfunction and financial problems were enough for Glover to leave Karibu. Once he did, the business fell deeper into financial disarray. And Sana couldn't handle it all. There was only one path forward, he reasoned. The book industry, and Karibu's customers, were all shocked when Sana announced in January 2008 that all the chain's stores would close by that February.

News articles were riddled with contradictions about the business's demise. In some, Sana blamed the closing on failed personal relationships, and in others, he cited financial issues. He blamed internal mismanagement and revealed that the company owed thousands to vendors. Sana had plans to file for bankruptcy. He told *The Baltimore Sun* that Karibu had been in a downward spiral and he "would need a miracle to pay back all the debt now."

Before calling it quits, Sana made a last-ditch effort to address his relationship with Glover and, in turn, save Karibu. If the former friends could reconcile, maybe there was a chance to replicate the success Karibu had seen in its most profitable years. He called a meeting of elders—respected mentors with no money invested in Karibu. The group became a sort of oversight board. They listened to both sides of various arguments and encouraged Glover and Sana to reconcile as "brothers." It didn't work. Glover recalled much of the group being Sana's close friends, and the meeting amounting to more of an ambush than anything else. It was difficult for him and Sana to return to a healthy working relationship amid allegations of unfair business practices, cheap insults, and violence, all while the bookstore chain fell deeper into debt. Karibu couldn't weather such a fierce storm. The book industry, and Karibu's customers, were all shocked when Sana announced in January 2008 that all the chain's stores would close by that February. Zane planned to continue her tradition of beginning her author tour at Karibu. She was confused when store managers couldn't schedule her for the tour stop. But it all began to make sense when Sana announced Karibu's closure.

The details of Karibu's downfall remained a mystery to the public. Writers, customers, publishers, and booksellers were simply sad to see the once-successful chain go. Leaders like Fugate and Coates regarded it as a major loss to Black booksellers, who were already on the margins of the book industry. Booksellers who knew and mentored Sana and Glover lamented the fractured relationship, even as they were left in the dark about the pair's personal issues.

All Karibu's stores soon had "Sale" and "Clearance" signs to unload their massive inventory. Customers drove from several states away to buy the last of Karibu's stock. They only had a few weeks to buy up what they could after the sudden closure announcement. Any profits that came from the sales went to paying off the chain's debts, Sana said. Despite the contradictions about the closure in news articles, Sana alluded to his failures as a leader at Karibu. His personal life and his business were crumbling at the same time—in addition to the chain's closure, he was in the middle of a divorce. He spent the next few years in limbo, "like a zombie," he said, as he worked to regain his footing and put his life back together. For Sana, Karibu's closing was a traumatic fall that he's still working to recover from. He tried to pour himself into things he loved, including managing boxers. He ended up chronicling his life and journey with Karibu in his 2017 memoir, *Never Stop.*

Many of Karibu's employees, some of whom remained close to Glover and Sana, went on to become respected writers and poets. But there were no stories of the Sana–Glover dispute or public declarations about the demise of the chain from them. The end of the most successful Black bookstore chain in the country would remain a mystery and steeped in contradiction for years to come. But this bitter end wouldn't tarnish Karibu's legacy. Booksellers, both Black and otherwise, would remember Karibu as a successful Black business that served its community with passion, intentionality, and care.

CHAPTER EIGHT

THE BATTLE AGAINST GENTRIFICATION

From left: Yao and Karla Glover, founders of Karibu Books; Ramunda and Derrick Young, owners of MahoganyBooks; and Shirikiana and Haile Gerima, owners of Sankofa Video, Books & Café.

SANA AND GLOVER SPENT THE NEXT FEW YEARS SEPA-rately repairing their finances and coming to terms with their fractured dream. Disillusionment set in for Glover. His relationship with both Sana and Karibu ended in financial loss and heartache that he was unsure how to recover from. He wondered if he'd been naïve to think he could build a lasting Black institution, one sustained by a commitment to Black freedom.

A poet first and foremost, Glover poured himself into his writing. He read poetry at local events and published his prose in journals. He maintained relationships with many of Karibu's employees and invited them along in a new online project he called *Free Black Space. Free Black Space* was an opportunity to duplicate the Karibu environment in a digital space amid the rise of the Internet. Glover entered the world of blogging and saw *Free Black Space* as a vehicle for making public the private conversations Black people were having among themselves every day. As the years passed, he published essays by friends and writers he'd met throughout his life. His writing proved to be a safe place to reflect on his time with Karibu. On the blog, and once in a literary journal, Glover shared the story of his early vending days with his wife, Karla, and his dashed hopes and dreams with Karibu. He did not write much about Sana and never explained the cause of their strained relationship. Glover resolved early on to remain silent about Karibu's end and his strife with Sana and allow his extroverted, charismatic former business partner to run with his account of what happened to Karibu—whether it was entirely accurate or not. This silence became the norm for Glover.

Glover may have lost a friend, a dream, and a business with Karibu's end, but he'd developed a wealth of knowledge. Karibu taught him the ways of the book industry and how to run and manage a book business. In the years after the chain shut down, it was W. Paul Coates who encouraged Glover to continue putting his skills to use. There was a struggling bookstore in Washington, DC, that could use his expertise, Coates said. Sankofa Video, Books & Café had been open for fifteen years when Glover began working with the owners, Shirikiana and Haile Gerima, in 2013. Sankofa sat nestled on Georgia Avenue Northwest, just a few blocks from Howard University. The Gerimas didn't think much about money. The filmmaking and bookselling duo focused on the community, rather than financial goals, when running the store. They put deep thought into the store's furniture, décor, and children's programs, and pushed thoughts of profits from their minds.

"The way the place became community rooted was slow and steady, but it happened from the beginning," Shirikiana recalled. "That community root is what let us know we were succeeding. Looking at the financial part was discouraging. Even now, if we were to have gone the route of trying to make benchmarks, I don't think we would have Sankofa now."

This community-over-money approach was both a flaw and an asset for Sankofa. And it was a consistent source of frustration when Glover began working as a consultant at the store. He was meticulous as he read through the store's financial records—or lack thereof—and taught the owners how to engage with vendors and record important data. Shirikiana and Haile practice Glover's advice even today.

||| ▰▰▰▰▰▰ |||

Sankofa was a keepsake of Black culture in DC as economic pressure threatened businesses in the city. It was a specialty store in a way, selling movies by Black filmmakers and sandwiches named after famous Black directors—like the Spike Lee Panini. Sankofa grew out of Shirikiana and Haile's love for film. They named the shop after their most successful movie, *Sankofa*, the story of a young woman transported back in time to the slave era. Mainstream distributors told the couple the movie wasn't marketable. So, they raised money on their own, securing small grants and later funding from the Ghana and Burkina Faso governments. From 1993 to 1995, the Gerimas and a group of dedicated supporters helped the couple screen *Sankofa* at theaters across the country, rallying communities to watch the film. They were still distributing *Sankofa*, their other films, and movies from other filmmakers through their distribution company, Mypheduh Films, when they bought the building that would become Sankofa Video, Books & Café in the late 1990s. The fraternity chapter that owned the space before left files and abandoned desks throughout the building. As Haile and Shirikiana's eyes wandered over the desolate office space, Haile said, "This would be good for a bookstore."

Their vision was to house books and movies by Black people on the same shelves. It didn't take much to determine their inventory. Both Haile and Shirikiana were Pan-Africanists, and they wanted the books on Sankofa's shelves to reflect that worldview. The couple reached out to an old friend, Nati Natakati, who ran both the Afrikan World Books wholesaler and Everyone's Place Bookstore in Baltimore. They loaded up their van with books from the wholesaler, and Natakati sent them on their way with a simple "Pay me when you sell them." The couple operated Mypheduh Films and their production company Negod Gwad Productions out of Sankofa's basement. Upstairs, books by Chancellor Williams and Haki Madhubuti sat next to films by obscure

Black artists. The Gerimas launched Sankofa with a gala. Poets Sonia Sanchez, Madhubuti, Toni Lightfoot, and Brian Gilmore performed, and locals got a taste of Sankofa's activities and children's story time. They advertised the event through local radio and flyers, but mainly through word of mouth. Haile and Shirikiana were amazed to see the opening packed with Black artists and community members. The success of the gala was an early sign to the Gerimas that the community would find a second home in Sankofa and come to regard it as a cultural staple in the city.

Young people especially were drawn to Sankofa. Howard students settled in on Sankofa's couches to talk and work in study groups. While other Black bookstores hosted authors, Sankofa held events with both writers and up-and-coming filmmakers who could talk about breaking into the industry. Local parents would bring their children to Sankofa for storytelling events or the occasional African dance class. From the time the store opened in 1998, the Gerimas knew they wanted Sankofa to be a communal space first and business second. The way to do this, they reasoned, was by holding these events. In the store's early days, Shirikiana sat in a used rocking chair and read books to children every Sunday. First, only three children showed up, then four, and soon the room would be filled weekly with children excited for their trip to Sankofa to hear a few stories.

Sankofa remained one of the few strongholds as both Black bookstores and their competition, bookstore chains, endured the wrath of the recession. This came after the demise of Borders, once a major enemy darkening indie bookshop doors. The chain announced the liquidation of its stores in 2011, blaming digital media and the volatile bookselling industry. And along with Borders went its massive, sometimes discounted selection of Black books. Black book industry leaders knew Black authors would likely feel the effects of the closure; they would lose a major retail space to sell their books. But the closure wasn't enough to send customers back to Black bookstores to find books from Black authors — Amazon and Barnes & Noble were still alive and well. And as a result, the number of Black bookstores was startlingly low.

There has never been a totally accurate picture of just how many of the shops existed in the country at any given time. But Troy Johnson has kept a list. Even though the American Booksellers Association was finally bouncing back from years of declining membership, the number of Black bookstores in total continued to decrease. Johnson, then a web designer, began attempting to track the number of Black bookstores in the country in the late 1990s, and he has admitted that his estimates may be off. But when he declared to the public in 2014, "Only 54 Black-owned bookstores remain in America," people listened. By Johnson's account, hundreds of stores had closed since the 1990s' surge of Black bookshops. He published the news in a post on his website, the African American Literature Book Club, and sounded the alarm in articles about the state of the Black book industry. This had become a familiar tale for Black booksellers, but the declaration of such a steep decline sent shock waves through the Black bookselling world. Whether the number was accurate, headlines about the state of Black bookselling certainly supported Johnson's claim. The Shrine of the Black Madonna had liquidated its store in Detroit and closed its Houston location for "restructuring," Marcus Books launched an unsuccessful fundraising campaign to buy back its San Francisco store from real estate developers, and several other booksellers were unsure of their fate. After hosting signings for luminaries like Maya Angelou, Toni Morrison, and both Bill and Hillary Clinton, Villarosa, then seventy-four, retired from Hue-Man Experience Bookstore in Harlem in 2004. Marva Allen took ownership of the store, and over the next few years, the shop struggled to stay afloat. Hue-Man in Harlem, once seen as the picture of a successful Black bookshop, was forced to close and go online in 2012. Allen weighed the pros and cons for years before breaking the news in an open letter to the community. "Faced with tremendous social pressures to deliver the next big idea, celebrity books have become the interim hype, yet even that is not a sustainable model for an industry in turmoil," Allen said.

Hue-Man was among several Black bookshops that just couldn't compete with new consumer technology and a fast-changing business environment. Glover used *Free Black Space* to lament the demise of so many Black bookstores. It was a post riddled with defeat. "They die along with people," Glover wrote of Black bookshops. "They die along with parts of the city where black folks used to live." Glover championed the library as a more sustainable way to get books to Black communities. By this time, Liberation in Harlem had closed and Una Mulzac herself had passed away, and Alfred Ligon, the last piece of the Aquarian Bookshop, died, too. There was a loss of landmarks: both stores and booksellers.

The situation wasn't much better in 2015. Hakim's Bookstore in West Philly was in such dire straits that locals did a double take when they walked past the location and saw the shop was still open. Yvonne Blake struggled to hold on to both the family business and her father's legacy after Dawud Hakim died in 1997. The store's hours were limited as Blake worked full-time and took care of her ailing mother. And the holiday season, once a sure source of meaty sales for the store, was becoming less lucrative. Meanwhile, many of the store's core, longtime customers had moved away or died, and technological advances like Amazon made it difficult to attract new ones. Even with help from local economic development groups, Blake couldn't scrape together enough money to hire employees to keep the store open more often. Hakim's was at death's door. It would take at least two years and a fundraising campaign before Blake would find the store on steadier financial ground. Articles about its potential closure served as a clarion call for Black communities across the country. A man who owned a computer-consulting firm heard about the store's misfortune and created a website for the shop, and put together a reorganization plan for the business. A young local activist visited Blake and offered some advice to attract young readers: get on social media and make the store visible. An air of accomplishment spread throughout the city as Hakim's began to recover. It had become commonplace for bookstores to rely on charity at one time or another to keep their doors open. This was both a testament to the power of community and an example of just how much Black bookshops struggled.

||| ▬▬▬▬▬ |||

Changes in the 2010s marked uncharted territory for Black booksellers, much like the rest of the country. Smartphones and social media were well into their ascent and would irreversibly alter American social life by the end of the decade. If Black booksellers were already feeling the effects of operating largely offline, the new digital age would demand more from them than ever before. Meanwhile, the symbolism of the first Black president, and the resulting backlash, would usher in a racial dynamic that sent Black communities and their supporters into Black bookshops. This wasn't the first time non-Black customers patronized Black bookstores, but the political climate of the 2010s brought on a visible solidarity. Barack Obama was less than a year into his presidency at the start of the decade, and the country was only just beginning to recover from the Great Recession. This repair, however, was unequal. While white households began to recover the wealth they'd lost, Black family wealth declined through the first three years of the decade. A narrative of victory swept through the country, even as Black communities struggled under debt, criminalization, and the remnants of the housing crisis. Conversations about reparations began in earnest but bumped up against a brewing right-wing nationalist backlash.

Obama's election launched a national debate about whether America had become a post-racial society, never mind the very real and foundational systemic racism embedded in every area of American life. This debate came and went swiftly with Donald Trump's birther conspiracy and a string of racist police and white vigilante killings. Technological advances of the decade made it easier to document the abuse Black people experienced. Social media live streams and smartphone videos, along with police body and dash cameras, led to unprecedented evidence of the police violence Black people had decried for centuries. And the police killings were almost constant. Black America could not recover from the killing of Trayvon Martin in 2012 before a string of other police murders followed in 2014: Michael Brown, an eighteen-year-old gunned down in the St. Louis suburb of Ferguson, Missouri; Eric Garner, a New York father; and Tamir Rice, a twelve-year-old boy holding a toy gun in a park. The next year, 2015, saw the deaths of Freddie Gray, Sandra Bland, and nine Black churchgoers at the Mother Emanuel AME Church in Charleston, South Carolina. A year later, a Minnesota police officer killed Philando Castile, and Castile's girlfriend streamed the altercation with police and Castile's death on Facebook Live.

Each death led to protests, and this time, mourners had access to several social media platforms where they could share their pain, express their frustrations, and amplify the voices of others like them. This was monumental for Black activism and, in turn, promoted an ever-increasing interest in race issues and Black consciousness. Protests only intensified when George Zimmerman, who murdered Martin in 2012, was acquitted of the killing. Martin's death marked the start of Black Lives Matter, a poignant hashtag that quickly became a rallying cry and social justice movement. Black bookstores, however few remained at the time, took on their historic role as educators. Donya and Donna Craddock, sisters who run The Dock Bookshop in East Fort Worth, Texas, welcomed a surge of customers amid Martin's death and the subsequent trial related to the killing. Fort Worth residents piled into the shop for town halls to voice their frustrations about everything from the killing itself, to the trial, to media coverage of the teen's death.

The Dock had opened four years earlier, in 2008, and had already cemented itself as a place to talk about political and social issues—locals would go to the store to watch Obama in the presidential debates. The controversy over Martin's death was a moment for Fort Worth residents to utilize The Dock's community hub. Elsewhere, Khamani Harrison was among countless people wanting to understand how Zimmerman could get away with what he'd done without serving any prison time. So, she went to Zahra's Books and Things in Inglewood, California.

"I felt like they had answers that somehow I wasn't getting in the mainstream," she said of Black bookstores. She bought *Survival Strategies for Africans in America* by Anthony Browder. The book helped her cope with seeing so much violence against Black Americans.

As the years passed, the lingering pain over the police killings continued to mix with economic frustrations. Gentrification was picking off small businesses one by one and replacing them with larger operations with dozens of employees. Higher rents and an ever-shifting Black community had always been cause enough for a Black bookseller to move their store. Booksellers saw their neighbors, often local mom-and-pop businesses, shuttered and neighborhoods become whiter, younger, and wealthier all before being pushed out themselves.

A racial reckoning was brewing within the American Booksellers Association, too. A group of Black and other booksellers of color spoke out during a town hall at the ABA's Winter Institute conference in 2017. Angela Maria Spring, a self-proclaimed "white-passing, white-privileged" Latina, along with Hannah Oliver Depp, a Black woman who now owns Loyalty Bookstores, led the charge. They read a statement calling for the ABA to support Black booksellers and booksellers of color and make the association's leadership more diverse and inclusive. As a result, the

ABA launched its Diversity Task Force, and Spring was elected to serve on the ABA board in 2018. The ABA would see a more diverse membership in the coming years, but it wouldn't shake the allegations of being a "white organization" among many Black booksellers. There was a period when the ABA saw more Black booksellers join its ranks—thanks to the likes of Villarosa and Rodgers—but white membership and support continued to outpace any other racial group in the organization. Through the end of the '90s and the years after, some Black booksellers said they were ignored when they requested to join the ABA. Others had long abandoned the idea of joining the ABA, not seeing much sense in aligning their Black bookshops with the overwhelmingly white organization. For the Gerimas, membership in the ABA didn't take up much space in their minds as they continued to endure racialized economic struggles.

Haile and Shirikiana watched with worry through the decades. More than a hundred businesses around Sankofa, many of them Black-owned, closed under the weight of rising operational costs in the rapidly changing city. A funk song conferred the moniker "Chocolate City" on DC back in the 1970s, when more than 70 percent of the city was Black. But decades of economic disparities and gentrification had pushed much of the population out, leaving the district with a less than 45 percent Black population by 2019. This exodus of Black residents meant the closure of respected Black establishments, like a sub shop and a clothing store near Howard where students loved to go. Sankofa was the last of these communal hangouts. If there were ever a time for the Gerimas to abandon their lackadaisical approach to the store's profits, this would have been it. Gentrification around Sankofa meant rising property value and, in turn, taxes. Sankofa was hit with a $30,000 tax bill in 2018, and the burden grew by the thousands as the months passed. Paying that kind of money would put the store in jeopardy and the community at risk of losing one of its last cultural hubs. Local, lesser-known artists, filmmakers, and authors would lose an important outlet for showcasing and selling their work.

"Gentrification in DC is like a wildfire," Shirikiana told a reporter. "People are looking for an oasis in the midst of a big, white snowstorm." The thousands the owners had already shelled out to relieve some of their tax burden took away from renovation projects and upgrades to their aging building. The community was eager to rally behind the Gerimas to fight for a tax abatement and, ultimately, save the store. Community members shared updates through email lists, social media, and local radio programs, and other supporters wrote op-eds with a simple declaration: "Gentrification is the villain." The Gerimas themselves held rallies outside Sankofa, speaking about the ills of gentrifying Black neighborhoods: the white people who walked down District streets with an air of entitlement, expecting everyone to move out of their way, and the city officials who pressured Black business owners to leave the area for the sake of "development."

"What we're facing now with gentrification is what we've been facing since we've been here—on steroids," Shirikiana told supporters at one rally in June 2019.

Shirikiana reached out to a council member, Brianne Nadeau, who agreed to sponsor a resolution, the Mypheduh Films DBA Sankofa Video and Books Real Property Tax Exemption Act. The tax abatement bill would exempt Sankofa from tax payments for ten years. The Gerimas weren't just making an appeal for Sankofa. They wanted to lead a charge to protect other Black businesses in the area at risk of closure. They understood that several small Black businesses in the city didn't have the notoriety or community support to hold rallies or appeal to council members for their cause. So, a fight for Sankofa needed to be a fight for all Black businesses in the district. To this end, the Gerimas hoped to find a way to create economic protections for what they called "legacy Black businesses." Thankfully, Haile and Shirikiana were fighting tax hikes in a new era. Social media platforms like Twitter and Instagram ruled the roost in 2019, giving them new, innovative ways to get the word out about their campaign. The couple promoted their cause on Twitter, sharing photos of the storefront alongside tweets like "Gentrification has raised Sankofa's property tax to a whopping $30,000 for 2019! This undermines our growth and sustainability (and many other small businesses, too)." "Are you a small, Black business?" "Is gentrification threatening you?" These were the questions the Gerimas raised to rally other small business owners to tackle the economic pressures as a united front.

Locals routinely gathered at Sankofa to talk about the issues and make plans to advocate for small businesses at city government meetings. It wasn't difficult to win residents to their cause at a time when gentrification was threatening more than just businesses. DC's distinct go-go music became an anti-gentrification battle cry among Black Washingtonians forced to watch their communities became whiter and wealthier. The fight began in the spring of 2019 when a resident in a shiny new luxury apartment building complained about the go-go music blasting from a nearby electronics store. Authorities told the owner to turn the music off. The sudden silence was deafening coming from a store known for blasting go-go music from its speakers for years. The backlash was swift. Residents took to the streets, started petitions, and launched the #DontMuteDC campaign to restore the shop's music, but also to challenge gentrification and the stripping of Black DC culture more broadly. The music was soon back on, but the situation was a tipping point for fed-up locals.

Sankofa's campaign was just another iteration of this battle. The fight to keep the store open was a struggle to maintain a sense of culture and identity as surrounding neighborhoods quickly became unrecognizable. Still reeling from the Go-Go fight, locals rallied behind Sankofa and geared up for the first hearing on the tax abatement bill. On June 3, 2019, customers, activists, authors, and artists who relied on Sankofa packed room 500 of the John Wilson government building for a hearing in front of the DC council's Committee on Business and Economic Development. It didn't faze Shirikiana when she saw Kenyan McDuffie was the only council member to show up for the hearing. Instead, she spoke forcefully about plans to make Sankofa more accessible for customers with disabilities, install HVAC upgrades, and continue footing the bill to host and promote local artists. None of these changes would be possible with a $30,000 tax bill hanging over the Gerimas' heads. Customers old and young spoke at the hearing of Sankofa's longevity and what a consistently operating Black institution meant for residents living through the city's reshaping. By the end of the hearing, the committee had heard from concerned customers and advocates who made it clear that the

#DefendSankofa campaign wasn't simply about the bookstore but a defense of all the small Black businesses being crushed under the weight of gentrification.

Local activists joined the Gerimas' cause, seeing Sankofa's troubles as both a manifestation of systemic racism and, ultimately, a political fight as much as a social one. W. Paul Coates, the Black publisher and former Black Panther, was among the activists who spoke of Sankofa's relevance to Black communities battered by displacement and economic pressure. The Gerimas waited with bated breath after the hearing to learn if the committee would approve the tax abatement and move the bill on to the full council. They found a foe in Jim Dewitt, then DC's chief financial officer, who objected to the tax abatement. But his objection was drowned out by the thousands of written testimonies from community members. The testimonies were enough to convince all but one of DC's council members to approve the tax abatement bill in 2019. Mayor Muriel Bowser signed the bill into law in what appeared to be a victory for Sankofa's anti-gentrification efforts across the city. There were years of back-and-forth as the Gerimas pushed the local government to uphold the new law amid slow-moving procedures. But by 2022, Sankofa's slate was wiped clean. The Gerimas don't pay property taxes for the store today.

|||▬▬▬▬|||

This support for Sankofa was proof that Black bookstores were finally getting their due. Customers wrote moving essays about their time at their favorite shops, and headlines about shuttered bookstores were inspiring a new generation of booksellers to open stores of their own. Poignant profiles remembered past shops like

Vaughn's Bookstore and veteran stores still in existence, like Eso Won. Customers and Black booksellers alike lauded booksellers of the last fifteen years who had powered through nationwide decline and had a wealth of knowledge to show for it. Perhaps one of the greatest examples of this fortitude is the Washington, DC–based MahoganyBooks. Derrick and Ramunda Young's strictly online shop was an innovative idea in 2007 when other bookstores struggled to stay afloat in their physical stores.

"We wanted to make Black books accessible no matter where you live. It was important to us then, and it's important to us now," Ramunda told WTOP News in 2024. Derrick added, "We wanted to make sure that people across the country, no matter if you're in Minnesota, West Virginia, would have access to the same quality books that I had access to."

Derrick grew up with access to Black books, able to read titles with images of children who looked like him. But Ramunda hadn't. She was among the many booksellers who recalled having few, if any, books about Black people as a child. This influenced the Youngs' mission for MahoganyBooks. Today, both new and old booksellers mention the Youngs when they talk about the leaders who inspired them and served as models for Black bookselling. MahoganyBooks still experienced struggles, though. The couple felt the strain of not having a physical location, a place to gather people and interact with them in person. And they wanted more than their successful Lit Lounge. After ten years in the business, the Youngs decided it was time to take their books to a physical location. But, like Sankofa, they confronted fierce gentrification in the DC area. They spent years searching for the perfect location for their store. Ultimately, MahoganyBooks landed in the predominately Black neighborhood of Anacostia in Southeast DC. Anacostia, too, was feeling the effects of gentrification, which made MahoganyBooks even more of a welcome addition to the neighborhood. It was considered Anacostia's first bookstore in twenty years. It was a five-hundred-square-foot store with an adjacent space for events. Rather than a single dusty, old computer, the Youngs filled the store with tablets customers could use to find books online while they browsed the shelves. Derrick called it "a bookstore 2.0."

The Youngs were certainly forward-thinking. They wanted to make the physical store a digital operation that would withstand economic downturn and periods of slow business. Their years of bookselling experience equipped them with the insights and wisdom required to successfully run a Black bookstore. Like several other community-oriented bookstore owners, the Youngs are known for hosting dozens of book and community events. And as their influence grew, so did their inventory. This would come in handy for booksellers' next challenge: a pandemic and racial uprising in 2020.

The 2010s was a decade marked by closings, openings, and reopenings. But it ended with more Black bookstores than it started with. The recession had subsided, and it finally looked like Black bookstores had found stable ground. A communal commitment to Black books and education became the norm among Black booksellers, even if they didn't know about stores like Drum and Spear or Liberation. In Missouri, Pamela Blair opened the Eye-SeeMe African American Children's Bookstore in 2015 to play an active role in local children's education. The shop regularly hosts online and in-school book fairs, donates books to schools and non-profit centers, and partners with local groups to host educational programs. The store even has a classroom designated for children's lessons, events, and talks. Meanwhile, Marc Lamont Hill launched Uncle Bobbie's Coffee and Books in 2017 to provide both Black books and a community space for Philadelphia's Germantown area. Noëlle Santos opened the Lit. Bar in 2019 in the Bronx's Mott Haven neighborhood, despite having no retail experience, to fill a void after the area's only bookstore—Barnes & Noble—closed. The Black activism of the 2010s, and the social media platforms that helped to fuel it, were cause for rejoicing. But it was born out of necessity, and no one could have predicted what was to come. Yes, people's voices were finally being heard, but it didn't exactly equate to progress or social advancement for Black people.

The country was still immersed in voter suppression, education and housing inequalities, and domestic terrorism from emboldened white nationalists. There was a clear backlash to Obama's presidency, and Trump's administration only empowered the host of white nationalist groups looking for permission to carry out their terrorism. As a result, readers were becoming increasingly interested in books about systemic racism and white supremacy. At Eso Won, customers ran to buy *When They Call You a Terrorist* by a cofounder of Black Lives Matter, Patrisse Khan-Cullors, and *Fire and Fury* by Michael Wolff, a book about the Trump White House. There was a budding desire among communities across the country to simply know more—more about the ways racism colors everyday life and the ways the powers that be worked to quell Black political movements. The deaths of Trayvon Martin, Michael Brown, Eric Garner, Alton Sterling, Philando Castile, and others were flashpoint moments only intensified by Trump's presidency. The nation was approaching a tipping point. Soon it would see again just how much massive Black movements and Black bookstores impacted each other.

When *The New York Times* asked a group of famous writers about their favorite bookstore, Ta-Nehisi Coates didn't hesitate to name Eso Won. He recalled visiting the store and perusing its aisles for an hour while on tour for his first book. As a child of the Black Power movement, he said, he was raised on authors like Zora Neale Hurston and C. L. R. James. To him, Eso Won watered the roots of the Black literary canon. His words, published about a month after Trump was elected president, positioned Black bookstores as a source of comfort and strength for the days ahead.

"In much the same way we need diversity among authors and editors, we need diversity among the ranks of booksellers," Coates said then. "They are the ultimate arbiters of our literary tradition. In these coming dark times, we can scarcely afford to be without them."

CHAPTER NINE

A BITTERSWEET RACIAL RECKONING

Akwete Tyehimba speaks with children at
the Pan-African Connection Bookstore.

AKWETE TYEHIMBA DIDN'T KNOW WHAT TO EXPECT WHEN
she reopened her Dallas bookstore, Pan-African Connection, for
walk-ins in late May 2020. The store had been closed for months

because of the Covid pandemic, and she wasn't sure how quickly business would bounce back—or whether it would pick up at all. Tyehimba's answer came in the form of a full store; lines wrapped around the corner. Customers shifted their masks to smell the essential oils for sale and sifted through the bookshop's tables to find their size in black T-shirts with George Floyd's face on the front. They stuffed books under their arms as they walked the store's aisles, looking through the African sculptures, drums, mudcloth, waist beads, and dashikis. At checkout, most bought a book or two along with a soap, body butter, sculpture, or essential oil. Typically, Pan-African Connection, in Dallas's Oak Cliff neighborhood, saw its biggest rush during its annual Juneteenth celebration. But the store owed this burst of business to tragedy. And Tyehimba knew it.

"George Floyd died, and people were upset. People were wanting justice," Tyehimba said. "People were determined to intentionally support Black businesses. It turned on a light inside of them that, 'Look, we are all we got. We have to support each other.'"

Pan-African Connection reopened just days after Minneapolis police officer Derek Chauvin knelt on Floyd's neck for nearly ten minutes, killing him, on May 25. The murder set off a string of protests across the country and Black people boiled with anger over the all-too-familiar racism that killed Floyd, Breonna Taylor, Ahmaud Arbery, and Tony McDade within months of one another. And, of course, Black Dallasites relied on Pan-African Connection as a place to voice their frustrations and support their communities; the beloved bookstore has been a fixture in the city for more than thirty years. Tyehimba and her bookselling family intentionally fashioned Pan-African Connection as a community resource center and art gallery. The store is known for its Sunday markets, where vendors from across the city can peddle their wares at the shop's entrance. Local leaders who run community gardens, back-to-school programs, and social justice groups routinely use the store's auditorium-esque side room to put on their programs. And stationed at the store's entrance are tables filled with flyers and pamphlets letting customers know about events and programs happening in the city. Anyone born and raised in northern Texas has at least heard of Pan-African Connection, if they aren't loyal customers already. And transplants new to the city, like me, find their way to the store almost immediately.

In 1989, Tyehimba founded the store with her husband, Bandele, both as a haven for people interested in African heritage and as a way to familiarize people with African history. At the time, they were members of the socialist All-African People's Revolutionary Party, founded by revolutionary and Ghanian politician Kwame Nkrumah, and saw bookstores as a tool for teaching and organizing people around African cultures and ideologies. The couple named the store to reflect these Pan-Africanist political beliefs. And they've stayed true to that goal through the decades. After Bandele's death in 2012, Tyehimba and their daughter, Adjwoa, continued the work the couple had started. These decades of community investment and cultural focus made Pan-African Connection the ideal place for locals to congregate and make sense of Floyd's murder. The summer of 2020 was Pan-African Connection's most successful period to date.

In the early days of the pandemic, W. Paul Coates called for a Zoom meeting of at least one hundred booksellers and other book industry officials. On that massive call, Black booksellers from across the country were able to commune, crafting their survival strategies and sharing their experiences and tips for getting through the pandemic with their stores intact. Some booksellers focused on providing schools with reading guides and at-home learning toolkits. Others, who were based in college towns, were launching YouTube channels to make up for losses due to a lack of in-person student customers. It was a moment of calm and community before the storms of 2020 swept through in full swing. Soon, these Black booksellers had stories like Tyehimba's: shops shuttered by Covid and facing uncertain futures were being inundated with requests for books about race, were overwhelmed with new customers, and were selling more books than ever before.

DeAndra Beard, who owns Beyond Barcodes in Indianapolis, told me of the nights she spent filling book requests behind her desk at home while protesters marched and chanted loudly outside her window. There were hundreds of orders. Her phone rang constantly, and online requests came in by the minute. One copy of Robin DiAngelo's *White Fragility* for a man in Ohio; three copies of Ijeoma Oluo's *So You Want to Talk About Race* for a woman in Mississippi and her daughters; and a bulk order of Ibram X. Kendi's *How to Be an Antiracist* for a school in Fort Wayne. Beard's hands were full. She was just as angry as the protesters making their way down the streets outside her home. Although she would have loved to be outside, walking arm in arm with the other angered marchers, she decided books would be her contribution to the political moment.

"I could see them. I could hear them," Beard recalled of the protesters. "And I had to make a decision. My work is right here. My part in the protest, my part in this movement, is right here where I am."

By then, it had been weeks since Floyd's murder, and months since Covid forced the country into shutdown. The protests were about more than just police violence, though. People were forced to think about systemic racism's violent nature, and the way it plays out in every area of American life. Black people were bearing the brunt of an unprecedented health crisis: more likely to get sick from Covid, more likely to lose their jobs, and less likely to recover fully from any of it. They were contracting the virus and dying from it at disproportionate rates, and it was nearly impossible to get adequate healthcare at overwhelmed hospitals. The role of racism in both the political deaths and Covid outcomes couldn't be ignored. White and other non-Black people were inspired to protest and learn more about the racism that colored their lives. Antiracist reading lists circulated on the Internet and calls to buy from Black businesses sent people to Black bookstores. *How to Be an Antiracist* was one of the biggest sellers for Black bookstores that summer. And customers bought up Oluo's *So You Want to Talk About Race*, DiAngelo's *White Fragility*, and *The New Jim Crow* by Michelle Alexander. It was hard to keep these titles stocked, and difficult to convince customers to buy lesser-known books about racism and Black life—ones you wouldn't find on the *New York Times*' bestseller list. Many of the white customers finding their way to Black bookstores sought out the easily digestible books about race targeted to them.

"I sold books that came out from the fifties up to the nineties, because I didn't want people to forget those authors either," said VaLinda Miller, who runs Turning Page Bookshop in South Carolina.

Just a state away from Beard, Janeice Haynes's Detroit home was in disarray. Books were piled on tables and chairs, packing labels sat in organized chaos, and boxes and packing paper were strewn across the floor. Haynes, her husband, and their daughter had formed a type of assembly line; one person gathered the books, one placed them in boxes, and another placed the packing labels. The Detroit Book City physical bookstore may have been closed, but business was booming. More customers than Haynes could fathom were placing orders online and by phone. The bookshop brought in at least $25,000 between May and August, a surge Haynes hadn't seen before and hasn't seen since. Like many Black booksellers at the time, Detroit Book City didn't have the infrastructure to meet the unprecedented demand. Thankfully, Haynes's long-ignored request to join the American Booksellers Association had finally been approved, allowing her to fulfill book orders through its online store, Bookshop.org, which the ABA co-owns.

In Boston, Frugal Bookstore had to release a statement asking customers to be patient while they worked to fill more than twenty thousand orders. At Turning Page Bookshop, Miller urged her customers to purchase other books while she waited for a shipment of four hundred copies of *White Fragility* to make it to the store. Marcus Books went from being on life support at the beginning of the year to having to recruit volunteers just to keep up with the store's phone calls. Public schools and other local institutions placed bulk book orders and established new relationships with their local Black bookstores. It was a time of collaboration and hope for Black booksellers. The tense political climate was the perfect storm for the book industry. In turn, authors were seeing unprecedented sales. In 2019, less than a year before the protests began, Kendi struggled to drum up interest in his book *How to Be an Antiracist*. He only sold about forty copies during a signing at Eso Won in Los Angeles, and there was just a spattering of orders for it in the months that followed. But by the summer of 2020, Black bookstores across the country were selling hundreds of copies of the book—Eso Won sold five hundred in a matter of weeks.

The moment was bittersweet, though.

Booksellers were happy to see more sales and jumped at the chance to talk about Black history and social issues with new customers. But they couldn't ignore the circumstances that led to the boom in business. Floyd's, Taylor's, and Arbery's deaths didn't just inspire a renewed interest in Black bookstores; they served as a sharp reminder of the injustices and inequities that characterize being Black in America. It wasn't lost on booksellers that it took police officers and white vigilantes murdering Black people to usher the nation into a racial reckoning and people of all races into Black bookstores. It was difficult to simply be happy for the success, especially as images and videos of Floyd's final moments played constantly on television and the Internet. Some booksellers, like Haynes, shied away from directly addressing the political turmoil on the bookstores' social media and messaging. Other booksellers, like Beard and Ali Nervis, owner of Grassrootz Books and Juice Bar in Phoenix, saw the moment as an opportunity to mobilize the community. Beard held virtual meetings for locals to vent and chart new paths forward. Nervis held virtual fundraisers to support other Black businesses and worked with a local non-profit to get food and resources to the pandemic-battered community. In Texas, Donna and Donya Craddock complied with shutdown orders and closed The Dock in Fort Worth. But that didn't stop the public from using the beloved bookstore as a meeting place during both the pandemic and the summer's uprisings. The doors remained locked, the inside was dark and empty, and old signs sat affixed to the exterior. But local students sat crisscross or brought cushions to spend their days on the small bit of concrete in front of the store, located in a strip mall. With schools shut down and in-person classes replaced with virtual lessons, Black children who didn't have access to the Internet from home needed a place to do their schoolwork and socialize with friends. The Dock was one of few places in the area with Wi-Fi available from the inside of the store to its proverbial stoop out front.

When the Craddock sisters would visit to check on the store, they'd have to step over dozens of Black children typing away on laptops or cell phones. The students would greet them with a wave, and the sisters would return a smile. They'd rather have had the community's Black youth at their store than anywhere else. When news of protests began to mix with news of the pandemic, more people made their way to the closed store. Black teens, adults, and other people of color gathered in front of the shop with signs and bullhorns. They used The Dock as a meeting place to organize and plan before marching through Fort Worth's streets in protest. The Craddock sisters would find the groups filling the sidewalk in front of the store, handing out masks and hand sanitizer as they charted their route through the city. As the months progressed, the state loosened its shutdown rules, allowing "essential" businesses that provided necessities to operate. The Craddocks resolved that books were certainly essential. Besides, they also sold hygiene products like natural soaps, shea butter, and chewing sticks.

So, they opened their shop with a bevy of Covid protocols—only ten people allowed in the store at a time, masks required, and a hand sanitizer dispenser at the store's entrance. This brought a sigh of relief to the community that had come to rely on The Dock since it first opened in 2008. People could finally enter the store to pick up a book or talk to the owners they'd come to know and love. And the Craddocks could finally put a face to the torrent of customers who were placing thousands of online and phone orders while the shop was closed, including a sprinkling of white customers and Black out-of-towners. The Dock was a regular on the myriad lists of Black bookstores to support. When the turmoil began to unfold that summer, you'd have been hard-pressed to find a major news outlet without a list of Black bookstores. "12 Black-Owned Bookstores You Can Support Right Now," read a BuzzFeed News headline; *Entertainment Weekly*, Refinery29, and several others also published lists of Black bookstores "you can support right now." Oprah Daily published a list of active Black bookstores across the country. Its estimations put the number of Black bookshops at 125, a comfortable figure that encouraged optimism after the shops hung in the double digits for years. But soon the headlines told a different story about the bookshops' sudden fame. A June *New York Times* headline read, "Overwhelmed with Orders, Some Black-Owned Bookstores Ask for Patience," and in *W* magazine, "Have Patience for the Owners of Black-Owned Bookstores."

If the summer's protests led to more interest in Black books and books about racism, it was only a matter of time before the spotlight turned to the publishing industry: the people who decided what books to publish and promote. Amistad Press launched a social media campaign, hashtagged #BlackoutBestsellerList and #BlackPublishingPower, to bring attention to Black writers and Black people working in the book industry. The goal for the campaign was simple: readers were instructed to buy any two books by Black writers from June 14 through June 20 to "Blackout bestseller lists with Black voices." Tracy Sherrod, a Black woman and veteran in the publishing industry, was behind the campaign. Having spent decades advocating for Black books at Simon & Schuster, HarperCollins, and Hachette Book Group, Sherrod herself was proof that hiring Black people in the publishing industry could lead to more support for Black books. Thanks to the campaign, Black-authored book sales increased by 10 percent, Sherrod said, noting that HarperCollins's director of marketing kept track of week-to-week sales. It seems the campaign made a difference in the *New York Times* bestseller list, as by mid-June, Black authors and books about racism did indeed dominate the list. From mid-June through July, *How to Be an Antiracist*, *White Fragility*, and *So You Want to Talk About Race* sat comfortably in the top five spots of the *New York Times* combined print and e-book nonfiction and paperback nonfiction lists. As the weeks passed, *The New Jim Crow*, Kendi's *Stamped from the Beginning*, Beverly Daniel Tatum's *Why Are All the Black Kids Sitting Together in the Cafeteria?*, and Layla F. Saad's *Me and White Supremacy* spent weeks in the top five.

The overwhelming whiteness of the book publishing industry has never been a secret. By 2020, while publishing houses were hiring more Black people in entry-level positions, most literary agents, executives, and marketing and editorial jobs remained overwhelmingly white. Any progress happening was coming slowly. This disparity trickled down into publishing houses' inventories, with white authors accounting for 95 percent of the thousands of books put out by major publishers from 1950 to 2018. The year 2020 ushered in a time of some much-needed transparency. When L. L. McKinney, a Black woman author, started the #PublishingPaidMe hashtag in June 2020 to bring attention to the chronic racial disparities in writers' advance payments, the world learned that beloved writers like Jesmyn Ward and Roxane Gay fought tooth and nail to see adequate advances while lesser-known white writers snagged $150,000 book deals for their debuts. As a result, more than a thousand workers across the publishing industry joined in collective action, taking a day off work and devoting that time and the day's pay to supporting the uprisings over the deaths of Floyd, Taylor, Arbery, and McDade. Their bosses seemed receptive. The "Big Five" publishing houses (Penguin Random House, Simon & Schuster, Hachette Book Group, HarperCollins, and Macmillan) all put out statements denouncing racism and expressing their support for racial justice. They also promised to publish more books by writers of color and implement inclusivity training. Between the #BlackoutBestsellerList and #Publishing-PaidMe campaigns, it was clear the industry had some work to do. The statements and verbal commitments to Black books sounded good. But only time would tell whether they would lead to meaningful and lasting equity or fade along with the protests.

In 2020, several publishing houses announced a slew of imprints that focused on prioritizing Black stories and the stories of people of color. Phoebe Robinson, a comedian, author, and actress, partnered with Plume and Penguin Random House to launch Tiny Reparations Books, an imprint dedicated to amplifying "diverse voices." Its first acquisitions were Lester Fabian Brathwaite's essay collection *Rage: On Being Queer, Black, Brilliant ... and Completely Over It* and the novel *What the Fireflies Knew* by Kai Harris, a Black woman educator from Detroit. Hachette launched Legacy Lit, the publisher's first imprint dedicated to books by people of color. It touted authors like Shanita Hubbard and Faith Jenkins. Simon & Schuster went a flashier route, tapping Charlamagne tha God to lead its Atria Books division's new imprint Black Privilege Publishing. These were seismic industry shifts that signified that, perhaps, the disproportionately white publishing field was turning over a new leaf. That summer, Dana Canedy made history as the first Black person appointed as senior vice president and publisher of Simon & Schuster. Penguin Random House tapped Lisa Lucas to lead their Pantheon and Schocken Books imprints, making her the first Black publisher in Pantheon's history.

In short, Black bookstores, writers, and publishers were all impacted by the 2020 uprisings. But independent Black publishing houses, which have historically operated in a zone of invisibility, didn't end up in news stories or on lists of businesses to support. And Black publishers like Kassahun Checole, Haki Madhubuti, and Coates, who have been in the business for decades, knew well that the sudden attention on and success of Black books and publishing was artificial and would end as quickly as it began. They did not have to put out statements of solidarity or vow to hire

Black people, because they were already doing that work. Black Classic Press saw an increase in orders for titles like *Blood in My Eye* by George Jackson, Ralph Ginzburg's *100 Years of Lynchings*, and *Why Should White Guys Have All the Fun* by Reginald Lewis and Blair Walker. The publishing company closed out 2020 with more sales than it had seen in years. Amid the newfound success, Black booksellers were looking toward the future, working to come up with plans to stay financially afloat after the surge died down. And those that had relied solely on book sales and business acumen were thinking of ways to transform their shops into community hubs that could serve as important third places during similar times of national crisis. It was a return to the original focus of Black bookselling: community and camaraderie.

It wasn't just publishers and bookstores. The entire Black book ecosystem was adapting to changes brought on by the pandemic and responding to the increased interest in Black and anti-racist books. Black-centered book clubs boosted their online presences, and 2020 brought a proliferation of new reading groups. These clubs were a reliable way for readers from all over to get together and make sense of all the new books they were buying on race, class, gender, and more. Well-Read Black Girl, launched in 2015, had four hundred thousand members and 150 book club chapters around the world by 2020. And the Noname Book Club, founded in 2019, was quickly growing its membership and solidifying its chapters. Clubs like Amerie's Book Club, launched by singer Amerie, and Kimm Lett's Flowers Bookclub were created before 2020 but became havens for even more readers confined to their homes and computers during the countrywide shutdown. Other, new clubs were small but mighty. A vlogger known as Jouelzy created the SmartBrownGirl club in 2020, and the #BlackLibLit hashtag represented an online community for Black people around the world to talk about books. Meanwhile, literary advocacy groups, not wanting to cancel their festivals and conferences, went online, too. The National Black Book Festival, the National Black Writers Conference, and the National Book Club Conference, all mainstays in the industry, decided to host their annual events virtually rather than canceling.

These organizers understood the importance of the literary communities, especially during 2020's upheaval. The National Black Book Festival launched its livestreamed show *Black Authors Matter TV* in July 2020 and spent the chaotic remaining months of the year interviewing authors and Black booksellers. Meanwhile, the National Black Writers Conference, a program out of the Center for Black Literature at Medgar Evers College, was determined to happen. Its organizers made the four-day conference fully virtual and pushed it from March to November. Even with the conference on the horizon, founder Brenda Greene saw the early days of the health crisis as the perfect time to send another offering out into the world: a book club.

"Being the literary activists that we are, and the book lovers, we knew rather intuitively that people were going to turn to the arts for comfort, and for healing, and to make things make sense," April Silver, the communications consultant for the conference, said of the monthly book club. The book club is still operating today.

Tyehimba continued facilitating community events and discussions as these questions filled her head. She tucked money from the bolstered sales away to use for the many rainy days to come. Tyehimba and her daughter worked the store's two registers with lines stretching down the street during the day. In the evenings, locals sat in chairs in Pan-African Connection's auditorium to lament police violence and shed tears over recent Black deaths. Juneteenth 2020 was Pan-African Connection's biggest day of sales in the store's history. Black locals and customers from surrounding cities spent hours at Pan-African Connection watching films, participating in the store's Juneteenth Bike Ride, and bearing the heat to be part of a day of activities and community. Tyehimba cherished the programs and the bolstered sales, but like her peers, she realized the excitement would be short-lived.

The chaos of 2020 led to moments of success and profits for Black booksellers and opportunities for social advancement within white institutions. But booksellers weren't naïve; they knew the passion for Black books, and buying from Black businesses, wouldn't last forever. Most of them hoped that the moment wouldn't begin and end with book sales but would turn into meaningful action and lasting change. Others questioned the authenticity of their new customers: Were they really interested in dismantling racism? Or would the books they'd bought just collect dust on their shelves? This reflected Black booksellers' loyalty to not just their stores but the work they did in them. Making a sale was a good thing, but seeing a person transformed and mobilized by what they'd read was what many booksellers were after.

CHAPTER TEN

A NEW GENERATION OF BOOKSELLERS

Nia-Tayler Clark outside her bookstore,
Blacklit, in Farmers Branch, Texas.

JUST AS BLACK BOOKSELLERS EXPECTED, THE FERVOR FOR supporting their bookstores dissipated. The famous Eso Won in South Los Angeles had gone from seeing a thousand orders daily in 2020 to about fifty a day in the years that followed. But, beyond just slower business, the Black bookselling landscape was changing. Veteran booksellers who helped shape the industry were retiring. The industry was dealt a serious blow when James Fugate announced in 2022 that Eso Won would close its physical store by the end of the year. Fugate and Hamilton had weathered storm after storm through decades as booksellers, so it wasn't the slow business that led them to close their store. They were simply tired.

"We've been working at it a long time and at some point, I think people reach that point where that daily grind of coming into the store, even though we're open a small amount of time, you want to end that," Fugate told the *Los Angeles Times* then.

He added to *Publishers Weekly* that neither he nor Hamilton had gone on vacation in at least two years. "I'm 67 and Tom is 68. I've been in the book business since 1980 when Reagan was elected president. Both of us are sort of tired of going to work every day," he said. Eso Won was a beacon in many ways, a literary sanctum that Black people could trust for books and community. Not just because it had seen nearly every notable Black author, but because of Fugate and Hamilton's unwavering passion for Black books. A passion that accompanied Eso Won for nearly thirty-four years, from Slauson Avenue east of Crenshaw to Inglewood, and finally to Leimert Park. And a grit that sustained Eso Won through competition from chains and a death knell from Amazon. The closure was a devastating loss for authors, locals, and customers alike, but the shop's enduring legacy is a shining example of the power of the Black bookstore.

Since they began in the 1800s, Black bookstores have fallen victim to the usual downsides of business amplified by systemic racism: lack of capital, poor sales, gentrification, and exorbitant operating costs. It was a breath of fresh air to see longtime owners of a Black bookstore close the store of their own volition. There is beauty in putting an end to a dream when you are satisfied with it. Few Black booksellers have come to a place where they could dictate their own end without pressure from external forces. Fugate lamented a lack of Black bookstores when he first started out as a bookseller, but by the time Eso Won ended, he was confident that Los Angeles was in good hands, especially with shops like Malik Books and Reparations Club in Los Angeles and Octavia's Bookshelf and Shades of Afrika nearby in Pasadena and Long Beach, respectively. The longtime booksellers were more than happy to pass the torch to a new generation. Young booksellers, who weren't alive for most of the history chronicled in this book, speak proudly about Drum and Spear, Una Mulzac, Eso Won, and many of their other predecessors. Meanwhile, customers have increasingly spent time writing poignant essays, articles, and more about their experiences in Black bookstores throughout their lives. These businesses are finally beginning to receive the place of reverence in media that they deserve. In the fall of 2023, some one hundred people gathered in Philadelphia's Fifty-Second Street business corridor to celebrate the city's oldest Black bookshop, Hakim's Bookstore. They crowded outside the store in front of its blue, newly installed historical marker. After more than sixty years in the community, the beloved shop was finally being recognized as a historic staple in the city. The marker shared a slice of the store's history that had been forgotten:

"Founded in the 1950s by Dawud Hakim, it was the first Black-owned bookstore in Philadelphia specializing in Black history and titles by Black authors. A civil rights and Black activism gathering space in the 1960s, it was surveilled by the FBI along with other Black bookstores."

The bulk orders and crowds of customers may have slowed, but the recognition Black booksellers enjoyed during 2020 remained even after the protests and after reading lists no longer circulated on the Internet. In the years that followed, celebrities and authors have increasingly made a point of highlighting their favorite Black bookstores. In 2022, Stacey Abrams was in the middle of her Georgia gubernatorial battle with Brian Kemp when she gushed about her favorite Georgia bookstores, For Keeps Books in Atlanta and Brave + Kind Bookshop in Decatur, to Oprah Daily. She praised For Keeps Books for stocking well-known authors like Richard Wright and James Baldwin and selling classic editions of *Jet* magazine and *Atlanta Daily World*. She lauded Brave + Kind as a thoughtfully curated space that uses children's books to bring families together. Black bookstores had slipped out of their historical zone of invisibility—it became cool to care about them. Nikole Hannah-Jones, fresh off her 2020 Pulitzer Prize win for *The 1619 Project*, voiced her love for MahoganyBooks and Semicolon Bookstore in Chicago: "They are both Black-women-owned bookstores that really cater to the community and have also clearly been very supportive of my work," she told Oprah Daily.

In March 2024, Deion Sanders made sure to stop at The Dock Bookshop to promote his book, *Elevate and Dominate: 21 Ways to Win on and off the Field*. Even writers who rose to fame in 2020 made a point of supporting Black bookstores. When Ijeoma Oluo released *Be a Revolution* in early 2024, she launched the book at

Café con Libros, a cherished Afro-Latinx, woman-owned book-store in Brooklyn. Some one hundred people bought tickets for the event, and at least eighty came out on a rainy January night to hear Oluo talk and ask her questions. Yona Deshommes was the PR veteran behind the event. She spends most of her time connecting Black authors with Black bookstores, so she didn't hesitate when HarperCollins officials called her to coordinate Oluo's stop at the bookshop. Often, Black writers seek her help themselves. Deshommes has done this work for years, but it kicked off after 2020. Before Oluo and Café con Libros, Deshommes sent authors and celebrities to MahoganyBooks, Marcus Books, Eso Won, The Dock, and other Black bookshops.

|||▬▬▬▬|||

Even though Black bookstores were getting their due respect, circumstances were much different in 2023 than in 2020. The protests were over, and politicians reminded the country that they were more committed to the status quo than ever. Cities went back on their promises to defund their police departments and instead expanded their budgets. Republican lawmakers introduced anti-protest bills to make sure such an uprising would never happen again. States restricted what educators could teach public school students about race, with some even twisting and watering down the violent truths about slavery. And, across the country, books about race and gender were banned from schools and challenged at public libraries. The hope for social advancement that swelled during 2020's racial reckoning fell away, right along with the success Black bookstores experienced. For VaLinda Miller, the surge began to wind down in September of 2020. The torrent of white customers who once flocked to Turning Page Bookshop in Goose Creek, South Carolina, had reduced to a trickle — and that's being generous. Meanwhile, the backlash to the 2020 uprisings was consistent; conservative lawmakers and activists wouldn't let up. Industry after industry experienced right-wing attacks. And in December 2023, a member of Moms for Liberty, a conservative group working to eradicate race- and gender-based equity initiatives in schools, visited Miller's shop.

"We're checking out books to see what's going on," the white man told the manager working the store at the time. He looked around and scoffed. "You only have Black books!" The manager told him Turning Page carried all types of books and invited him to look around. He wandered around the store, picking up title after title and angrily stuffing it back on the shelf. He ultimately gave up and stormed out of the store.

"When the surge happened, I said, 'Let's enjoy it as long as we can because it's not gonna last,'" Miller recalled. "George Floyd brought on all this DEI. I kept saying to myself, '[Conservatives] are up to something. It's only a matter of time.' And now we see it."

Beginning in 2021, school officials, lawmakers, and parents set out on a mission to rid the country of books about the lived experiences of Black and queer people. Schools and public libraries were ground zero for this culture war. Republican lawmakers and conservative groups said books about racism and LGBTQIA+ people weren't appropriate for students. More than 1,600 books were banned in over 5,000 schools during the 2021–2022 school year. There were 1,269 attempts to censor library books and resources in 2022, the highest number of book challenges since the American Library Association began keeping tabs. This was double the 729 book challenges reported in 2021. And in 2023, the number of books challenged in libraries across the country increased again, by 65 percent—setting a new American Library Association record for the second year in a row. Book bans are common in the United States and have been for centuries. But there was something more sinister about this wave of censorship in the aftermath of 2020. Librarians and literacy advocates alike warned that these sweeping bans were simply a political strategy. Looking at the reasons for banning certain books made this even more clear. George M. Johnson's *All Boys Aren't Blue* was sexually explicit and talked so much about a Black, queer boy's life that it was criminal, according to one Florida school board member. *The Bluest Eye* by Toni Morrison talked about sexual abuse and had too much of that diversity stuff; it should certainly be gone from any public library shelf. *The 1619 Project* had no place in public school curriculums with its dangerous and divisive subject matter. Books were caught up in the manufactured conservative panic over what young people should learn about race and sexuality.

The publishing industry stood at attention. Publishers, libraries, and literacy advocacy groups shared banned-book reading lists and published action plans for readers to push back against the censorship. Celebrities joined campaigns to speak out against book bans and LeVar Burton, the famed *Reading Rainbow* host, lent his star power to the movement. RuPaul even launched the Rainbow Book Bus and later an online store to sell banned and challenged books. Thankfully, independent Black bookstores weren't beholden to state laws that declared Black books inappropriate. Trenessa Williams, who runs Kizzy's Books and More in Winter Garden, Florida, dedicated a part of her online bookstore to banned or challenged books by Black authors. Black bookstores like Turning Page and the Ujamaa Community Bookstore in Indianapolis have "banned books" sections in their stores to push back against the racial censorship. As much as conservatives thought about the kinds of books people had access to, Black book peddlers did, too. Although Fatimah Warner, a musician and poet who goes by Noname onstage, doesn't run a bookstore per se, her Radical Hood Library, in Los Angeles's predominately Black—but rapidly gentrifying—Jefferson Park neighborhood, is part of the radical bookstore tradition. When she opened the library in 2021, locals were hard-pressed to find more than a single copy of Mumia Abu-Jamal's book *Live from Death Row* at any public library in the city. Members of Noname's eponymous book club wanted to read and discuss the memoir, so the Radical Hood Library helped fill the gap.

This, to Warner and her collaborators, was the importance of having what she called a "free space" like the Radical Hood Library. Libraries, she reasoned, are an important intervention in political culture wars. How much more would a Black-centered, fiercely anti-capitalist, "hood" library disrupt this organized attempt to cut off people's access to books? The library is committed to books with radical political ideas, and its categories make that plain. "Global Black Resistance," "Prison Writings," and "How the US F*cked Up Everything" are just a few sections readers can browse. Warner, with her book club and library, is representative of this new generation.

No, the Radical Hood Library is *not* a bookstore. But it's this kind of innovation that moves forward the Black book ecosystem. If you ask any Black bookseller in the country, they'll tell you that new, fresh ideas will secure the Black bookstore's longevity. If the goal is to get Black books to the masses consistently, it will take imagination to do it. The community library project sounds a lot like the movement bookstores of sixty years ago: offering classes, sending books to incarcerated people, and distributing radical literature on socialism and revolution at a time when the country is reckoning with its racist past and present. To Warner, the venture is more than a simple reading room—it's a vehicle for building community solidarity through group study and organizing. Warner is no stranger to entrepreneurship. Her mother, Desiree Sanders, ran the Afrocentric Bookstore in Chicago's Bronzeville neighborhood for nearly twenty years, from 1990 to 2008. She would visit her mother's shop often as a child and seeing the communal business model helped shape her as a young reader. She has lamented that her mother's shop shuttered "because of institutions that created a consumer model and environment that makes it almost impossible for brick-and-mortar establishments to compete."

As a result, Warner has fashioned the Radical Hood Library as a community tool, bringing in volunteers and tapping into social media to engage customers. There are open mic nights, author talks, movie nights, and workshops on everything from gun safety to harm reduction. Shortly after launching the book club, Warner thought about abolition and the prison industrial complex, and ways she could build a bridge between readers behind bars and those on the outside. In less than a year, library volunteers managed to send at least five thousand books to people in US prisons. The efforts call to mind the George Jackson Prison Movement of some fifty years before. The Black Panther–turned–book peddler Coates understood that any Black liberation would have to push back against attempts to disappear people inside prisons and jails. Once a person is incarcerated, they are often seen as disposable and no longer deserving of humanity. Activist booksellers throughout the decades—from those who ran Drum and Spear to the Marcus Books owners—understood this and prioritized incarcerated people in ways that fostered connection. All these years later, the Radical Hood Library operates with the same mission. When you walk into the library, it's hard to miss the black-painted map of the United States hanging on the wall. It's riddled with small flags, one for each prison chapter of the Noname Book Club.

On the other side of the country, OlaRonke Akinmowo is dealing books her own way, too. Like the Radical Hood Library, Akinmowo's Free Black Women's Library isn't a bookstore. Books aren't sold and marketed. Instead, it's both a traveling library and reading room where people can trade one book by a Black woman or queer author and get another. There's no money involved in the trading, yet another anti-capitalist commitment in the Black book ecosystem. The Free Black Women's Library is the only bookshop, reading room, and traveling library of its kind in the nation. Akinmowo's journey with the traveling library began in 2015. Worn out from doing social justice work to fight police brutality, Akinmowo decided to continue serving her community through books. So, every so often, she'd lug a hundred books by Black women authors to a Brooklyn brownstone stoop, hoping to make trades with other Black women and girls. Her first trade was with an eight-year-old girl who sauntered up to the porch one summer day.

"What are you doing with all these books?" the little Black girl asked.

"These are books written by Black women, and I want to share them with people like you and me," Akinmowo replied. Akinmowo asked the girl if she liked to read.

"She said, 'Yes, I love books!'" Akinmowo recalled of the exchange. "I said, 'Perfect, so do I! If you see anything you like, if you want, I will trade you. If you have a book by a Black woman writer, you can bring it to me, and we'll trade!'"

The little girl ran home, returning less than an hour later. As Akinmowo promised, she swapped the little girl a novel from her collection. That was ten years ago. Today, Akinmowo operates the library out of a shop in Brooklyn and still holds monthly pop-ups throughout the city, setting up in museums, creative spaces, theaters, art galleries, churches, and festivals. She's become a fixture in Brooklyn, and well-known to artists and fellow bookshop owners. The Free Black Women's Library functions as a reading room, a co-working space, and a house for the project's four thousand books. I first met Akinmowo in 2019, when I learned about the project and wanted to write about it. We sat down at a rickety table outside a restaurant in downtown Brooklyn, where she told me all about the library's beginnings and her vision for its future. Her voice was calm, and her demeanor was reserved, but I could see the fire in her eyes as she talked about her dream. It was a passion I've come to associate with Black booksellers. The familiar look of excitement, adventure, and possibility. Then, the library was still just a traveling pop-up and Akinmowo's name was spreading across the city—slowly but surely. She gushed about her ultimate goal of having a brick-and-mortar home for the library and a van that would function as a bookmobile. By 2021, other people saw Akinmowo's vision, too. Dozens donated more than $100,000 in just a few months to help bring Akinmowo's dream for the library to life.

Today, people are almost constantly at the reading room to attend events, to trade books, or simply to hang out. And even more follow the library around, eager to attend its famous monthly pop-ups. What started as a community-building, "social art project" has grown into a cultural staple that exists in the tradition of Black activist booksellers. Bibliophiles have launched chapters of the library in Detroit, Houston, and Los Angeles. Akinmowo, who still considers the library a social art project, encourages the community to collaborate. Each month, she invites the public to the reading room to talk about everything from books to social justice issues. She uses the shop's influence to provide for community members through the library's Sister Outsider Relief Grant, a mutual aid grant for single Black mother artists, writers, activists, and cultural workers. The library has given more than $40,000 in grant funding. When she isn't manning the library or planning the pop-ups, Akinmowo is making sure those who support the library have a wealth of resources at their disposal. Her free Patreon is full of reading challenges, flyers for events, and articles and videos she simply wanted to share. Akinmowo has used her creativity as an artist and her love for Black communities to create an appealing, unprecedented way of distributing Black books. Projects like Noname's Radical Hood Library and Akinmowo's Free Black Women's Library give a glimmer of what's to come from the young, wide-eyed booksellers breaking into the industry.

||| ▬▬▬▬ |||

I made a point of visiting the Black-owned bookstores around me when I moved to Dallas in 2020. At first, I spent most of my time at Pan-African Connection, appreciating its deep Pan-African aesthetic and the mix of new and old Black books on its shelves. Then, Nia-Tayler Clark opened Blacklit in 2022 in Farmers Branch, on the opposite end of the city. I'd visit both stores and marvel at the clear distinctions between them, one that showed a marked difference between the new generation of Black bookstores and those around for decades. The Pan-African Connection is delightfully crowded with books, body care products, and African art. At Blacklit, there is a café and a carefully designed event space where young, Black Dallasites filed in with their Birkenstocks and vape pens for poetry slams. When you walk into Blacklit, you see a wide, open space with bookshelves and shelves with shirts, stickers, and cards along the walls. Glance to your right, and you'll see a brown wall with the names of Black authors written in white. In front of it, a platform and microphone; it's a stage where Black writers, poets, and thinkers can share their work. There is art along the walls, some simple printouts from Etsy and others Basquiat-esque paintings from local artists. The name Blacklit is on the store's door, with the shop's Instagram handle underneath. Blacklit and Pan-African Connection are different branches of a single tree. Despite their differences, Tyehimba and Clark share similar ideas of what it will take to make sure Black bookstores stay open and successful.

One, the shops may need to expand their inventory to appeal to a broader audience, while still staying true to their core Black roots. And two, they need to brainstorm new, imaginative ways to court customers and establish their shops as cool, interesting hangouts. These ideas aren't exactly new. Black booksellers have spent years, decades even, weighing whether to sell more general titles rather than focusing on books by and about Black people, and how to do this without betraying their commitment to Black literature and communities. It's a conundrum that we can trace back to the 1960s and 1970s.

Clark, a twentysomething Black woman, was surprised that when she set out to open Blacklit, potential investors told her repeatedly, "You're not going to survive with just a bookstore." She was offended. She had spent most of her adult life teaching English to high schoolers and started Blacklit to encourage reading and sell the very Black books investors told her weren't enough to sustain a bookstore. Clark quickly learned they were right, though. Mailing books from her home, with little help and profit, wasn't sustainable. So, she opened Blacklit's storefront in July 2022 with a temporary café and rented out its event space for everything from podcast meetups to baby showers. She and her small team often carry books to and from community events for pop-ups and partner with local groups to sell books wherever they can.

Blacklit originally started back in 2019 as a subscription box service. Clark would sit in her tiny one-bedroom apartment with her young son on her hip and fill boxes with books by and about Black people to mail out to whoever wanted them. So, she had a few years of bookselling under her belt before her brick-and-mortar shop came along, but she still didn't know quite where to start. She saw Pan-African Connection as a model for the community-oriented approach she wanted to take to her own store. It was a model she wanted to build on, not replicate exactly. Clark's first two years in business were full of struggle and trial and error—but also some unimaginable highs. The store went from facing eviction in 2023 to securing a vendor spot at the BET Awards a year later. Clark, like other new booksellers, was able to leverage social media, a beneficial resource that many of her predecessors hadn't had. Now, a well-curated Instagram feed or a few engaging TikToks can lead to more sales and recognition for a Black business. Even with the instantaneity of social media, Clark didn't begin to gain her footing until about a year into the new venture. Joining the ranks of a new generation of Black booksellers was overwhelming for the young mom of one, and it took a veteran in the industry to strengthen Clark through her toughest moments.

Years after closing her Black Images Book Bazaar, Emma Rodgers visited Blacklit. She *had* to see this new Black bookstore for herself. Clark, admittedly, didn't know who "Miss Emma" was before she waltzed into the store. It was Rodgers's son who shared his mother's story with Clark in Blacklit that day and made known her stature in the bookselling industry. Immediately, Clark found a mentor in Rodgers. Rodgers taught her how to set up book signings and other author events, and encouraged her to join the American Booksellers Association and take advantage of its online selling tool, Bookshop.org. Clark saw a bit of herself in Rodgers, too; both women started bookselling with small children. And their relationship has motivated Clark, though she's still a young bookseller, to think through her own legacy and impact on the industry in the years and decades to come.

"Emma Rodgers found me and poured into me in a way that I would never forget and I'm so excited to do for the next generation," Clark said. "She's had events here, she's hosted her book club here. She truly has been a phone call or a text away and she's shared with me resources I didn't even know about! I see what it's gonna look like to pass the torch."

Succession is a long way away for Clark, but she sees herself as a newcomer in an industry with deep roots. And she has grand plans for Blacklit's future. Clark wants to start a Blacklit literary festival, hold even more community events, and eventually turn Blacklit into a franchise, much like Hodari Ali's Pyramid Books and the Karibu Books chain.

It is yet to be seen what the future holds for the Black book ecosystem, but historical patterns give us an idea. If history is any indicator of the future, Black bookstores may continue to exist on the margins of the larger book industry, but they will play a part that can't be discounted. Many will close, as is the nature of the volatile industry, but many more will open, full of innovation, and they'll survive. And the communities they serve will benefit— Black bookstores are embedded in schools, local community groups, and prison programs. The story of Black bookstores, as I've laid out in these pages, is a tale not only of a revolutionary swath of businesses but of resilience. Through racist targeting, troubling economic times, and changing cultural interests, Black bookstores have persisted. This reflects not only entrepreneurial activism but what it means to be Black in America in general: pushing through adversity, holding on to values, and bending without breaking. The shops' branches reach every area of society. And this, I've learned, is part of the beauty of Black bookstores. Some branches bend and others twist, but they all exist as part of a singular root system—one grounded in community, passion, and a commitment to Black books.

"I'm really hopeful for the future of Black-owned bookstores in the country. I think this generation and the next has a level of resilience that's not going anywhere," Clark said. "The same way people before us pushed through, now we have a couple of more people about to push through. And by being dedicated to completing my assignment, I'm going to make sure there's a couple more Black bookstore owners. If I have something to do with it, there will be more than there were yesterday."

CONCLUSION

SINCE I BEGAN REPORTING ON BLACK BOOKSTORES IN 2019, and especially since starting this book, every bookseller I've talked to has told me they're glad this story is finally being told. And I was eager to listen.

When I interviewed the former owners of the Hub in Kansas, they spoke with glee for hours about the joy of running a bookstore with their friends. The Craddock sisters spoke passionately about their time as booksellers and plans for The Dock's sixteenth anniversary—I recommended a block party. Even over the phone, I could feel James Fugate's excitement about running Eso Won, supporting writers, and sometimes quarreling with them, too. In my last phone conversation with Simba Sana about Karibu's end, he laughed at his long-windedness. "Have I given you enough dysfunction?" he joked. There was an underlying current in my conversations and visits with them. They spoke about invisibility, the fact that Black bookstores and their fraught histories were forgotten or considered unimportant. From Los Angeles to New York, booksellers both old and new shared similar sentiments that it was time to tell the story of the businesses. And there was certainly a lot of ground to cover.

The entire Black book industry collaborated to make this book possible. In between stocking shelves, planning events, and working with publishers, so many Black booksellers sat with me excitedly in person, on Zoom, or over the phone for hours of reminiscing. Almost every conversation I've had ended with the interviewee pointing me in a new direction—"Have you talked to Ramunda Young?" "You must read Colin Beckles!" And "You gotta talk to the folks over at Sankofa!" They wanted to make sure I told the story in its entirety.

Black booksellers' commitment to community stretched beyond putting on events for people in their respective neighborhoods. It meant a reliance on one another. They know one another, and their stories are riddled with praise for the Black wholesalers, publishers, booksellers, and other book professionals that they credit with aiding in their success. It was no surprise that so many of them rallied around me and helped me however they could. Before I knew it, I was part of the Black book ecosystem myself. I've likened the Black book industry to a tree, with many branches and leaves representing everyone from Black publishers to teens who sweep their local bookshop each night before closing. And they are all connected in ways that prop one another up and support one another in times of hardship and success even amid friendly— and not-so-friendly—competition. W. Paul Coates was a major part of this effort. In writing this book, I spoke with him perhaps more than any other person in the industry. After all, he *is* considered the Black book industry's unofficial historian. He never failed to indulge my questions or connect me with others in the field. He shepherded me through the process from start to finish. I am eternally grateful to him for his help and guidance. As our relationship developed, he certainly wasn't shy about telling me which of my conclusions were wrong—though he was too polite to state that outright. Instead, he'd simply say, "I disagree," before setting me straight. I knew I could trust him because he'd seen it all. He was immersed in Black Power movements and he was using books for political missions long before I was born. And he'd never fallen away from books as a political tool. He went from Black Panther to bookseller to publisher. A casual historian, he provided me with his own research and notes stretching back decades. He is just as committed to telling these stories as I am. He wanted to make sure I got this history right and answered the tough questions necessary to do so.

||| ▬▬▬▬▬ |||

Readers will notice that at no point in this book do I present a clear definition of what I consider a "Black bookstore." I use "Black bookstore" and "Black-owned bookstore" interchangeably. This was purposeful, not a glaring omission. Coates, Troy Johnson (creator of the African American Literature Book Club), and I had a lengthy discussion about the distinction between a Black bookstore and a Black-owned bookstore, and what characteristics define each. The question of distinction consumed me for months after the conversation, and I wondered how I'd tackle it in this book. I define a Black bookstore as a shop owned by a Black person that specializes in books by and about Black people. It is defined by both its ownership and its inventory. But a Black-owned bookstore is simply a shop owned by a Black person, no matter the nature of their inventory.

Stores like Loyalty Bookstore in DC and Turning Page Bookshop would, by my definition, be considered Black-owned bookstores and not technically "Black bookstores" because they sell a wide variety of books, rather than primarily those by and about Black people. Meanwhile, Marcus Books and MahoganyBooks would be, by my definition, Black bookstores. This distinction is important, and it becomes more so as moments of political turmoil thrust Black businesses into the spotlight. It is worth noting, though, that some Black booksellers who do not specialize in Black books in their shops may balk at being consistently described as "Black bookstore owners" or at their shops' being described as "Black-owned."

I did not present a clear definition in the book because I wanted to immerse readers in the commonalities between Black and Black-owned bookstores—what makes them similar, rather than highlighting what makes them different.

Besides, many Black-owned bookstores only expanded their inventory to sell more general titles to stay afloat. If you ask VaLinda Miller of Turning Page, her choice to sell more than just Black books was more of a business decision than a personal one. And the Craddock sisters, whose shop is very Black both visually and in its inventory, said themselves that Black booksellers would have to think long and hard about whether to focus their inventory on Black books or work to appeal to customers of different races and backgrounds.

To base this book on the narrow definition of a "Black bookstore" would mean excluding Black-owned shops that exist in the same mission-driven tradition. *That* would have been a glaring omission. Therefore, I use "Black bookstore" and "Black-owned bookstore" interchangeably.

CONCLUSION

This book is not simply a comprehensive history but an account of the ways Black bookstores have served as the communal backbone pivotal to moments throughout our nation's history. From the 1960s, when the US government worked to squash liberation movements, to the '90s, when videos of police brutality began to spread, Black bookshops have always been present. They were places of refuge and political action, where people felt safe to gather and make plans for radical demonstrations. Now Black-owned bookstores have reclaimed their place not simply as a part of Black culture but as a centerpiece of Black resistance. At first glance, bookselling may seem like an understated response to white supremacy compared to protests, boycotts, and public calls for police reform and abolition. But their most recent boom in business and innovation in 2020 was no coincidence; Black-owned bookstores have been at the forefront of Black politics for centuries, and their responses have been equally effective as (or more effective than) headline-making protests. This latest crossroads in the fight for justice and equity means we've entered another chapter in Black America's long, rich, and perilous history of bookstores supporting and empowering Black radical movements. The story of Black bookstores isn't some dull account of forgotten business owners and old tomes collecting dust. It is an exciting account of resistance, violence, espionage, community, and joy.

Most of what we know about the political lives of Black-owned bookstores has come from sporadic interviews with owners, old newspaper clips, and some work from historians and scholars that usually only mentions specific Black bookstores and focuses more on the circumstances surrounding their existence than on the stores' role in history. *Black-Owned* weaves together the scattered, forgotten, and usually vague pieces of this history to finally tell the full story of Black-owned bookstores in America. We can learn a lot from the life of the Black-owned bookstore, and those lessons can empower us all for the future. This most recent racial reckoning won't be the nation's last, and whether the next revolution comes in ten years or one hundred years, Black-owned bookstores will remain at the foundation of change.

Writing this book brought so many joys, but I loved sitting and talking with booksellers the most. Clara Villarosa, with her sharp business acumen and thirst for new ideas, made the Hue-Man Experience Bookstore the most influential and successful Black bookshop of the 1980s. I visited Villarosa at her New York home in 2023. We sat with her daughter Alicia at Villarosa's kitchen table and talked about Hue-Man. Villarosa, now in her nineties, laughed and smiled as she recalled her early days as a bookseller: her brief spat with Maya Angelou, a fateful phone call from Terry McMillan, and seeking advice from her own daughters as they grew in the business.

"I was trying to think of something concrete, and a bookstore is concrete," Villarosa said of her decision to open the store. "Bookstores are substantive."

We were surrounded by her own paintings, sculptures she'd acquired over the years, and plaques and statuettes awarded to her for her work as a bookseller. We snapped photos and looked at images of the family Villarosa built while working full-time in the book industry. I sat listening, and laughing, too, with a deep awareness that Villarosa would one day join Mulzac, Richardson, Hakim, the Ligons, and other influential booksellers who had passed on. This only bolstered my sense of responsibility to share her story.

Perhaps the most challenging part of crafting *Black-Owned* was keeping up with the almost constant developments in the Black book industry while writing. Several brick-and-mortar shops shifted to online stores and others found pop-ups to be a more sustainable way to distribute books. Ramunda Young of Mahogany-Books and Kalima DeSuze of Café con Libros launched the Black Bookstore Coalition as a result of the 2020 uprising and pandemic. The coalition is a collective of more than forty Black-owned bookstores focused on partnering with one another and sharing resources. After the chaos of 2020 died down, after Black booksellers held the country's hand through the turmoil, they got to work on a different project. In 2022, Black booksellers and publishers like W. Paul Coates, Shirikiana and Haile Gerima, Wade and Cheryl Hudson, sisters Donna and Donya Craddock, James Fugate and Thomas Hamilton, and several others banded around a single cause: Marcus Garvey's exoneration. By that point, it had been almost a hundred years since the US government imprisoned Garvey for mail fraud in 1923. It was a controversial conviction and Black people protested Garvey's imprisonment. A century later, they rallied around him again. The group, alongside Garvey's son, Julius Garvey; the Caribbean-American Political Action Committee; and other supporters, launched the Justice4Garvey movement to secure one hundred thousand signatures to present to President Biden to have Garvey pardoned. The booksellers, who carried his books, saw the imprisonment as a stain on his legacy that was, in essence, a wrong committed against the global Black community. Biden pardoned Garvey in January 2025, more than one hundred years after his imprisonment. Their efforts are a reminder of just how Black booksellers have historically rallied around political causes. In 2024, they published a book about the exoneration movement, *Justice for Marcus Garvey*, with writing from the likes of W. Paul and Ta-Nehisi Coates and Maulana Karenga.

This movement was "the first time that Black book publishers and Black bookstores combined in a political expression to use their base of support to come together around any Black issue," Coates said. "Black booksellers have done it, Black publishers have done it, but we've never done it together. It represents a singular act. That's as political as you get."

When I wasn't sitting with booksellers or keeping up with current events in the industry, I was thinking through just how to address the number of Black bookstores in the country in the last century. In one of our many phone calls, Coates asked—more accurately, implored—me not to repeat what he considered an inaccurate claim about Black bookstores: that almost two hundred of them operated in the 1990s, and that number dwindled drastically to fifty-four by 2014. In actuality, Black bookstores have constantly opened, closed, reopened, and shifted throughout history. It would be misguided to imply that some three hundred stores popped up in a single decade and all faded into obscurity in fifteen years' time. The truth is more complex than that. As mentioned, no one has kept a reliable list of operating Black bookstores throughout history. So, painful as it is to accept, we will never know exactly how many new Black bookstores opened, reopened, or closed at any given time.

|||▬▬▬▬|||

After 2020 sent scores of new customers to Black bookstores, the shops are now back to modest sales and the usual struggles of securing their longevity. This will not be the end of Black-owned bookstores, though. As long as the fight for Black liberation exists, so will these shops. The Black bookstore has seen cycles of success and struggle for nearly two hundred years. This is a trend that likely won't go away, but the recent transformation in bookselling could serve to quell moments of downturn and lead to more sustained success for the shops. As the new owners, younger and more in tune with pop culture, tailor their selling approach to readers immersed in a world of fast-changing cultural (and social media) trends, bookstores will go from reliable but seemingly antiquated resources to culturally relevant and potent gathering centers.

The story of Black bookstores is empowering as much as it is inspiring. This is not due solely to their fortitude, their survival through times of struggle, or even their inventory. Black bookstores are impactful because of the people who run them. I spent time with booksellers who smiled and remained as bright and energized as ever as they talked about running stores that were locally impactful yet received little national recognition. It is the booksellers' passion and their love for the work they do that carries them through. This assures me that the Black bookstore will always exist in some form. Some have questioned whether such an institution can survive, and see longevity, in a country built on white supremacy and oppression. But this history is full of stories and single moments that meant the difference between victory and defeat. It is unclear what the future holds, but history has proved that the country will always need Black bookstores, and they'll always be here.

ACKNOWLEDGMENTS

To thank each person who made this book possible would require a chapter of its own. *Black-Owned* would not be possible without my family, my friends, and my community. I'm grateful for everyone who supported me through this process, giving me encouragement when I needed it, and giving me a kick in the butt when I needed that, too. I am eternally grateful for the way you all have loved me through this journey, which often included me canceling plans and being holed up in my home to write. My heart is full of gratitude.

My spectacular agent Justin Brouckaert and my wonderful editors Emi Ikkanda and Grace Layer guided me through the creation of this book with thoughtfulness and care. They consistently pushed me to dig deeper and asked critical questions that have made this book what it is today. I needed their guidance, and *Black-Owned* wouldn't be what it is without them.

I could not have asked for a better publishing team. There are so many people who helped bring this book from its inception to its finality. Designers Dana Li, Jenni Surasky and Lorie Pagnozzi created such a beautiful cover and interior, and Alice Dalrymple oversaw the production editing process. I'm so grateful for their hard work and the intentionality of the entire team at Tiny Reparations Books. The imprint has taken such great care of me and *Black-Owned*; working with TRB on my debut book is an experience I'll cherish forever.

I want to thank everyone who shared their stories with me. I am honored that you all trusted me with them. I've connected with more Black booksellers than I can count—elders who have decades of experience in the industry, and young booksellers still trying to find their way—each with a unique, inspiring story of their own.

The stories and accounts in this book build on the research so many people have done before me. I'm especially grateful to W. Paul Coates, Joshua Clarke Davis, Graham Hodges, and Colin Beckles. Coates, you were patient with me and carefully shepherded me through a book you've been waiting to see written. I could not have completed it without your guidance.

Davis, it was your work that inspired me to explore Black bookstores to begin with, and I thank you for sharing your research with me and selflessly supporting me.

It is because of Graham Hodges that we know all that we do about David Ruggles. Thank you for diligently uncovering his life and, in doing so, helping to lay the groundwork for this book.

Lastly, so many of us who love Black bookstores and are interested in their stories have Beckles to thank for all we've learned. Beckles died in 1999 after spending years publishing comprehensive, holistic research about Black bookstores. He was among the first to prove that these stores have a history of resistance. I am grateful for his work and for his passion. May he rest in peace.

BOOKS BLACK BOOKSELLERS WANT EVERYONE TO READ

Black booksellers always have a reading recommendation. Over the years, I've asked them about the books they consider essential reading—their lists were long and diverse. But two books came up most, *The Autobiography of Malcolm X* and *The Mis-Education of the Negro*. Here are ten books Black booksellers want everyone to read:

1. *The Autobiography of Malcolm X* by Malcolm X and Alex Haley
2. *The Mis-Education of the Negro* by Carter G. Woodson
3. *The New Jim Crow* by Michelle Alexander
4. *100 Years of Lynching* by Ralph Ginzburg
5. *Assata: An Autobiography* by Assata Shakur
6. *Beloved* by Toni Morrison
7. *How the Word Is Passed: A Reckoning with the History of Slavery Across America* by Clint Smith
8. *How Europe Underdeveloped Africa* by Walter Rodney
9. *Their Eyes Were Watching God* by Zora Neale Hurston
10. *The Price of the Ticket* by James Baldwin

BLACK-OWNED BOOKSTORES IN THE US BY STATE

I'm excited to share this list of Black-owned bookstores, though of course new stores are opening all the time. For a more up-to-date list, please visit my website at charadams.com.

ARIZONA
- Grassrootz Books and Juice Bar — Phoenix, AZ

ARKANSAS
- Pyramid Art, Books & Custom Framing — Little Rock, AR

CALIFORNIA
- Ashay by the Bay — Vallejo, CA
- Chukaruka — Fontana, CA
- Get Lit Books & Things — Moreno Valley, CA
- Malik Books — Los Angeles, CA
- Marcus Books — Oakland, CA
- Mija Books — Lakewood, CA
- Moments Co-Op — Oakland, CA

- Multicultural Children's Bookstore and Gifts—Richmond, CA
- Octavia's Bookshelf—Pasadena, CA
- Old Capitol Books—Monterey, CA
- Reparations Club—Los Angeles, CA
- Shades of Afrika—Long Beach, CA
- Underground Books—Sacramento, CA

COLORADO

- The Shop at Matter—Denver, CO
- Townie Books—Crested Butte, CO

CONNECTICUT

- Kindred Thoughts—Bridgeport, CT
- Obodo Serendipity Books—Stratford, CT

DELAWARE

- MeJah Books, Inc.—Claymont, DE

FLORIDA

- Best Richardson African Diaspora Literature & Culture Museum—St. Augustine, FL
- Black English Bookstore—Tampa, FL
- Cafe Resistance Bookstore & Coffee Shop—Jacksonville, FL
- Cultured Books Literacy Foundation—St. Petersburg, FL
- Dare Books—Longwood, FL
- Eden Books—Newberry, FL
- Erudite Encounters—Pembroke Pines, FL

- Essence of Knowledge — Cocoa, FL
- Pyramid Books — Boynton Beach, FL

GEORGIA

- 44th & 3rd Bookseller — Atlanta, GA
- All Things Inspiration — Mableton, GA
- Black Dot Cultural Center and Bookstore — Lithonia, GA
- The Book Worm Bookstore — Powder Springs, GA
- Brave + Kind Bookshop — Decatur, GA
- For Keeps Books — Atlanta, GA
- The Listening Tree — Decatur, GA
- Medu Bookstore — Atlanta, GA
- Nubian Bookstore — Morrow, GA
- Onyx Bookstore Café — Covington, GA
- Rejoice Christian Books & Gifts — Snellville, GA
- Yes, Please Books — Scottdale, GA

ILLINOIS

- AfriWare Books, Co. — Oak Park, IL
- Da Book Joint — Chicago, IL
- The Last Chapter Book Shop — Chicago, IL
- Semicolon Books — Chicago, IL
- The Underground Bookstore — Chicago, IL
- Zora's Place — Evanston, Illinois

INDIANA

- Akoma Books — Evansville, IN
- Beyond Barcodes Bookstore — Kokomo, IN
- Black Worldschoolers — Indianapolis, IN

- The Brain Lair Books—Sound Bend, IN
- Ink Drinkers Anonymous—Muncie, IN
- Loudmouth Books—Indianapolis, IN
- Ujamaa Community Bookstore—Indianapolis, IN

IOWA

- Soul Book Nook—Waterloo, IA

KANSAS

- Left on Read—Wichita, KS

LOUISIANA

- Baldwin & Co.—New Orleans, LA
- Community Book Center—New Orleans, LA
- Umoja Books and Products—Lafayette, LA

MARYLAND

- Everyone's Place—Baltimore, MD
- MahoganyBooks—Oxon Hill, MD
- Red Emma's—Baltimore, MD
- Urban Reads Bookstore—Baltimore, MD
- Vision Christian Store—Clinton, MD

MASSACHUSETTS

- Frugal Bookstore—Roxbury, MA
- JustBook-ish—Dorchester, MA
- Olive Tree Books-n-Voices—Springfield, MA
- Susie's Stories—Rockport, MA

MICHIGAN

- Black Stone Bookstore and Cultural Center—Ypsilanti, MI
- Comma Bookstore & Social Hub—Flint, MI
- God's World Superstore—Detroit, MI
- Nandi's Knowledge Café—Highland Park, MI
- Source Booksellers—Detroit, MI
- We Are LIT—Grand Rapids, MI

MINNESOTA

- Babycake's Book Stack—Twin Cities, MN
- Black Garnet Books—St. Paul, MN
- Planting People Growing Justice—St. Paul, MN
- Strive Bookstore—Minneapolis, MN

MISSISSIPPI

- Marshall's Music and Book Store—Jackson, MS

MISSOURI

- Bliss Books & Wine—Kansas City, MO
- EyeSeeMe—University City, MO
- Little Readers—St. Louis, MO
- Progressive Emporium & Education Center—St. Louis, MO
- Willa's Books & Vinyl—Kansas City, MO

NEBRASKA

- Aframerican Bookstore—Omaha, NE
- The Book Nook—Papillion, NE

NEVADA

- The Analog Dope Store—Las Vegas, NV

NEW JERSEY

- La Unique African American Bookstore & Cultural Center—Camden, NJ
- The Little BOHO Bookshop—Bayonne, NJ
- Source of Knowledge Bookstore—Newark, NJ
- Watchung Booksellers—Montclair, NJ

NEW MEXICO

- Prana Blessings Metaphysical Shop—Santa Fe, NM

NEW YORK

- Adanne Bookshop—Brooklyn, NY
- Archivist Books—Rochester, NY
- Blenheim Hill Books—Hobart, NY
- The Bronx is Reading—Bronx, NY
- Café con Libros—Brooklyn, NY
- Grandma's Place—New York, NY
- Kulture Café—Harriman, NY
- The Lit. Bar—Bronx, NY
- Liz's Book Bar—Brooklyn, NY
- Revolution Books—New York, NY
- Sadie's Books & Beverages—Middletown, NY
- The Schomburg Shop—New York, NY
- Sister's Uptown Bookstore—New York, NY
- Taylor & Co. Books—Brooklyn, NY
- Zawadi Books—Buffalo, NY

NORTH CAROLINA

- Fulfillity Books & More — Hope Mills, NC
- Liberation Station Bookstore — Raleigh-Durham, NC
- Noir Collective AVL — Asheville, NC
- Red Rice Books — Charlotte, NC
- The Roasted Bookery — Wilmington, NC
- Rofhiwa Book Café — East Durham, NC

OHIO

- Elizabeth's Bookshop & Writing Centre — Akron, OH
- ThirdSpace Reading Room — Cleveland, OH

OKLAHOMA

- Fulton Street Books and Coffee — Tulsa, OK

OREGON

- Sunrise Books — Portland, OR
- Third Eye Books Accessories & Gifts — Portland, OR

PENNSYLVANIA

- Atomic City Comics — Philadelphia, PA
- Black and Nobel — Philadelphia, PA
- The Black Reserve Bookstore — Lansdale, PA
- Hakim's Bookstore — Philadelphia, PA
- Harriett's Bookshop — Philadelphia, PA
- The Print Factory — Bellefonte, PA
- Read Rose Books — Lancaster, PA
- The Tiny Bookstore — Pittsburgh, PA
- Uncle Bobbie's Coffee and Books — Philadelphia, PA

TENNESSEE

- The African Place—Memphis, TN
- Alkebu-Lan Images Book Store—Nashville, TN
- Bo Society & Books—Clarksville, TN
- The Bottom Knox—Knoxville, TN

TEXAS

- Black Pearl Books—Austin, TX
- The Book Readers Venue—Humble, TX
- Cibolo Chicks Bookstore—Selma, TX
- CLASS Bookstore—Houston, TX
- The Dock Bookshop—Fort Worth, TX
- Enda's Booktique—Duncanville, TX
- Kindred Stories—Houston, TX
- LIT Java Coffee & Books—Pearland, TX
- Pan-African Connection Bookstore—Dallas, TX
- SOA Co. Books—Houston, TX

VIRGINIA

- Harambee Books and Artworks—Alexandria, VA
- House of Consciousness Bookstore—Norfolk, VA
- Paperbacks Ink—Newport News, VA
- Positive Vibes—Virginia Beach, VA
- The Printed Word Bookstore—Portsmouth, VA
- Resist Booksellers—Petersburg, VA

WASHINGTON

- Estelita's Library—Seattle, WA
- LEMS Bookstore—Seattle, WA

WASHINGTON, DC

- Loyalty Bookstore—Washington, DC
- Pages & Volumes Bookstore—Washington, DC
- Sankofa Video, Books & Cafe—Washington, DC
- Solid State Books—Washington, DC

WISCONSIN

- Darick Books—Milwaukee, WI
- Niche Book Bar—Milwaukee, WI
- Rooted MKE—Milwaukee, WI

FORMER BRICK-AND-MORTAR SHOPS NOW ONLINE

- African Bookstore—Plantation, FL
- Aya Coffee and Books—Kansas City, MO
- Baltimore Read Aloud—Baltimore, MD
- Bard's Towne Books & Bourbon—Nashville, TN
- Beyond This February—Greenville, SC
- Bingham's Books & Culture—Hamden, CT
- Black Ethos Bookstore—Detroit, MI
- Blacklit—Dallas, TX
- The Book Bar—Richmond, VA
- Books & Bagels—Wilmington, DE
- Books and Crannies—Martinsville, VA
- Conquest Books—Ashland, KY
- D3 Comic Book Spot—Richmond, CA
- Detroit Book City—Southfield, MI
- Footprints Bookshop—New Bedford, MA
- Frontline Book Publishing—Chicago, IL

- Good Books—Atlanta, GA
- Heart & Soul Books—Harrisburg, PA
- Helping Kids Rise—Columbia, SC
- House of Pages—Peachtree Corners, GA
- The Key Bookstore—Hartford, CT
- Kizzy's Books and More—Winter Garden, FL
- Little Visioneers—Los Angeles, CA
- Loving Room—Seattle, WA
- Miranda Writes Bookstore—Bronx, NY
- Multiverse—Philadelphia, PA
- The Noir Bookshop—St. Louis, MO
- Page 1 Books—Evanston, IL
- The Pouring Pages—Jersey City, NJ
- Riches in Reading—Virginia Beach, VA
- The Salt Eaters Bookshop—Inglewood, CA
- Scribes & Vibes—Conyers, GA
- Shelves Bookstore—Charlotte, NC
- Sistah Scifi—Oakland, CA
- Socialight Society—Lansing, MI
- Tuma's Books—New York City, NY
- Turning Page Bookshop—Goose Creek, SC
- Urban Moon Books—Chesapeake, VA
- Wise Acre Comics—Goodyear, AZ
- Wow Book and Toy Store—Gulfport, MS

PHOTOGRAPH CREDITS

p. 92: Clara Villarosa (Courtesy of Clara Villarosa)

p. 109: Hue-Man Experience Bookstore Denver storefront
(Courtesy of Clara Villarosa)

p. 127: Thomas Hamilton and James Fugate in Eso Won Books
(Photograph by Ken Hively/*Los Angeles Times* via Getty Images)

p. 157: Walter Mosley at Karibu Books (Photograph by Bill
O'Leary/*The Washington Post* via Getty Images)

p. 183: Yao and Karla Glover, founders of Karibu Books;
Ramunda and Derrick Young, owners of MahoganyBooks; and
Shirikiana and Haile Gerima, owners of Sankofa Video, Books &
Café (Courtesy of Yao Glover and Ramunda Young)

p. 203: Akwete Tyehimba (Tyehimba family/Pan-African
Connection Bookstore)

p. 219: Blacklit (Courtesy of Nia-Tayler Clark, founder/CEO of
Blacklit)

NOTES

CHAPTER ONE: FIRST OFFICER OF THE UNDERGROUND RAILROAD

12 **He rushed to the door:** Graham Russell Gao Hodges, *David Ruggles: A Radical Black Abolitionist and the Underground Railroad in New York City* (Chapel Hill: University of North Carolina Press, 2010).

12 **Men who were more than happy:** Jonathan Daniel Wells, "The Black New Yorker Who Led the Charge Against Police Violence in the 1830s," *Time*, June 17, 2020.

14 **He considered his shop:** Dorothy B. Porter, "David Ruggles, an Apostle of Human Rights," *Journal of Negro History* 28, no. 1 (January 1943).

17 **"Let him be Lynched!":** David Ruggles, "'Southern Chivalry': To the Public," *Liberator*, September 26, 1835.

17 **weren't allowed to use public:** Maurice Wheeler, Debbie Johnson-Houston, and Billie E. Walker, "A Brief History of Library Service to African Americans," *American Libraries* 35, no. 2 (February 2004).

19 **Black people who couldn't read:** Abiola Sinclair, "David Ruggles of the Underground Railroad: Black History Special," parts 1 and 2, *New York Amsterdam News*, February 6, 1988.

20 **"Whatever necessity requires, let that":** David Ruggles, "Kidnapping in the City of New York," *Liberator*, August 6, 1836.

21 **He wrote in his autobiography:** Frederick Douglass, *My Bondage and My Freedom* (New York: Auburn Miller, Ortan, and Mulligan, 1855), 340–43.

24 **Black people able to read:** Elinor Des Verney Sinnette, W. Paul Coates, and Thomas C. Battle, *Black Bibliophiles and Collectors: Preservers of Black History* (Washington, DC: Howard University Press, 1990).

24 **By 1908, he'd outlasted:** Booker T. Washington, *The Story of the Negro* (New York: Doubleday, Page & Company, 1909).

25 **Young's Book Exchange was perhaps:** "George Young Dead: Had Book Exchange," *New York Times*, April 19, 1935.

25 **In its first year:** Cleveland G. Allen, "New York City Has Book Exchange," *Chicago Defender*, May 29, 1915.

25 **Young was born in Virginia:** "Rare Books for Negroes," *Baltimore Sun*, November 20, 1921.

26 **Michaux saw education:** C. Gerald Fraser, "Lewis Michaux, 92, Dies; Ran Bookstore in Harlem," *New York Times*, August 27, 1976.

27 **A sign outside the bookstore:** Vaunda Micheaux Nelson, *No Crystal Stair* (Minneapolis: Carolrhoda Lab, 2012).

29 **leading groups of Black people:** "Nationalists Heading Up Drive," *New York Amsterdam News*, September 1, 1962.

29 **open a Black-owned-and-operated:** "Nationalists Entering Politics," *New York Amsterdam News*, March 16, 1963.

CHAPTER TWO: A BOOKSTORE UNDER SIEGE

33 **Charlie Cobb thought about Black:** Charlie Cobb, in-person interview by historian Joshua Clark Davis, October 16, 2015, https://www.crmvet.org/nars/cobb2015.pdf.

34 **He'd spent years organizing:** Charlie Cobb, "Where Do We Go from Here?," SNCCDigital.org, accessed October 15, 2022, https://snccdigital.org/inside-sncc/the-story-of-sncc/where-do-we-go-from-here/.

34 **Cobb was the one who:** Daniel Perlstein, "Teaching Freedom: SNCC and the Creation of the Mississippi Freedom Schools," *History of Education Quarterly* 30, no. 3 (Autumn 1990): 303.

35 **He enlisted the help:** Judy Richardson, video interview by author, November 15, 2019.

35 **With some seed money from:** Colin Beckles, "PanAfrican Sites of Resistance: Black Bookstores and the Struggle to Re-Present Black Identity," PhD diss., University of California, Los Angeles, 1995, 186–87.

35 **create a haven for Black:** Charlie Cobb, interview by Joshua Clark Davis, October 16, 2015.

35 **drum in Drum and Spear:** SNCC Digital Gateway, "Drum and Spear Books Founded," SNCCDigital.org, accessed October 15, 2022, https://snccdigital.org/events/drum-and-spear-books-founded/.

37 **Columbia Heights was a risky:** Stanley Marcuss, Victòria Alsina Burgués, and Rachael Stephens, "The Riots and the Slums: Comparing Public and Private Sector–Led Redevelopment in Washington, D.C.," M-RCBG Associate Working Paper no. 74, May 3, 2017.

37 **match for the urban renewal:** Margaret Farrar, *Building the Body Politic* (Champaign: University of Illinois Press, 2008), 103.

37 **closed for good:** Patricia Camp, "4th St. Struggles Back from Riot: Government Gets Blame for Slowness," *Washington Post*, April 3, 1978.

37 **heart of a Black neighborhood:** Judy Richardson, phone interview by author, January 24, 2023.

37 **Richardson was immediately in:** Richardson, interview by author, January 24, 2023.

38 **Gittens had been a major student leader:** Orville Green, "Howard U. Closes in Student Siege," *Baltimore Afro-American*, March 23, 1968; Jim Hoagland, "Board Plan Ends Sit-In at Howard," *Washington Post*, March 24, 1968; Todd Zwillich, "The Howard University Takeover, Fifty Years Later," *Takeaway*, WNYC, March 19, 2018.

38 **The movement arguably began:** Ibram Rogers, "The Black Campus Movement and the Institutionalization of Black Studies, 1965–1970," *Journal of African American Studies* 16, no. 1 (2012): 21–40.

38 **nearly a thousand schools:** Rogers, "The Black Campus Movement."

38 **Gittens and Adrienne Manns Israel:** Rick Massimo, "Leaders of

Howard University Takeover Reflect 50 Years Later," *Los Angeles Sentinel* / WTOP-FM, March 23, 2018.

39 **One night, the pair sat:** Tony Gittens, "Drum and Spear Bookstore by Tony Gittens," *Black Power Chronicles*, accessed November 5, 2022, https://blackpowerchronicles.org/cool_timeline/drum-and-spear-bookstore/.

39 **Richardson first saw the shop:** Richardson, interview by author, January 24, 2023.

39 **Gittens had some accounting experience:** Gittens, "Drum and Spear Bookstore by Tony Gittens."

39 **"They had just tear-gassed":** Richardson, interview by author, January 24, 2023.

39 **The activists wanted Drum and Spear:** Cobb, interview by Davis.

40 **Richardson and Gittens rented:** Richardson, interview by author, January 24, 2023; Gittens, "Drum and Spear Bookstore by Tony Gittens"; Joshua Clark Davis, *From Head Shops to Whole Foods: The Rise and Fall of Activist Entrepreneurs* (New York: Columbia University Press, 2017), 58.

40 **"two young Black people":** Richardson, interview by author, November 15, 2019.

40 **By the summer, Drum:** US Department of Justice, Federal Bureau of Investigation, "Drum and Spear Bookstore," July 22, 1968.

41 **Members of the Black Panther:** Cobb, interview by Davis.

41 **"What's the point of having":** Cobb, interview by Davis.

41 **Locals came in to read:** Richardson, interview by author, November 15, 2019.

41 **flew off the shelves:** Gittens, "Drum and Spear Bookstore by Tony Gittens."

42 **"What was amazing was that":** Beckles, "PanAfrican Sites of Resistance," 192.

43 **"It was doing exactly what":** Gittens, "Drum and Spear Bookstore by Tony Gittens."

43 **The first book released under:** Donald Joyce, *Gatekeepers of Black Cul-*

ture: Black-Owned Book Publishing in the United States 1817–1981 (Westport, CT: Greenwood Press, 1983), 92.

43   **The group even hosted:** Drum and Spear, "Areas of Interest and Accomplishment," *Drum and Spear Bookstore, 1968–1978*, undated, Courtland Cox Papers, Duke University.

43   **the Center for Black Education:** John Lewis, "Black Voices," *Baltimore Afro-American*, August 9, 1969.

44   **Once, troops lined the sidewalk:** Gittens, "Drum and Spear Bookstore by Tony Gittens."

44   **the FBI agents' job was simple:** "Article 5—No Title," *Washington Post, Times Herald*, March 12, 1972; FBI Director to Washington Field Office Secret Agent, "Drum and Spear Bookstore Racial Matters," Federal Bureau of Investigation, June 18, 1968.

44   **FBI director Hoover issued:** J. Edgar Hoover, "Black Nationalist Movement in the United States—Racial Matters," memo, October 9, 1968, FBI File 157-WFO-368, National Archives and Records Administration.

45   **Richardson was manning the store:** Richardson, interview with author, November 15, 2019; "Article 5—No Title."

45   **Federal agents had been spying:** FBI Director, "Drum and Spear Bookstore Racial Matters."

46   **Howard students were at Drum:** US Department of Justice, Federal Bureau of Investigation, "Drum and Spear Bookstore," FBI File 157-9594-6, October 22, 1968.

46   **informal lessons, or "dual degrees":** Maisha T. Fisher, "Earning 'Dual Degrees': Black Bookstores as Alternative Knowledge Spaces," *Anthropology & Education Quarterly* 37, no. 1 (2006): 83–99.

47   **Muse worked long hours:** Daphne Muse, telephone interview by author, July 9, 2022.

47   **A supervisor ordered one agent:** "Article 5—No Title."

47   **Agents even lured customers into:** US Department of Justice, Federal Bureau of Investigation, "Drum and Spear Bookstore," memo, September 4, 1968.

48   **Featherstone had joined SNCC in:** Carl Bernstein, "Bomb Blast Victim Was a Bitter Rights Activist," *Washington Post*, March 11, 1970.

48   **spending over a week:** Ralph Featherstone, "The Stench of Freedom," February 20, 1965, Wisconsin Historical Society, https://content .wisconsinhistory.org/digital/collection/p15932coll2/id/35321.

48   **"Never talk to the FBI":** Daphne Muse, "Drum and Spear Bookstore (1968–1971) by Daphne Muse," Black Power Chronicles, accessed November 10, 2022, https://blackpowerchronicles.org/cool_time line/drum-and-spear-bookstore-1968-1971/.

48   **On a Monday night in:** Kelly Gilbert, "Many Questions Still Posed in Bel Air Deaths," *Evening Sun* (Norwich, NY), March 17, 1970.

48   **was to be tried:** Jim Mann, "No Sign of Rap Brown on Bel Air Trial Eve," *Washington Post*, March 16, 1970.

48   **explosive was planted to kill:** "Black Psychology," *Black Scholar* 1, no. 5 (March 1970).

49   **The explosion led to heightened:** Beckles, "PanAfrican Sites of Resistance," 232–35.

49   **Federal agents knew Featherstone:** US Department of Justice, Federal Bureau of Investigation, "Drum and Spear Bookstore," memo, January 30, 1970.

49   **Protecting the store:** Muse, interview by author.

50   **By the time Drum and Spear:** Davis, *From Head Shops to Whole Foods*, 58.

50   **Richardson led the charge:** Judy Richardson, telephone interview by author, February 8, 2023; Judy Richardson, "Black Children's Books: An Overview," *Journal of Negro Education* 43, no. 3 (Summer 1974); Adrienne Manns, "Writing a New Chapter in Black Children's Books," *Washington Post*, December 18, 1973.

50   **the store's children's section:** Drum and Spear, "Areas of Interest and Accomplishment."

50   **This incentivized schools to prioritize:** Richardson, interview by author, February 8, 2023.

50   **It was Richardson who opened:** Richardson, interview by author, January 24, 2023; Judy Richardson, "Cultural Production, Activism,

and a Creative Hub: The Drum and Spear Bookstore," Library of
Congress, September 24, 2018, 2:34–2:45, https://www.loc.gov
/item/webcast-8548; "Judy Richardson papers, 1963–2014," Duke
University Libraries Archives & Manuscripts, accessed November 12,
2022, https://archives.lib.duke.edu/catalog/richardsonjudy.

51 **One day, a salesman from:** Richardson, interview by author, January
24, 2023; Richardson, "Cultural Production, Activism, and a Creative Hub."

51 **The idea for the center:** Cobb, interview by Davis; Beckles, "Pan-
African Sites of Resistance," 197–99; Lewis, "Black Voices"; "USD's
History," University of the District of Columbia, accessed November 12, 2022, https://www.udc.edu/about/history-mission/; HBCU
Library Alliance, "Federal City College: Land Grant College 1968
District of Columbia," Celebrating the Collections of Historically
Black Colleges and Universities, accessed November 12, 2022,
https://hbcudigitallibrary.auctr.edu/digital/collection/UDCW/id
/174/; SNCC Digital Gateway, "Pan-Africanism," SNCCDigital.org,
accessed November 12, 2022, https://snccdigital.org/our-voices
/internationalism/part-2/.

52 **The teachers sought more power:** Cobb, interview by Davis; Lewis,
"Black Voices."

52 **The activists and booksellers taught:** Richardson, interview by au-
thor, November 15, 2019; Cobb, interview by Davis; Lewis, "Black
Voices"; SNCC Digital Gateway, "Drum and Spear Books Founded";
Beckles, "PanAfrican Sites of Resistance," 197–99.

52 **Drum and Spear staffers were developing:** Beckles, "PanAfrican
Sites of Resistance," 199–200.

52 **"We realize that there is":** Lewis, "Black Voices"; Richardson, interview by author, November 15, 2019.

52 **"Drum and Spear Complex":** Seth Markle, "Book Publishers for a
Pan-African World: Drum and Spear Press and Tanzania's 'Ujamaa'
Ideology," *Black Scholar* 37, no. 4 (Winter 2008): 18.

52 **Drum and Spear was more:** Beckles, "PanAfrican Sites of Resistance";

Richardson, interview by author, January 24, 2023; Muse, interview by author; Cobb, interview by Davis.

53 **Drum and Spear members consistently:** Markle, "Book Publishers for a Pan-African World."

53 **On May 27, 1972, thousands:** George Musgrove, "50 Years Ago, DC's First African Liberation Day Launched a Movement," *Washington Post*, May 28, 2022.

54 **"Africa For The Africans":** Fanon Che Wilkins, "'In the Belly of the Beast': Black Power, Anti-Imperialism, and the African Liberation Solidarity Movement 1968–1975," PhD diss., New York University, 2001, 167, 124.

54 **The Black Panther Party was:** Jessica C. Harris, "Revolutionary Black Nationalism: The Black Panther Party," *Journal of Negro History* 86, no. 3 (Summer 2001).

55 **Columbia Heights neighborhood was in:** Patricia Camp, "14th St. Struggles Back from Riot: Government Gets Blame for Slowness," *Washington Post*, April 3, 1978.

55 **"They were also discounting in":** Richardson, interview by author, January 24, 2023.

55 **In 1972, Black studies programs:** Robert Allen, "Politics of the Attack on Black Studies," *Black Scholar* 6, no. 1 (September 1974).

55 **This served as another financial:** Richardson, interview by author, January 24, 2023; Beckles, "PanAfrican Sites of Resistance," 227.

56 **Even at Maelezo, Richardson saw:** Richardson, interview by author, November 15, 2019.

56 **Between refusing to carry popular:** Beckles, "PanAfrican Sites of Resistance," 235–36.

56 **In 1974, the nation learned:** "IRS Targets Under Nixon Are Identified," *Hartford Courant*, November 18, 1974.

56 **The unit existed from 1969:** "Groups Targeted by Secret IRS Unit," *Baltimore Afro-American*, December 7, 1974.

57 **Drum and Spear was evicted:** Judy Richardson, email interview by author, March 25, 2023; Judy Richardson, emails to author, March 25 and 29, 2023.

57 **In a 1974 article:** Gerard Burke, "Hard Times for Drum and Spear," *Baltimore Afro-American*, March 23, 1974; Cobb, interview by Davis.

CHAPTER THREE: LIBERATION COULD GET YOU IN TROUBLE

59 **"What are you trying to":** Beryle Banfield, "Liberation Bookstore: A Community Institution," *Interracial Books for Children Bulletin* 16, no. 7 (1985).

60 **"Liberation" would only invite trouble:** Abiola Sinclair, "Liberation Bookstore—15th Anniversary," *New York Amsterdam News*, November 20, 1982.

60 **Though major publishers shunned her:** Federal Bureau of Investigation, "Una Godfrey Muckram Memorandum," March 17, 1969.

62 **Hugh Mulzac was blacklisted:** Herb Boyd, "Captain Hugh Mulzac, Distinguished Merchant Marine and Activist," *New York Amsterdam News*, August 13, 2015; Tony Pecinovsky, "Torpedoing Black Radicalism: The Case of Hugh Mulzac," *Black Perspectives*, October 28, 2021.

63 **"Building up the shop":** Federal Bureau of Investigation, "Una Godfrey Muckram Memorandum," May 28, 1967.

63 **The horrors made it:** "Terrorist Blast Shakes Up Wife of Guiana Premier," *Morning Call* (Pittsburg, KS), July 18, 1964.

64 **"I am deeply sorry":** Federal Bureau of Investigation, "Una Godfrey Muckram Memorandum," May 28, 1967.

65 **"Black Nationalist activity":** Federal Bureau of Investigation, "Louis Michaux Memorandum," June 28, 1968.

67 **People of African descent:** Maisha T. Fisher, "Earning 'Dual Degrees': Black Bookstores as Alternative Knowledge Spaces," *Anthropology & Education Quarterly* 37, no. 1 (2006): 83–99.

67 **"They often acted"**: Abiola Sinclair, "Liberation Bookstore—15th Anniversary," *New York Amsterdam News*, November 20, 1982.

69 **While Michaux promoted a traditional**: Colin Beckles, "PanAfrican Sites of Resistance: Black Bookstores and the Struggle to Re-Present Black Identity," PhD diss., University of California, Los Angeles, 1995, 203–5; Bill Crawford and Miriam Crawford, "If These Walls Could Talk . . . Bill and Miriam Crawford's Dining Room," Philadelphia Folklore Project, interviewed by Teresa Jaynes and Nancy Yan, 1997 and 2004; Judy Richardson, interview by author, January 24, 2023.

71 **"I thought they would"**: Michel Marriott, "Bookseller's Paging All Blacks," *Philadelphia Daily News*, February 9, 1987: 8.

71 **Business picked up drastically**: Joshua Clark Davis, *From Head Shops to Whole Foods: The Rise and Fall of Activist Entrepreneurs* (New York: Columbia University Press, 2017), 55.

72 **A headline in the *Philadelphia***: Laurence Geller, "FBI Documents List Many Black 'Informants': Key Organizations, Book Stores, Bars Were Also Probed," *Philadelphia Tribune*, April 10, 1971.

72 **In FBI files, agents insisted**: Dennis Kirkland, "Media Files Reveal FBI Spied on CORE; Members Not Surprised," *Philadelphia Inquirer*, April 18, 1971.

72 **create the Revolutionary Action Movement**: Amy Cohen, "Honoring Hakim's, a West Philadelphia Landmark," *Hidden City*, April 21, 2023.

73 **Just a few years after**: Moritz Kuhn, Moritz Schularick, and Ulrike I. Steins, "Income and Wealth Inequity in America, 1949–2016," Opportunity & Inclusive Growth Institute, Federal Reserve Bank of Minneapolis, June 2018, 4; Beckles, "PanAfrican Sites of Resistance," 203–5; Crawford and Crawford, "If These Walls Could Talk"; Richardson, interview by author, January 24, 2023.

CHAPTER FOUR: BOOKS THROUGH THE REBELLION

76 **But Sostre kept his bookstore**: Vincent Copeland, *The Crime of Martin Sostre* (New York: McGraw Hill, 1970), 15–16.

77   He'd spent his time behind: Warren L. Schaich and Diane S. Hope, "The Prison Letters of Martin Sostre: Documents of Resistance," *Journal of Black Studies* 7, no. 3 (March 1977); Alexandria Symonds, "Overlooked No More: Martin Sostre, Who Reformed America's Prisons from His Cell," *New York Times*, April 24, 2019.

77   moment he opened the shop: Schaich and Hope, "The Prison Letters of Martin Sostre"; Symonds, "Overlooked No More."

77   warned Sostre to stop selling: Joseph Shapiro, "How One Inmate Changed the Prison System from the Inside," *Code Switch*, NPR, April 17, 2017; Copeland, *The Crime of Martin Sostre*, 19.

78   Forty-three people died during the: Robyn Meredith, "5 Days in 1967 Still Shake Detroit," *New York Times*, July 23, 1997.

78   headed to New Jersey: Ed Vaughn, interview by author, March 27, 2023.

78   "We were quite concerned, worried": Ed Vaughn, interview by Sam Pollard for *Eyes on the Prize II: America at the Racial Crossroads, 1965–1985* (documentary film), transcript, Washington University in St. Louis, June 6, 1989, http://repository.wustl.edu/downloads/m326 m552r.

78   After making sure his family: Chad Livengood, "Still Rebuilding: Detroit's Nascent Comeback Hinges on Rebuilding a Vast Network of Small Businesses That Were Lost in the Aftermath of 1967," *Crain's Detroit Business*, June 26, 2017.

78   Vaughn's good fortune seemed to: Vaughn, interview by author; Ed Vaughn, interview by Joshua Clark Davis, June 5, 2013; Livengood, "Still Rebuilding."

79   Vaughn called Detroit mayor: Vaughn, interview by Pollard.

79   Neighbors told him: Vaughn, interview by author; Vaughn, interview by Davis; Livengood, "Still Rebuilding."

79   leaders held a public tribunal: Vaughn, interview by author; Livengood, "Still Rebuilding."

79   Word spread across the country: Vaughn, interview by author; Livengood, "Still Rebuilding."

80 **Black nationalist critic Louis Lomax:** Louis E. Lomax, "Bookstore Pros Mapped Detroit Riots," *Vancouver Sun*, August 8, 1967.

80 **Vaughn had a reputation:** Vaughn, interview by Davis.

80 **established his eponymous bookshop:** Vaughn, interview by author; Livengood, "Still Rebuilding."

81 **Black Detroiters knew:** Matthew D. Lassiter and the Policing and Social Justice History Lab, "The Summer of 1963," *Detroit Under Fire*, accessed December 10, 2022, https://policing.umhistorylabs.lsa .umich.edu/s/detroitunderfire/page/the-summer-of-1963.

81 **In reality, Black communities were:** Char Adams, "Groups Across the Country Are Fighting Efforts to Expand 'Harmful' Highways," NBC News, October 15, 2022.

81 **Residents viewed the Detroit Police:** Vaughn, interview by author; Meredith, "5 Days in 1967 Still Shake Detroit"; Vaughn, interview by Pollard.

81 **Hundreds of protesters gathered in:** "Detroit Citizens to Protest Exoneration in Scott Killing," *Baltimore Afro-American*, August 17, 1963.

81 **"There was a consciousness that":** Jeroslyn JoVonn, "Detroit's First Black Owned Bookstore Receives $15,000 Preservation Grant from National Park Service," *Black Enterprise*, January 7, 2022.

82 **For years, Vaughn's Bookstore was:** Grace Lee Boggs, *Living for Change: An Autobiography* (Minneapolis: University of Minnesota Press, 1998), 120.

82 **Black people in the city:** Vaughn, interview by Pollard.

82 **Garveyite and Nation of Islam:** Joshua Clark Davis, *From Head Shops to Whole Foods: The Rise and Fall of Activist Entrepreneurs* (New York: Columbia University Press, 2017), 50.

82 **"the consciousness was being developed":** Vaughn, interview by Pollard.

82 **Vaughn emerged as a major:** Boggs, *Living for Change*, 118.

82 **Vaughn largely surrounded himself with:** Edward Vaughn, in-person interview by historian Joshua Clark Davis, June 5, 2013.

83 the Freedom Now political party: "Freedom Now Party Platform, 1964," *Illustrated News*, September 28, 1964, *12th Street Detroit*, Walter P. Reuther Library, accessed April 3, 2023, https://projects.lib .wayne.edu/12thstreetdetroit/items/show/368.

83 The all-Black party was a: Robert Shann, "250 Hear DeBerry at Detroit Student Rally; Rev. Cleage Urges Vote for Negro Nominee," *Militant*, November 2, 1964.

83 get 2 percent: George Breitman, "Further Discussion on Freedom Now Party," *Militant*, December 21, 1964.

83 with candidates up for offices: "Freedom NOW Party Candidates in Michigan Election," *Baltimore Afro-American*, November 7, 1964.

83 "It scared the daylights": Vaughn, interview by Davis.

83 "favor an all-colored party": "Dr. King Disturbed by FNP Tactics," *Baltimore Afro-American*, November 7, 1964.

83 Black Detroiters felt a sense: Vaughn, interview by Pollard.

83 Rebellion-torn areas fell into disrepair: Kevin Boyle, "The Ruins of Detroit: Exploring the Urban Crisis in the Motor City," *Michigan Historical Review* 27, no. 1 (Spring 2001).

84 He became executive director of: "Edward Vaughn Is Chosen CCAC Executive Director," *Michigan Chronicle*, December 9, 1967.

84 It became a vehicle: Paul Lee, "Prophet of Possibility," *Michigan Citizen*, June 22, 2008.

85 caused distance between Vaughn: Boggs, *Living for Change*, 136.

85 Vaughn didn't mince words: Vaughn, interview by Davis; Vaughn, interview by author; Vaughn, interview by Pollard.

86 Broadside Press was considered the: James Sullivan, "Real Cool Pages: The Broadside Press Broadside Series," *Contemporary Literature* 32, no. 4 (Winter 1999).

86 The Black Arts Movement, with: Larry Neal, "The Black Arts Movement," *The Drama Review: TDR* 12, no. 4 *Black Theatre* (Summer 1968).

86 "New Black Renaissance": Arthur P. Davis, "Novels of the New Black Renaissance (1960–1977): A Thematic Survey," *CLA Journal*

21, no. 4 (June 1978); Holly Bast, "Black Arts Movement Poets," *Washington Post*, November 26, 1996.

86 **spoke of this revolution:** Mel Watkins, "Hard Times for Black Writers," *New York Times*, February 22, 1981.

87 **Vaughn's Bookstore was among the:** Lolita Standifer, "The Man Behind the Pen," *Michigan Chronicle*, August 23, 2000.

87 **Vaughn made the shop a:** Margaret Boone-Jones, "Detroiter Author's Book for Children About Dr. King Jr.," *Michigan Chronicle*, November 2, 1968; "Autograph Party Slated for Vaughn's Book Store May 31," *Michigan Chronicle*, May 31, 1975.

87 **Black locals would flock to:** "School Crisis Is Subject of CCAC Meeting," *Michigan Chronicle*, November 11, 1967.

87 **"inflame the Negro community":** FBI Director to Detroit Field Office, "Counterintelligence Program Black Nationalist—Hate Groups Racial Intelligence," memo, April 3, 1968, National Archives and Records Administration; FBI Director to Detroit Field Office, "Counterintelligence Program Black Nationalist—Hate Groups Racial Intelligence," memo, March 22, 1968, National Archives and Records Administration.

87 **harassing the Detroit Police Department:** FBI Director to Detroit Field Office, "Counterintelligence Program Black Nationalist—Hate Groups Racial Intelligence," memo, April 3, 1968.

88 **"When they came to bust":** Vaughn, interview by Davis.

89 **"When the oil embargo came":** Vaughn, interview by Davis.

89 **numerology, astrology, and herbology:** Thomas Johnson, "A Parking Lot Is to Replace the Tree of Life in Harlem," *New York Times*, January 24, 1976.

90 **showed up to public hearings:** Ruby Dee, "... Swingin' Gently," *New York Amsterdam News*, November 19, 1977.

90 **He shut down the shop:** Vaughn, interview by author.

90 **But for Vaughn, the effect:** Vaughn, interview by author.

91 **the George Jackson Prison Movement:** W. Paul Coates, interview by author, October 30, 2022; US Department of Justice, Federal Bureau of Investigation, "RE: George Jackson Prison Movement also known

as Black Book Store George Jackson Prison Movement," November 7, 1973, FBI File 157-HQ-26110, National Archives and Records Administration.

91 **"We'd be getting books into":** Coates, interview by author.

91 **famed Black journalist Earl Caldwell:** Earl Caldwell, "Black Bookstores Creating New Best-Seller List," *New York Times*, August 20, 1969.

CHAPTER FIVE: BLACK BOOKS WITHOUT BLACK POWER

93 **"start a Black Tattered Cover":** Clara Villarosa and Linda Villarosa, video interview by author, June 12, 2023.

93 **She had no experience running:** "Linda and Clara Villarosa: How Books Shaped Their Experiences," *Shelf Awareness*, April 19, 2022, https://www.shelf-awareness.com/issue.html?issue=4214#m 55881.

93 **working her way up:** Kevin Simpson, "The SunLit Interview: Clara Villarosa's Hue-Man Experience Finds Unexpected New Life," *Colorado Sun*, March 13, 2021; Clara Villarosa, *Down to Business: The First 10 Steps to Entrepreneurship for Women* (New York: Avery, 2009), 1, 84, 156, 157.

94 **And she watched their influence:** Manning Marable, *Race, Reform, and Rebellion: The Second Reconstruction and Beyond in Black America, 1945–2006*, 3rd edition (Jackson: University Press of Mississippi, 2007), 146–82, 194–95.

94 **Estimates at the time put:** Joshua Clark Davis, *From Head Shops to Whole Foods: The Rise and Fall of Activist Entrepreneurs* (New York: Columbia University Press, 2020), 71; Juana Duty, "Age of Aquarian Book Shop: Bookstore Still Surviving in 'Starvation Business,'" *Los Angeles Times*, March 24, 1982.

94 **Soon she began dating:** Mary Luins Small, "Denver's Black 'Bookstore and More,'" *American Visions*, February 1, 1989.

95 **block or so from Five:** Denver Public Library, "Five Points–Whittier Neighborhood History," Denver Public Library, https://history.denverlibrary.org/five-points-whittier-neighborhood-history.

95 **Paintings and Afrocentric murals:** Anonymous, "Book Biz: A Community Best-Seller," *Ms.*, September 1989.

96 **She'd been a social worker:** Alex Miller, "The Hue-Man Experience Bookstore," in *Strategic Management* (Boston and Burr Ridge, IL: Irwin/McGraw Hill, 1998), C221–C234.

96 **Villarosa used her severance:** Nicholas Siropolis, *Small Business Management*, 3rd edition (Boston: Houghton Mifflin Company, 1998), 85.

97 **African American business can't be:** Stuart Leuthner, "Buy the Book: Confounding Racial and Retail Stereotypes," *Emerge*, November 1990, 19.

97 **She knew none would approve:** Shawn Rhea, "Buy the Book," *Black Enterprise*, February 1999: 175.

99 **And Hue-Man found a longtime:** Lynn Cald, "The Hue-Man Experience: Black Bookselling in the Rockies," *ABBWA Journal* 3, no. 1 (Fall/Winter 1989).

101 **a book club at the:** Alicia and Clara Villarosa, in-person interview by author, July 21, 2023.

102 **Alice Walker had published:** Jacqueline Trescott, "The Stories That Cry to Be Read Caught in the Truths of 3 Unconventional Booksellers," *Washington Post*, July 2, 1992.

102 **"African American women developed":** Carolyn Brown, "Writing a New Chapter in Book Publishing," *Black Enterprise*, February 1995: 108.

102 **Villarosa recognized this pattern early:** Steven Rosen, "Book-Group Scene Adds a Dimension to Black Awareness," *Denver Post*, February 26, 1993.

103 **Villarosa recalled getting a letter:** Monte Young, "A Renaissance for Black Authors," *Newsday*, July 6, 1994.

103 **The author asked if she:** Daniel Max, "McMillan's Millions," *New York Times*, August 9, 1992.

103 **Hue-Man became a regular:** "Calendar of Book-Related Events," *Denver Post*, September 3, 1989.

104 **The decade saw what's believed:** Gwendolyn Osborne, "How Black

Romance—Novels, That Is—Came to Be," *Black Issues Book Review*, January/February 2002: 50; Yvonne Ann White, "Cultural Representation and the Production of African American Romance Novels," PhD diss., University of Iowa, 2008, 6; Mimi Swartz, "Vivian Stephens Helped Turn Romance Writing into a Billion-Dollar Industry. Then She Got Pushed Out," *Texas Monthly*, September 2020.

104 **Hue-Man stocked Black history:** Benjamin Chavis, "Where Are African American Children's Books?," *Civil Rights Journal / New Journal and Guide*, October 21, 1987: 5.

107 **The nation collectively shifted:** Graham Kinloch, "Black America in the 1980s: Theoretical and Practical Implications," *Humboldt Journal of Social Relations* 14, nos. 1 and 2 (Fall/Winter and Spring/Summer 1986–87): 1–7.

107 **The narrative of the decade:** Richard Lowy, "Yuppie Racism: Race Relations in the 1980s," *Journal of Black Studies* 21, no. 4 (June 1991): 455.

107 *The Cosby Show*'s **popularity:** Leslie Inniss and Joe Feagin, "*The Cosby Show*: The View from the Black Middle Class," *Journal of Black Studies* 25, no. 6 (July 1995): 692.

108 **Controversial journalist Tony Brown:** Joel Kotkin, "Why Blacks Are Out of Business," *Washington Post*, September 7, 1986: C1.

108 **Not only did Black people:** Sam Fulwood III, "Business Owners Narrow Gap with Majority-Owned Firms," *Los Angeles Times*, September 18, 1990.

108 **Ed Vaughn continued running his:** Phyllis Lynn Burns, "Activist Ed Vaughn Joins Council Race: Stresses Economic Development," *Michigan Chronicle*, July 29, 1989; M. A. Goodin, "Black Literature Was a Vital Part of the Movement," *Michigan Chronicle*, February 15, 1986: 4D.

109 **Book publishing in the United:** Richard Jean So and Gus Wezerek, "Just How White Is the Book Industry?," *New York Times*, December 11, 2020.

109 **The '60s and '70s were:** Concepción de León, Alexandra Alter, Elizabeth A. Harris, and Joumana Khatib, "'A Conflicted Cultural Force': What It's Like to Be Black in Publishing," *New York Times*, July 1, 2020.

109 **Morrison joined Random House:** Mel Watkins, "Hard Times for Black Writers," *New York Times*, February 22, 1981.

110 **The 1980s served as:** Connie Goddard, "Aiming for the Mainstream," *Publishers Weekly*, January 20, 1992: 28; Donald Joyce Franklin, *Gatekeepers of Black Culture: Black-Owned Book Publishing in the United States 1817–1981* (Westport, CT: Greenwood Press, 1983), 126–37.

110 **Haki Madhubuti cemented himself:** Haki Madhubuti, telephone interview by author, November 11, 2022; Catherine Daniels Hurst, "Haki R. Madhubuti (Don L. Lee)," in *Afro-American Poets Since 1955*, edited by Trudier Harris and Thadious M. Davis (Farmington Hills, MI: Gale, 1985), 222–25; "Third World Press: Thirty Years of Book Publishing," *Journal of Blacks in Higher Education* 18 (Winter 1997–1998).

112 **both had presses in their:** S. Pearl Sharp, phone interview by author, June 11, 2023.

112 **He was one of the:** Bill Alexander, "New Bookstore Fills Void," *Washington Post*, December 10, 1981.

113 **Charles F. Harris's Amistad Press:** "Amistad," HarperCollins Publishers Celebrating 200 Years of Great Books, accessed June 12, 2023, https://200.hc.com/stories/amistad/#menu; Diane Patrick, "At 30, Amistad Press Looks Ahead," *Publishers Weekly*, October 10, 2016.

113 **Harris was a veteran:** Calvin Reid, "Obituary: Charles F. Harris," *Publishers Weekly*, December 22, 2015; "*Essence* Purchases 35% of Amistad Press," *Los Angeles Sentinel*, December 24, 1987.

114 **The flood of Black children's:** Rudine Sims, "Where Have All the Black Children Gone?," *Christian Science Monitor*, August 3, 1984: B5.

114 **The couple started the press:** "Couple Produces Afro-Centric Books," *Standard-Freeholder*, August 2, 2004: 14.

114 **they'd published thousands of copies:** Claire Serant, "Success in Kids Books," *Black Enterprise*, March 1991: 21.

117 **Villarosa made a lifelong friend:** Alicia and Clara Villarosa, in-person interview by author, July 21, 2023.

118 **Alfred opened the Aquarian Bookshop:** Claire Luna, "Alfred Ligon, 96; Started Oldest Black Bookstore," *Los Angeles Times*, August 16,

2002: B12; Alisa Samuels, "Black Bookstore Renaissance," *Los Angeles Times*, February 10, 1990.

118 **He'd started the business with:** Luna, "Alfred Ligon, 96."

118 **He convinced Bernice to:** Alfred Ligon, "All the Lights the Light: Alfred Ligon," interview by Ranford B. Hopkins, Department of Special Collections, University of California, Los Angeles, February 10 and 17 and March 24, 1982.

118 **Black Angelenos headed to the:** Juana Duty, "Aquarian Book Shop Survives but 'It's a Starvation Business,'" *Los Angeles Times*, May 4, 1982.

118 **Alfred wasn't a Black Nationalist:** Jessica C. Harris, "Revolutionary Black Nationalism: The Black Panther Party," *Journal of Negro History* 86, no. 3 (Summer 2001).

119 **Earl Ofari Hutchinson was one:** Earl Ofari Hutchinson, email to author, July 7, 2023.

122 **Chains like Waldenbooks:** Ryan L. Raffaelli, "Reinventing Retail: The Novel Resurgence of Independent Bookstores," Harvard Business School Working Paper, No. 20-068, January 2020.

122 **They took advantage of the:** Peter Osnos, "How Book Publishing Has Changed Since 1984," *Atlantic*, April 12, 2011.

123 **"Crown, a Washington-area discount bookstore":** "Black-Owned Bookstore Was Born Out of a Need," *Washington Informer*, April 30, 1981.

125 **While mainstream news outlets:** Richard Harrington, "Rap of Rages: Public Enemy's Assault on the Airwaves," *Washington Post*, July 31, 1988.

125 **Hakim's Bookstore in Philadelphia:** Ron Harris, "Echoes of the '60s Black Youth: Assertive New Pride," *Los Angeles Times*, March 9, 1989.

CHAPTER SIX: THE GOLDEN AGE OF BOOKSELLING

128 **Gunfire rang out and smoke:** Richard Serrano, "All 4 in King Beating Acquitted: Violence Follows Verdicts; Guard Called Out," *Los Angeles Times*, April 30, 1992: VYA1.

128 **Protesters marched to Martin Luther:** Edward Boyer, "Black-Owned Businesses Pay a Heavy Price," *Los Angeles Times*, May 8, 1992: SBA1.

128 "There's no need to go": Seth Mydans, "Los Angeles Journal; Riot Leveled a Font of Black Culture," *New York Times*, August 5, 1992: 14.

128 The shop buzzed with loyal: S. Pearl Sharp, phone interview by author, June 11, 2023.

129 weeks before the Aquarian burned: Carol Byrne, "Questions Burn in L.A. Hearts," *Star Tribune*, May 10, 1992: 1A.

129 The burning wasn't just some: Sharon Jones, "The New Age of Aquarian: A Phoenix Is Stirring in Ashes of Riot," *San Diego Union-Tribune*, March 22, 1993: E1.

130 Ligons continued providing books: Claire Luna, "Alfred Ligon, 96; Started Oldest Black Bookstore," *Los Angeles Times,* August 16, 2002: B12.

130 Aquarian's debts and donate books: Karen Idelson, "Out of the Ashes—Donations Pour in to Rebuild Black Bookstore Gutted During L.A. Riots," *Houston Chronicle*, May 28, 1992.

131 the number of books purchased: Brenda Mitchell-Powell, "The Trouble with Success," *Publishers Weekly*, December 12, 1994: 33.

131 "boom in books for Blacks": Mary Corey, "A Boom in Books for Blacks: From Best-Seller Lists, to Romance Novels, to More Shelf Space at Book Stores, Black Literature Is Proliferating," *The Sun* (Baltimore, MD), November 1, 1991: 1E.

131 considering Black books a lucrative: Carol Taylor, "A Diverse Market for African-American Books Keeps Growing," *Publishers Weekly,* December 13, 1999.

131 The Shrine of the Black: Shelia M. Poole, "Black Bookstores in the Black," *Atlanta Journal-Constitution*, August 31, 1991.

132 Childs surveyed more than forty: Elizabeth Chur, "Giving Black Books a Boost," *Chicago Tribune,* July 21, 1992: 1.

132 The list became a de facto: Hillel Italie, "Best-Seller List Tracks Sales of Black Books," *New York Beacon*, June 17, 1994: 4.

134 There were a lot of firsts: Elizabeth Bernstein, "National Black Bookstore Week Planned for June," *Publishers Weekly*, March 24,

1997: 40; "Stores Celebrate First Black Bookstore Week," *Michigan Chronicle*, June 18, 1997: 4A.

134 **Black Angelenos found solace:** James Fugate, phone interview with author, September 5, 2023; Erin Aubry, "Culture Club: James Fugate and Tom Hamilton Share a Passion: Books," *Los Angeles Times*, February 6, 1995: 1.

135 **Fugate's bookselling career began:** James Fugate, phone interview, September 5, 2023; Lindsay Blakely, "The Founder of This Beloved L.A. Institution Reflects on Being Black and a Business Owner in America," *Inc.*, September 3, 2020.

136 **Former Black Panther Elaine Brown:** Charisse Jones, "Rage Motivates Former Black Panther to Pen 'Taste of Power,'" *Las Vegas Review-Journal*, March 28, 1993: 11b.

136 **Former gang members and Black:** Charisse Jones, "Memories of the Revolution: Elaine Brown Has Examined Her Years as a Black Panther," February 24, 1993.

137 **Shahrazad Ali had just published:** Njeri Itabari, "Off the Cuff Books: A 'Guide' Urging Submission of Black Women to Black Men Is Selling Briskly Despite Its Message of Oppression," *Los Angeles Times*, July 30, 1990: 1.

138 **Fugate and Hamilton appealed to:** Theresa Drew, "A Proud Heritage," *Los Angeles Times*, February 14, 1993: 10.

138 **Akbar Watson never imagined that:** Akbar Watson, phone interview by author, December 13, 2019; Sabirah Rayford, "Black Bookstore Owner Says for the First Time in 30 Years He's Selling Out of Books," WPTV, June 9, 2020.

139 **W. Paul Coates brought together seven:** "7 Black Book Publishers Set Up Trade Association," *Atlanta Daily World*, June 2, 1994: 1.

140 **Once totally absent from ABA:** Ethan Michaeli, "African American Press Alive and Well: Publishers Report Big Gains at Booksellers' Convention," *Chicago Defender*, June 17, 1996: 3.

140 **Checole told the *Chicago Defender*:** Michaeli, "African American Press Alive and Well."

140 **Hudsons, of Just Us Books:** Connie Goddard, "Aiming for the Mainstream," *Publishers Weekly*, January 20, 1992: 28; Wade and Cheryl Hudson, phone interview by author, August 28, 2023.

142 **Ken Lombard, then president:** Edward Boyer, "Bookstore Lands in Lease Limbo," *Los Angeles Times*, September 23, 1996.

143 **"back when nobody knew who":** Fugate, phone interview by author, September 5, 2023; Eugene Holley Jr., "PW Bookstore of the Year Finalist: Eso Won Books," *Publishers Weekly*, May 14, 2021.

144 **Kareem Abdul Jabbar and B. B. King:** "Black Bookstores Booming: Sales and Touring Authors," *Sun-Reporter*, November 6, 1997.

144 **coveted book-signing with Colin Powell:** Andrea Adelson, "Black-Owned Bookstores Defend Niche," *New York Times*, October 6, 1997.

145 **The mayor welcomed King:** Elize Dowdy, "Coretta Scott King Visits San Bernardino," *Precinct Reporter*, October 16, 1997: A3.

145 **The Robertses topped off the:** Adelson, "Black-Owned Bookstores Defend Niche."

145 **Lonnice Brittenum Bonner went from:** "African American Bookstores Go to Bat for Black Writers," *Milwaukee Journal*, August 16, 1994: D2.

146 **In a 1997 interview:** Karen Angel, "Black Booksellers Aim to Get Their Groove Back," *Publishers Weekly*, September 15, 1997.

146 **Marcus Books celebrated its thirty-fifth:** Teresa Moore, "Marcus Books Celebrates 35 Years / Key Outlet for Writings by and About Blacks," *San Francisco Chronicle*, November 27, 1995: A13.

147 **Hakim's Bookstore in Philadelphia rang:** Kendall Wilson, "Dawud Abdul Hakim, 65, Scholar, Publisher, Bookseller," *Philadelphia Tribune*, April 29, 1997.

147 **As Black booksellers enjoyed business:** Ryan L. Raffaelli, "Reinventing Retail: The Novel Resurgence of Independent Bookstores," Harvard Business School Working Paper, No. 20-068, January 2020: 6–7.

148 **Johnson watched with dread:** Tania Padgett, "Black Bookstore Takes on Mainstream Giant," *Network Journal*, February 28, 1995.

149 **Shahrazad Ali declared:** Shahrazad Ali, "White-Owned Chains Wage War on Black Bookstores," *Chicago Independent Bulletin*, August 29, 1996: 9.

149 **His sales once exceeded:** Denise R. Barnes, "Local Black Bookstores Win Award in Anti-Trust Settlement," *Washington Informer*, August 5, 1998: 15.

149 **Pyramid's Baltimore location was:** Wiley A. Hall, "A Black-Owned Bookstore Toils in the City That Reads," *Evening Sun* (Norwich, NY), June 3, 1993: 2A.

149 **By 1998, competition had ground:** Barnes, "Local Black Bookstores Win Award in Anti-Trust Settlement."

149 **As independent bookstores shuttered:** Patricia Holt, "Book Brawl: Independent Bookstores, the Internet, Chain Stores, and Discount Houses Duke It Out," *Whole Earth*, July 1999: 64–67.

149 **ABA membership began to decline:** Raffaelli, "Reinventing Retail."

149 **booksellers put up a fierce:** Rachel Beck, "Barnes & Noble Opts Not to Buy Ingram, Barnes & Noble Decides Merger Not Worth Effort," *Austin American-Statesman*, June 3, 1999: C1.

150 **The accusations were bolstered by:** Barnes, "Local Black Bookstores Win Award in Anti-Trust Settlement"; Holt, "Book Brawl."

150 **the ABA sued Penguin USA:** "Penguin Settlement Doled Out: 9 Months After Deal, Booksellers Get Paid," *Newsday*, July 11, 1998: A23.

150 **The ABA would go on:** Jeff Harrington, "Independent Booksellers Sue Big Chains," *St. Petersburg Times*, March 19, 1998.

150 **"It really bothered me":** Steven Zeitchik, "S&S Title Only at Barnes & Noble; Black Booksellers Irked," *Publishers Weekly*, December 15, 1997: 11.

151 **Amazon.com sold books in every:** Brad Stone, *The Everything Store: Jeff Bezos and the Age of Amazon* (New York: Little, Brown and Company, 2013).

151 **The ABA knew it had:** Sharon Gaudin, "Independents Take Aim at Amazon," *Computerworld*, May 17, 1999.

151   **Coffer criticized Penguin:** Lorraine Kee, "Author Bows Out of Book Signing: Terry McMillan Caught in Bookshop Rivalry," *St. Louis Dispatch*, May 20, 1997.

152   **death threats over the cancellation:** Gregory Freeman, "Flap over Author Upsets Many People," *St. Louis Post-Dispatch*, May 22, 1997.

153   **"relevant to the struggle of Black":** Mary Corey, "A Boom in Books for Blacks: From Best-Seller Lists, to Romance Novels, to More Shelf Space at Book Stores, Black Literature Is Proliferating," *Baltimore Sun*, November 1, 1991: 1E.

154   **Mulzac up to fifty summonses:** James C. McIntosh, "Is the City Trying to Close Liberation Bookstore?," *New York Amsterdam News*, March 11, 1995: 19.

154   **When asked in the late:** Simba Sana, "African-Centered Bookstores as Weapons of Culture: Applying the Thought of Amilcar Cabral to the Development of Black Cultural Institutions in the US," PhD diss., Howard University, 1998.

CHAPTER SEVEN: THE EARLY AUGHTS AND THE KARIBU BOOKSTORE CHAIN

158   **Simba Sana and Yao Glover:** Steven Zeitchik, "From Incense to Book Sense: Ex–Street Vendors' Black Bookstore Flourishes," *Publishers Weekly*, October 12, 1998.

158   **they'd sit on the phone:** James Fugate, phone interview by author, October 13, 2023.

158   **Hamilton watched Sana from:** Fugate, interview by author; Simba Sana, phone interview by author, October 24, 2023; Simba Sana, "African-Centered Bookstores as Weapons of Culture: Applying the Thought of Amilcar Cabral to the Development of Black Cultural Institutions in the US," PhD diss., Howard University, 1998, 93–95.

158   **"You should not go":** Fugate, interview by author.

160   **soon found the African Development:** Simba Sana, *Never Stop: A Memoir* (Evanston, IL: Agate Publishing, 2017).

161   **Sana got a glimpse:** Zeitchik, "From Incense to Book Sense."

163 **"They are calling it Hue-Man"**: Herb Boyd, "We Are Liberated at Liberation," *New York Amsterdam News*, July 12, 2001.

164 **"Race/Culture," "Revolutionary," "Caribbean Studies"**: Linton Weeks, "The Niche with a Mile of Shelves: Karibu Books Goes from Kiosk to Chain," *Washington Post*, March 17, 2003.

166 **Nkiru Books in Brooklyn was**: Herb Boyd, "Another Black Bookstore Faces Extinction," *New York Amsterdam News*, September 21, 2000.

167 **The September 11 attacks prompted**: Tracy Sherrod, phone interview by author, February 20, 2024.

168 **MahoganyBooks as an online bookstore**: Lauren Poteat, "SE Black Bookstore Holds Grand Opening," *Washington Informer*, March 15, 2018.

170 **"We came up together, right"**: Sana, interview by author.

171 **Rodgers was a sort**: Scott Goldstein, "Oak Cliff Loses an Anchor: Black Images Book Bazaar Played a Vital Role, Supporters Say," *McClatchy Tribune Business News*, December 24, 2006.

173 **At the beginning of the nineteenth**: Laura J. Miller, *Reluctant Capitalists: Bookselling and the Culture of Consumption* (Chicago: University of Chicago Press), 34.

174 **The booksellers hadn't marketed**: Emma Rodgers, phone interview by author, November 16, 2023.

175 **customers crammed into Black Images**: Andre Coe, "Interrupting Author Terry McMillan," *Louisville Defender*, August 25, 2005.

177 **Fugate mentioned Eso Won's woes**: Fugate, interview by author.

180 **The book industry, and Karibu's**: Laura Barnhardt, "Readers Say Goodbye to a Friend," *Baltimore Sun*, September 30, 2021.

180 **Sana made a last-ditch effort**: Yao Glover, "FBS Remix—the Fifty Four," *Free Black Space*, July 10, 2017.

CHAPTER EIGHT: THE BATTLE AGAINST GENTRIFICATION

184 **In the years after the**: Shirikiana Gerima, phone interview by author, December 12, 2023.

186 **Ghana and Burkina Faso governments:** Carrie Rickey, "A Filmmaker's Continuing Struggle to Bring His Slave Story to Audiences," *Philadelphia Inquirer*, August 25, 1994.

189 **Glover used *Free Black Space*:** Yao Glover, "FBS Remix—the Fifty Four," *Free Black Space*, July 10, 2017.

190 **Hakim's was at death's door:** Valerie Russ, "New Chapter: Pioneer Bookstore on Steadier Financial Ground," *Philadelphia Inquirer*, December 29, 2017.

193 **Zahra's Books and Things:** Courtney Vinopal, "How Black Bookstore Owners See the Flood of Requests for 'Anti-Racist' Reading," PBS News, June 23, 2020.

193 **ABA to support Black booksellers:** Angela Maria Spring, "It's Past Time for the Bookselling Industry to Reckon with Its Institutional Racism," Literary Hub, July 23, 2020.

195 **"Gentrification in DC is like":** Judith Rosen, "A Glimmer of Hope for Black-Owned Bookstores," *Publishers Weekly*, February 19, 2016.

197 **turn the music off:** Marissa Lang, "'The Music Will Go On': Go-Go Returns Days After a Complaint Silenced a DC Store," *Washington Post*, April 10, 2019.

202 **He recalled visiting the store:** "7 Writers on Their Favorite Bookstores," *New York Times*, December 7, 2016.

CHAPTER NINE: A BITTERSWEET RACIAL RECKONING

203 **Akwete Tyehimba didn't know:** Akwete and daughter Adjwoa Tyehimba, Zoom interview by author, August 23, 2024.

206 **Beard's hands were full:** DeAndra Beard, phone interview by author, February 15, 2024.

208 **formed a type of assembly line:** Janiece Haynes, phone interview by author, January 27, 2024.

208 **At Turning Page Bookshop:** VaLinda Miller, phone interview by author, January 22, 2024.

209 **He only sold about forty:** Natalie Escobar, "A Bittersweet Moment for Black Bookstore Owners," *Code Switch*, June 27, 2020.

209 **Nervis held virtual fundraisers:** Ali Nervis, phone interview by author, January 24, 2024.

210 **In Texas, Donna and Donya:** Donna and Donya Craddock, phone interview by author, February 23, 2024.

212 **Thanks to the campaign:** Tracy Sherrod, phone interview by author, February 20, 2024.

213 **accounting for 95 percent:** Richard Jean So and Gus Wezerek, "Just How White Is the Book Industry?," *New York Times*, December 11, 2020.

215 **Black-centered book clubs:** Khalisa Rae, "'Seen, Known and Heard': Black Readers Find Education and Healing in Book Clubs," NBC News, November 5, 2020.

216 **"Being the literary activists that":** April Silver, phone interview by author, February 29, 2024.

CHAPTER TEN: A NEW GENERATION OF BOOKSELLERS

222 **Brave + Kind Bookshop in Decatur:** "12 Authors Share Their Favorite Black-Owned Bookstores," Oprah Daily, February 18, 2022.

224 **He ultimately gave up:** VaLinda Miller, phone interview by author, January 22, 2024.

225 **made this even more clear:** Nicole Chavez, "A Florida School Board Member Filed a Criminal Complaint over a Black Queer Memoir," CNN, November 18, 2021.

229 **"'Perfect, so do I!'":** Char Adams, "This Traveling Library Is Making Sure 'Black Women's Literature Has the Place It Deserves,'" Oprah Daily, May 1, 2019.

232 **Clark, a twentysomething Black woman:** Nia-Tayler Clark, Zoom interview by author, August 27, 2024.

CONCLUSION

244 **"Black booksellers have done it":** W. Paul Coates, phone interview by author, November 21, 2023.

ABOUT THE AUTHOR

Char Adams is a journalist and editor who covers race, gender, and class. She has worked with NBC News and *People*, and her writing has appeared in *The New York Times*, *The New Republic*, Oprah Daily, *Vice*, *Teen Vogue*, and elsewhere. She is a proud Philadelphia native and now lives in the Dallas–Fort Worth area.